◁ W9-BPJ-522

J.K. Lasser's
Business Forms
for Managing
the Smaller Business

ARNOLD GOLDSTEIN, EDITORIAL CONSULTANT

Prentice Hall
New York • London • Toronto • Sydney • Tokyo • Singapore

Certain of the forms in this book appear with the permission of Caddylak Systems, Inc.

Second Edition

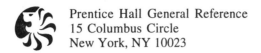 Prentice Hall General Reference
15 Columbus Circle
New York, NY 10023

A J.K. Lasser™ Book

J.K. LASSER and PRENTICE HALL are registered trademarks
of Prentice-Hall, Inc.
Colophon is a trademark of Prentice-Hall, Inc.

Library of Congress Cataloging-in-Publication Data

J.K. Lasser's business forms for managing the smaller business /
   Arnold Goldstein, editorial consultant.—2nd ed.
     p.   cm.
   Includes index.
   ISBN 0-671-88328-3
   1. Business—Forms. 2. Small business—Forms. 3. Time
management—Forms. I. Goldstein, Arnold S. II. J.K. Lasser
Institute. III. Title: Business forms for managing the smaller
business.
HF5371.J18   1994
651'.29—dc20   93-48505
                                        CIP

Manufactured in the United States of America

1 2 3 4 5 6 7 8 9 10

This book is sold with the understanding that neither the author nor the publisher is engaged in rendering legal advice. If legal advice is required, the services of an attorney should be sought. Publisher and author cannot in any way guarantee that the forms in this book are being used for the purposes intended and, therefore, assume no responsibility for their proper and correct use.

LIST OF FORMS

Section 2   General Planners   B 109

Section 3   Projects   B 127

Section 4   Executive and Administrative   B 149

Section 5   Accounting and Finance   B 201

Section 6 Purchasing and Shipping B 241

Section 7 Sales and Marketing B 297

Section 8   Personnel   B 329

Section 9   Graphs and Charts   B 391

Section 10 Maps   B 443

ABOUT THIS BOOK

Even the smallest business needs hundreds of different forms to run smoothly. The forms in this book are specifically designed to help you increase efficiency, improve productivity, and organize yourself for peak managerial performance. You'll find forms for just about every need and function—forms for setting goals, defining projects, organizing important records, documenting business transactions, hiring or firing employees, and much more. With *J.K. Lasser's Business Forms for Managing the Smaller Business*, you can set up a personalized planning system that will help you take control of the one commodity you can't afford to waste—your time.

Now with this complete business and executive form-file, you'll have the most extensive compilation of management forms available. With over 450 pages of forms for every business need, you'll have a complete and valuable collection of ready-to-use forms to help you make running your business more . . .

Convenient: No more searching for those hard-to-find or only rarely used forms. This book puts virtually every needed form at your fingertips.

Economical: No more expensive form suppliers, printers, or designers, who can charge $100 or more to prepare even **one** form found in this book. *J.K. Lasser's Business Forms for Managing the Smaller Business* is the low-priced alternative, with each master form available for pennies.

Efficient: No more tying up valuable storage space and money with unused or seldom used forms. Whether you need one form or dozens of copies, now you can print precisely the number of forms you need . . . when you need them.

Effective: No more doing without important forms or patching together makeshift forms. Now J.K. Lasser offers these professionally designed forms to help every size and type of organization get much more done in less time. You'll find . . .

* Over 200 business forms to improve every phase of operations—personnel, sales, credit and collection, bookkeeping, inventory and purchasing, expense control, routine office procedure . . . and much more.

* Over 200 of the most effective time management forms created exclusively for this book by a leading systems analyst. Form day organizers to project planners, these time savers belong on the desk of every manager who wants to increase efficiency and improve productivity.

* The bookkeeping department will welcome the more than 40 data sheets and columnar forms proven ideal for the collection, analysis, and review of operating data. Whether it be daily or annual summaries, these multi-purpose forms quickly put the numbers into focus.

* The business and executive form-file is an instant source of charts, graphs, and tables. These popular graphics give every presentation the perfect professional touch.

* To plan and review activities geographically, this book also includes world and state maps. These master maps encompass the key areas of interest to most organizations.

Browse though this book and discover for yourself the many useful forms you can put to work today.

HOW TO USE THIS BOOK

The form-file has been thoughtfully designed for convenient, professional use.

* Durable, heavy-stock paper allows long use, clear, crisp copies, and easy perforation. Perforation is fast—just fold along the perforated line to ensure a clean tear, then pull, gently starting at the top. Store the original after use, so that it can be located easily for reuse when needed. Wide margins allow forms to be hole-punched for binder storage.

* Every form can be quickly and easily modified or customized to specific needs. Use the forms "as is" or as a reference for designing your own forms, easily created by desktop publishers or typesetters.

* Appropriate forms can be personalized with your company name, address, logo, etc. simply by typeset, rubber stamp, or overlay on your business card.

* Just as these forms can be customized and personalized to match your particular needs, your plain paper copier can be loaded with a variety of paper stocks to give you added flexibility. This will enable you to copy your forms on colored paper, letterhead, or special paper stock.

Now you are all set—simply push the copier button to enjoy the easiest and most economical way to produce the forms your company needs.

THE FORM YOU NEED IS EASY TO FIND

The forms in this book are grouped by section. It's easy to find just the form you need:

Section 1: Administrative & Planning

Section 2: General Planners

Section 3: Projects

Section 4: Executive and Administrative

Section 5: Accounting & Finance

Section 6: Purchasing & Shipping

Section 7: Sales and Marketing

Section 8: Personnel

Section 9: Graphs & Charts

Section 10: Maps

There may be several formats for the more popular forms, so check and compare the various forms to find the one most appropriate for your purposes. Once you have selected the forms you will be using, set them up in a file or notebook at your desk and see how productive they will be in making time work for you.

Administrative
and
Planning

APPOINTMENTS

	APPOINTMENT	NOTES
7:00		
7:15		
7:30		
7:45		
8:00		
8:15		
8:30		
8:45		
9:00		
9:15		
9:30		
9:45		
10:00		
10:15		
10:30		
10:45		
11:00		
11:15		
11:30		
11:45		
12:00		
12:15		
12:30		
12:45		
1:00		
1:15		
1:30		
1:45		
2:00		
2:15		
2:30		
2:45		
3:00		
3:15		
3:30		
3:45		
4:00		
4:15		
4:30		
4:45		
5:00		
5:15		
5:30		
5:45		
6:00		
6:15		
6:30		
6:45		

DAILY PLANNER

DATE _____

THINGS TO DO	✔

APPOINTMENTS	✔

PHONE CALLS	✔	REMINDERS	✔

DAILY DIARY

DATE_____

TIME	ACTIVITY

PROFESSIONAL CHARGE SHEET

HOUR	CLIENT/ACTIVITY	TIME	
		HRS.	MIN.

DAILY NOTES

FOR TOMORROW

DATE _____

1 - URGENT   2 - HIGH PRIORITY   3 - LOW PRIORITY

PRIORITY		✔

MEETING NOTICE AND AGENDA

Group _____   Date _____

Title of meeting _____   **Starting time** _____

Called by _____   **Place** _____

Purpose of meeting _____

Background materials _____

Please bring _____

Comments _____

_____

_____

Agenda items	Time allocated
1. _____	
2. _____	
3. _____	
4. _____	
5. _____	

MEETING AGENDA

Location: _____ *Date* _____

Time: _____

Participants: _____

_____

_____

_____

_____

Meeting items:	*Action taken:*

MEETING PLAN

Purpose: _____   Location: _____

Date: _____   Time: _____

8:00 - 8:30	_____
8:30 - 9:00	_____
9:00 - 9:30	_____
9:30 - 10:00	_____
10:00 - 10:30	_____
10:30 - 11:00	_____
11:00 - 11:30	_____
11:30 - 12:00	_____
12:00 - 12:30	_____
12:30 - 1:00	_____
1:00 - 1:30	_____
1:30 - 2:00	_____
2:00 - 2:30	_____
2:30 - 3:00	_____
3:00 - 3:30	_____
3:30 - 4:00	_____
4:00 - 4:30	_____
4:30 - 5:00	_____
5:00 - 5:30	_____
5:30 - 6:00	_____
6:00 - 6:30	_____
6:30 - 7:00	_____
7:00 - 7:30	_____
7:30 - 8:00	_____
8:00 - 8:30	_____
8:30 - 9:00	_____

MEETING PLANNER

_____ Meeting   Date _____   Time _____

ITEMS	PRIORITY	RESULTS EXPECTED	PROBLEMS/ DECISIONS/ PLANS	INFO REQUIRED	PERSONS INVOLVED	TIME

Follow-Up

ITEMS	PERSONS RESPONSIBLE	RESULT	DUE DATE

DAILY GOALS

DATE _____

	PRIORITY	GOAL	✔
1			
2			
3			
4			
5			
6			
7			
8			
9			
10			

	GOAL #	ACTIVITY	DUE DATE	✔
1				
2				
3				
4				
5				
6				
7				
8				
9				
10				
11				
12				
13				
14				
15				
16				
17				
18				
19				
20				
21				
22				
23				
24				

DAILY PRIORITY PLANNER

DATE_____

MUST DO	COMPLETED ✔	FOLLOW-UP
1.		
2.		
3.		
4.		
5.		
6.		
7.		
8.		
9.		
10.		

CAN WAIT	COMPLETED ✔	FOLLOW-UP
1.		
2.		
3.		
4.		
5.		
6.		
7.		
8.		
9.		
10.		

TODAY'S ACTIVITIES

DATE _____

NOTES

1.
2.
3.
4.
5.
6.
7.
8.
9.
10.
11.
12.
13.
14.
15.
16.
17.
18.
19.
20.

EXPENSES	AMOUNT

DAILY PLANNER AND APPOINTMENTS

DATE _____

UNFINISHED FROM YESTERDAY	✔	SCHEDULE
		6:00
		6:30
		7:00
		7:30
		8:00
TODAY'S ACTIVITIES ✔		8:30
		9:00
D O		9:30
		10:00
		10:30
		11:00
		11:30
P H O N E		12:00
		12:30
		1:00
		1:30
		2:00
W R I T E		2:30
		3:00
		3:30
		4:00
		4:30
OTHER FOLLOW-UP ✔		5:00
		5:30
		6:00
		6:30
		7:00
		7:30
DO TOMORROW		NOTES

THINGS TO DO TODAY

DATE _____

MEET WITH:	✔

PHONE:	✔

WRITE TO:	✔

DAILY PLANNER AND APPOINTMENTS

DATE _____

FROM YESTERDAY	✔	TIME SCHEDULE
		6:00
		6:30
		7:00
		7:30
		8:00
		8:30
TODAY'S PRIORITIES	✔	9:00
		9:30
		10:00
D O		10:30
		11:00
		11:30
		12:00
P H O N E		12:30
		1:00
		1:30
		2:00
		2:30
W R I T E		3:00
		3:30
		4:00
		4:30
FOLLOW-UP	✔	5:00
		5:30
		6:00
		6:30
		7:00
		7:30

FOR TOMORROW	NOTES

URGENT ACTIVITIES

DATE _____

TIME REQUIRED	PRIORITY	ACTIVITY	✔

TIME ANALYSIS

DATE ______________

SCHEDULED TIME		ACTUAL TIME		ITEM	✓
TOTAL TIME	% OF TIME	TOTAL TIME	% OF TIME		

DAILY TIME SHEET

EMPLOYEE		DEPARTMENT		LOCATION	
DATE	EMPLOYEE NUMBER	SOCIAL SECURITY		PAYROLL CLASSIFICATION	

TIME RECORD FOR:
☐ SHIFT ☐ JOB ☐ CONTRACT ☐ _____ COMMENTS: _____

	CUSTOMER	SERVICE	SCHEDULED APPOINTMENT	TIME BEGAN	TIME STOPPED	TOTAL TIME	NEXT APPOINTMENT DAY/TIME
1							
2							
3							
4							
5							
6							
7							
8							
9							
10							
11							
12							
13							
14							
15							
16							
17							
18							
19							
20							

SUMMARY OF SERVICES RENDERED

☐ _____ # APPOINTMENTS _____ TIME _____

☐ _____ # APPOINTMENTS _____ TIME _____

☐ _____ # APPOINTMENTS _____ TIME _____

☐ _____ # APPOINTMENTS _____ TIME _____

☐ _____ # APPOINTMENTS _____ TIME _____

EMPLOYEE SIGNATURE   DATE

_____

SUPERVISOR SIGNATURE   DATE

_____

DATE

DAILY TRACKING

COMMITTEE/GROUP

Committee: _____ Date _____

Functions: _____

Specific Objectives: _____

Chair: _____

Participants:

Name:	Address	Phone

COMMITTEE REPORT

Items Accomplished: *Date*

_____

_____

_____

_____

_____

_____

_____

_____

_____

Future Activities:

_____

_____

_____

_____

_____

_____

_____

_____

_____

_____

_____

_____

_____

_____

_____

_____

_____

_____

_____

_____

_____

_____

_____

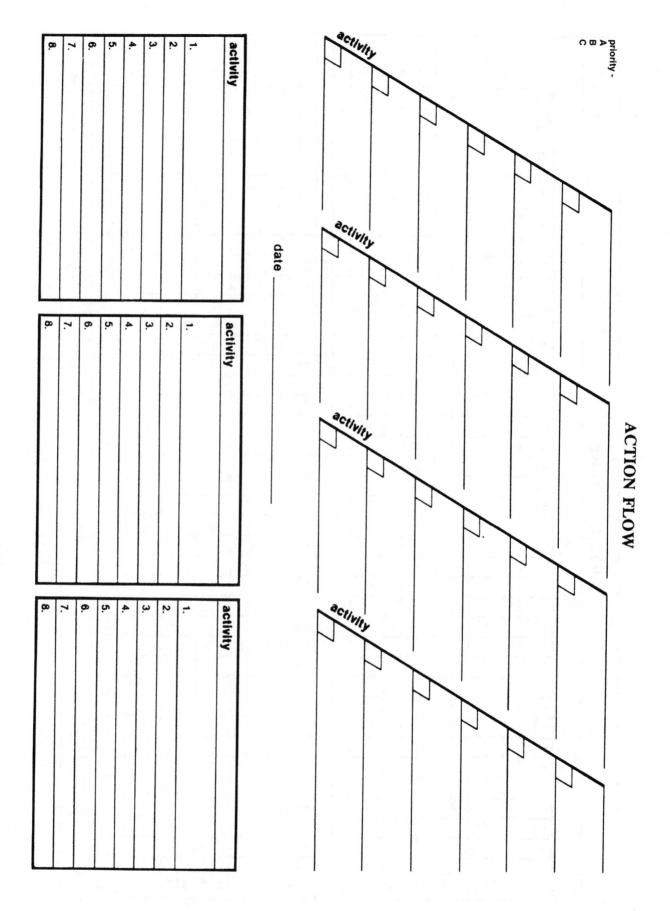

ACTION FLOW

priority -
A
B
C

activity

activity

activity

activity

activity

date _____

activity

1.
2.
3.
4.
5.
6.
7.
8.

activity

1.
2.
3.
4.
5.
6.
7.
8.

activity

1.
2.
3.
4.
5.
6.
7.
8.

HOURS WORKED

NUMBER

NAME

19	1	2	3	4	5	6	7	8	9	10	11	12	13	14	15	16	17	18	19	20	21	22	23	24	25	26	27	28	29	30	31	LATE HRS	LATE MIN	SICK	DAYS ABSENT EXC	DAYS ABSENT INEXC
JAN.																																					
FEB.																																					
MARCH																																					
APRIL																																					
MAY																																					
JUNE																																					
JULY																																					
AUG.																																					
SEPT.																																					
OCT.																																					
NOV.																																					
DEC.																																					
TOTAL																																					

19	1	2	3	4	5	6	7	8	9	10	11	12	13	14	15	16	17	18	19	20	21	22	23	24	25	26	27	28	29	30	31	LATE HRS	LATE MIN	SICK	DAYS ABSENT EXC	DAYS ABSENT INEXC
JAN.																																					
FEB.																																					
MARCH																																					
APRIL																																					
MAY																																					
JUNE																																					
JULY																																					
AUG.																																					
SEPT.																																					
OCT.																																					
NOV.																																					
DEC.																																					
TOTAL																																					

CODE: I – INEXCUSED ABSENCE V – VACATION L – LATE (SHOW NO. OF MINUTES LATE)

E – EXCUSED ABSENCE S – SICK

COMMENTS:

PERSONAL ATTENDANCE

WEEK ENDING _____

	HOURS WORKED						
	SUN	MON	TUE	WED	THU	FRI	SAT

OVERTIME SUMMARY

Day																

Date

Employee	Began Work	End Work	Over Time	Comments

DAILY TIME AND EXPENSE LOG

DATE _____

CLIENT/CUSTOMER	SERVICES RENDERED	TIME	
		HRS.	MIN.

EXPENSE	AMOUNT	COMMENTS
Travel		
Breakfast		
Lunch		
Dinner		
Lodging		
Tips		
Auto		
Tolls/Parking		
Telephone		
Entertainment		
TOTAL		

FOR TODAY

DAY _____

Appointments/Telephone Calls/Meetings:

_____   _____
_____   _____
_____   _____
_____

Item: Completed

1. _____ ☐

2. _____ ☐

3. _____ ☐

4. _____ ☐

5. _____ ☐

6. _____ ☐

7. _____ ☐

8. _____ ☐

9. _____ ☐

10. _____ ☐

11. _____ ☐

12. _____ ☐

13. _____ ☐

14. _____ ☐

15. _____ ☐

DAILY TIME AND EXPENSE LOG

DATE_____

SERVICES RENDERED	TIME	
	HRS.	MIN.

EXPENSE	AMOUNT	REASON FOR EXPENSE
Travel		
Breakfast		
Lunch		
Dinner		
Lodging		
Tips		
Auto		
Tolls/Parking		
Telephone		
Entertainment		
TOTAL		

PROFESSIONAL CHARGE SHEET

HOUR	DIARY	TIME	
		HRS.	MIN.

PROFESSIONAL TIME RECORD

	CLIENT	CHARGES		PAID		BALANCE	
7:00							
7:15							
7:30							
7:45							
8:00							
8:15							
8:30							
8:45							
9:00							
9:15							
9:30							
9:45							
10:00							
10:15							
10:30							
10:45							
11:00							
11:15							
11:30							
11:45							
12:00							
12:15							
12:30							
12:45							
1:00							
1:15							
1:30							
1:45							
2:00							
2:15							
2:30							
2:45							
3:00							
3:15							
3:30							
3:45							
4:00							
4:15							
4:30							
4:45							
5:00							
5:15							
5:30							
5:45							
6:00							
6:15							
6:30							
6:45							

30 MINUTE TIME LOG

7:00	
7:30	
8:00	
8:30	
9:00	
9:30	
10:00	
10:30	
11:00	
11:30	
12:00	
12:30	
1:00	
1:30	
2:00	
2:30	
3:00	
3:30	
4:00	
4:30	
5:00	
5:30	

THIS WEEK'S DEADLINES

WEEK OF _____

DAY								TIME NEEDED	ITEM	FOLLOW-UP	✔
S	M	T	W	T	F	S					

WEEKLY ORGANIZER

DATE _____

GOALS FOR WEEK

GOAL	✔	GOAL	✔		✔		✔

MONDAY

DO

PHONE

WRITE

TUESDAY

DO

PHONE

WRITE

WEDNESDAY

DO

PHONE

WRITE

THURSDAY

DO

PHONE

WRITE

FRIDAY

DO

PHONE

WRITE

SATURDAY/SUNDAY

DO

PHONE

WRITE

WEEKLY GOALS

WEEK OF _____

	PRIORITY	GOAL	✔
1			
2			
3			
4			
5			
6			
7			
8			
9			
10			

	GOAL #	ACTIVITY	DUE DATE	✔
1				
2				
3				
4				
5				
6				
7				
8				
9				
10				
11				
12				
13				
14				
15				
16				
17				
18				
19				
20				
21				
22				
23				
24				

WEEKLY PROJECTS

WEEK OF ___

DAY								ITEM	DATE NEEDED	FOLLOW-UP	FOLLOW-UP DATE	✔
S	M	T	W	T	F	S						

THIS WEEK'S PLANS

MONDAY   Date: ✔   ✔

1. _____ ☐   7. _____ ☐
2. _____ ☐   8. _____ ☐
3. _____ ☐   9. _____ ☐
4. _____ ☐   10. _____ ☐
5. _____ ☐   11. _____ ☐
6. _____ ☐   12. _____ ☐

TUESDAY   Date: ✔   ✔

1. _____ ☐   7. _____ ☐
2. _____ ☐   8. _____ ☐
3. _____ ☐   9. _____ ☐
4. _____ ☐   10. _____ ☐
5. _____ ☐   11. _____ ☐
6. _____ ☐   12. _____ ☐

WEDNESDAY   Date: ✔   ✔

1. _____ ☐   7. _____ ☐
2. _____ ☐   8. _____ ☐
3. _____ ☐   9. _____ ☐
4. _____ ☐   10. _____ ☐
5. _____ ☐   11. _____ ☐
6. _____ ☐   12. _____ ☐

THURSDAY   Date: ✔   ✔

1. _____ ☐   7. _____ ☐
2. _____ ☐   8. _____ ☐
3. _____ ☐   9. _____ ☐
4. _____ ☐   10. _____ ☐
5. _____ ☐   11. _____ ☐
6. _____ ☐   12. _____ ☐

FRIDAY   Date: ✔   ✔

1. _____ ☐   7. _____ ☐
2. _____ ☐   8. _____ ☐
3. _____ ☐   9. _____ ☐
4. _____ ☐   10. _____ ☐
5. _____ ☐   11. _____ ☐
6. _____ ☐   12. _____ ☐

WEEKLY WORKSHEET

MONDAY																
TUESDAY																
WEDNESDAY																
THURSDAY																
FRIDAY																

APPOINTMENTS THIS WEEK

	MONDAY	TUESDAY	WEDNESDAY	THURSDAY	FRIDAY
8:00					
8:30					
9:00					
9:30					
10:00					
10:30					
11:00					
11:30					
12:00					
12:30					
1:00					
1:30					
2:00					
2:30					
3:00					
3:30					
4:00					
4:30					
5:00					
5:30					

WEEKLY PLANNER

MONDAY	TUESDAY	WEDNESDAY	THURSDAY	FRIDAY

WEEKLY WORKSHEET

MON				
TUE				
WED				
THU				
FRI				

	MONDAY	TUESDAY	WEDNESDAY	THURSDAY	FRIDAY

WEEKLY WORKSHEET

WEEK-TO-WEEK ACTIVITIES DATE _____

1 - URGENT   **2 - HIGH PRIORITY**   **3 - LOW PRIORITY**

FROM LAST WEEK

PRIORITY		✔	PRIORITY		✔

FOR THIS WEEK

PRIORITY		✔	PRIORITY		✔

FOR NEXT WEEK

PRIORITY		✔	PRIORITY		✔

52 WEEK RECORD

1							1
2							2
3							3
4							4
5							5
6							6
7							7
8							8
9							9
10							10
11							11
12							12
13							13
14							14
15							15
16							16
17							17
18							18
19							19
20							20
21							21
22							22
23							23
24							24
25							25
26							26
27							27
28							28
29							29
30							30
31							31
32							32
33							33
34							34
35							35
36							36
37							37
38							38
39							39
40							40
41							41
42							42
43							43
44							44
45							45
46							46
47							47
48							48
49							49
50							50
51							51
52							52

TWO WEEK WORKSHEET

		MONDAY	TUESDAY	WEDNESDAY	THURSDAY	FRIDAY		MONDAY	TUESDAY	WEDNESDAY	THURSDAY	FRIDAY

14 DAY PLANNER

	SUNDAY	MONDAY	TUESDAY	WEDNESDAY	THURSDAY	FRIDAY	SATURDAY
	SUNDAY	MONDAY	TUESDAY	WEDNESDAY	THURSDAY	FRIDAY	SATURDAY

TWO WEEK PLANNER

SUNDAY	MONDAY	TUESDAY	WEDNESDAY	THURSDAY	FRIDAY	SATURDAY

SUNDAY	MONDAY	TUESDAY	WEDNESDAY	THURSDAY	FRIDAY	SATURDAY

TWO WEEK PLANNER

	MONDAY	TUESDAY	WEDNESDAY	THURSDAY	FRIDAY

MONDAY	TUESDAY	WEDNESDAY	THURSDAY	FRIDAY

TWO WEEK TRACKING

1											
2											
3											
4											
5											
6											
7											
8											
9											
10											
11											
12											
13											
14											

TWO WEEK TRACKING

1		
2		
3		
'4		
5		
6		
7		
8		
9		
10		
11		
12		
13		
14		

WEEKLY CALENDAR

DO THIS WEEK

☐ 1990
☐ 1991
☐ 1992
☐ 1993
☐ 1994
☐ 1995
☐ 1996
☐ 1997
☐ 1998
☐ 1999
☐ 2000
☐ 2001

☐ JANUARY
☐ FEBRUARY
☐ MARCH
☐ APRIL
☐ MAY
☐ JUNE
☐ JULY
☐ AUGUST
☐ SEPTEMBER
☐ OCTOBER
☐ NOVEMBER
☐ DECEMBER

FIND WHICH DAY THIS, THE PREVIOUS AND THE FOLLOWING MONTH BEGAN ON AND LABEL MONTHS BELOW

M		T	
T		F	
W		S	
		S	

MONDAY — DATE

TUESDAY — DATE

WEDNESDAY — DATE

THURSDAY — DATE

FRIDAY — DATE

SATURDAY — DATE

SUNDAY — DATE

B 53

100-YEAR CALENDAR

To use the 100-year calendar find the proper year in question. It is listed in the table on the facing page. The months of the year are identified by numbers 1-7. Select the desired month and refer to the corresponding tables.

Calendar 1

S	M	T	W	T	F	S
			1	2	3	4
5	6	7	8	9	10	11
12	13	14	15	16	17	18
19	20	21	22	23	24	25
26	27	28	29	30	31	

(Calendar 1 — month begins Sunday)

S	M	T	W	T	F	S
1	2	3	4	5	6	7
8	9	10	11	12	13	14
15	16	17	18	19	20	21
22	23	24	25	26	27	28
29	30	31				

Calendar 2

S	M	T	W	T	F	S
	1	2	3	4	5	6
7	8	9	10	11	12	13
14	15	16	17	18	19	20
21	22	23	24	25	26	27
28	29	30	31			

Calendar 3

S	M	T	W	T	F	S
		1	2	3	4	5
6	7	8	9	10	11	12
13	14	15	16	17	18	19
20	21	22	23	24	25	26
27	28	29	30	31		

Calendar 4

S	M	T	W	T	F	S
			1	2	3	4
5	6	7	8	9	10	11
12	13	14	15	16	17	18
19	20	21	22	23	24	25
26	27	28	29	30	31	

Calendar 5

S	M	T	W	T	F	S
				1	2	3
4	5	6	7	8	9	10
11	12	13	14	15	16	17
18	19	20	21	22	23	24
25	26	27	28	29	30	31

Calendar 6

S	M	T	W	T	F	S
					1	2
3	4	5	6	7	8	9
10	11	12	13	14	15	16
17	18	19	20	21	22	23
24	25	26	27	28	29	30
31						

Calendar 7

S	M	T	W	T	F	S
						1
2	3	4	5	6	7	8
9	10	11	12	13	14	15
16	17	18	19	20	21	22
23	24	25	26	27	28	29
30	31					

Year Tables

YEAR	JAN	FEB	MAR	APR	MAY	JUNE	JULY	AUG	SEPT	OCT	NOV	DEC
1900	2	5	5	1	3	6	1	4	7	2	5	7
1901	3	6	6	2	4	7	2	5	1	3	6	1
1902	4	7	7	3	5	1	3	6	2	4	7	2
1903	5	1	1	4	6	2	4	7	3	5	1	3
1904	6	2	3	6	1	4	6	2	5	7	3	5
1905	1	4	4	7	2	5	7	3	6	1	4	6
1906	2	5	5	1	3	6	1	4	7	2	5	7
1907	3	6	6	2	4	7	2	5	1	3	6	1
1908	4	7	1	4	6	2	4	7	3	5	1	3
1909	6	2	2	5	7	3	5	1	4	6	2	4
1910	7	3	3	6	1	4	6	2	5	7	3	5
1911	1	4	4	7	2	5	7	3	6	1	4	6
1912	2	5	6	2	4	7	2	5	1	3	6	1
1913	4	7	7	3	5	1	3	6	2	4	7	2
1914	5	1	1	4	6	2	4	7	3	5	1	3
1915	6	2	2	5	7	3	5	1	4	6	2	4
1916	7	3	4	7	2	5	7	3	6	1	4	6
1917	2	5	5	1	3	6	1	4	7	2	5	7
1918	3	6	6	2	4	7	2	5	1	3	6	1
1919	4	7	7	3	5	1	3	6	2	4	7	2
1920	5	1	2	5	7	3	5	1	4	6	2	4
1921	7	3	3	6	1	4	6	2	5	7	3	5
1922	1	4	4	7	2	5	7	3	6	1	4	6
1923	2	5	5	1	3	6	1	4	7	2	5	7
1924	3	6	7	3	5	1	3	6	2	4	7	2
1925	5	1	1	4	6	2	4	7	3	5	1	3
1926	6	2	2	5	7	3	5	1	4	6	2	4
1927	7	3	3	6	1	4	6	2	5	7	3	5
1928	1	4	5	1	3	6	1	4	7	2	5	7
1929	3	6	6	2	4	7	2	5	1	3	6	1
1930	4	7	7	3	5	1	3	6	2	4	7	2
1931	5	1	1	4	6	2	4	7	3	5	1	3
1932	6	2	3	6	1	4	6	2	5	7	3	5
1933	1	4	4	7	2	5	7	3	6	1	4	6

YEAR	JAN	FEB	MAR	APR	MAY	JUNE	JULY	AUG	SEPT	OCT	NOV	DEC
1934	2	5	5	1	3	6	1	4	7	2	5	7
1935	3	6	6	2	4	7	2	5	1	3	6	1
1936	4	7	1	4	6	2	4	7	3	5	1	3
1937	6	2	2	5	7	3	5	1	4	6	2	4
1938	7	3	3	6	1	4	6	2	5	7	3	5
1939	1	4	4	7	2	5	7	3	6	1	4	6
1940	2	5	6	2	4	7	2	5	1	3	6	1
1941	4	7	7	3	5	1	3	6	2	4	7	2
1942	5	1	1	4	6	2	4	7	3	5	1	3
1943	6	2	2	5	7	3	5	1	4	6	2	4
1944	7	3	4	7	2	5	7	3	6	1	4	6
1945	2	5	5	1	3	6	1	4	7	2	5	7
1946	3	6	6	2	4	7	2	5	1	3	6	1
1947	4	7	7	3	5	1	3	6	2	4	7	2
1948	5	1	2	5	7	3	5	1	4	6	2	4
1949	7	3	3	6	1	4	6	2	5	7	3	5
1950	1	4	4	7	2	5	7	3	6	1	4	6
1951	2	5	5	1	3	6	1	4	7	2	5	7
1952	3	6	7	3	5	1	3	6	2	4	7	2
1953	5	1	1	4	6	2	4	7	3	5	1	3
1954	6	2	2	5	7	3	5	1	4	6	2	4
1955	7	3	3	6	1	4	6	2	5	7	3	5
1956	1	4	5	1	3	6	1	4	7	2	5	7
1957	3	6	6	2	4	7	2	5	1	3	6	1
1958	4	7	7	3	5	1	3	6	2	4	7	2
1959	5	1	1	4	6	2	4	7	3	5	1	3
1960	6	2	3	6	1	4	6	2	5	7	3	5
1961	1	4	4	7	2	5	7	3	6	1	4	6
1962	2	5	5	1	3	6	1	4	7	2	5	7
1963	3	6	6	2	4	7	2	5	1	3	6	1
1964	4	7	1	4	6	2	4	7	3	5	1	3
1965	6	2	2	5	7	3	5	1	4	6	2	4
1966	7	3	3	6	1	4	6	2	5	7	3	5

YEAR	JAN	FEB	MAR	APR	MAY	JUNE	JULY	AUG	SEPT	OCT	NOV	DEC
1967	1	4	4	7	2	5	7	3	6	1	4	6
1968	2	5	6	2	4	7	2	5	1	3	6	1
1969	4	7	7	3	5	1	3	6	2	4	7	2
1970	5	1	1	4	6	2	4	7	3	5	1	3
1971	6	2	2	5	7	3	5	1	4	6	2	4
1972	7	3	4	7	2	5	7	3	6	1	4	6
1973	2	5	5	1	3	6	1	4	7	2	5	7
1974	3	6	6	2	4	7	2	5	1	3	6	1
1975	4	7	7	3	5	1	3	6	2	4	7	2
1976	5	1	2	5	7	3	5	1	4	6	2	4
1977	7	3	3	6	1	4	6	2	5	7	3	5
1978	1	4	4	7	2	5	7	3	6	1	4	6
1979	2	5	5	1	3	6	1	4	7	2	5	7
1980	3	6	7	3	5	1	3	6	2	4	7	2
1981	5	1	1	4	6	2	4	7	3	5	1	3
1982	6	2	2	5	7	3	5	1	4	6	2	4
1983	7	3	3	6	1	4	6	2	5	7	3	5
1984	1	4	5	1	3	6	1	4	7	2	5	7
1985	3	6	6	2	4	7	2	5	1	3	6	1
1986	4	7	7	3	5	1	3	6	2	4	7	2
1987	5	1	1	4	6	2	4	7	3	5	1	3
1988	6	2	3	6	1	4	6	2	5	7	3	5
1989	1	4	4	7	2	5	7	3	6	1	4	6
1990	2	5	5	1	3	6	1	4	7	2	5	7
1991	3	6	6	2	4	7	2	5	1	3	6	1
1992	4	7	1	4	6	2	4	7	3	5	1	3
1993	6	2	2	5	7	3	5	1	4	6	2	4
1994	7	3	3	6	1	4	6	2	5	7	3	5
1995	1	4	4	7	2	5	7	3	6	1	4	6
1996	2	5	6	2	4	7	2	5	1	3	6	1
1997	4	7	7	3	5	1	3	6	2	4	7	2
1998	5	1	1	4	6	2	4	7	3	5	1	3
1999	6	2	2	5	7	3	5	1	4	6	2	4
2000	7	3	4	7	2	5	7	3	6	1	4	6

THIS MONTH'S DEADLINES

MONTH _____

DATE NEEDED	TIME REQUIRED	ITEM	FOLLOW-UP	✔

MONTHLY CHECKLIST

MONTH OF	1	2	3	4	5	6	7	8	9	10	11	12	13	14	15	16	17	18	19	20	21	22	23	24	25	26	27	28	29	30	31

ONE MONTH RECAP

DAY	ITEM														
1															
2															
3															
4															
5															
6															
7															
8															
9															
10															
11															
12															
13															
14															
15															
16															
17															
18															
19															
20															
21															
22															
23															
24															
25															
26															
27															
28															
29															
30															
31															

ONE MONTH RECAP

1					
2					
3					
4					
5					
6					
7					
8					
9					
10					
11					
12					
13					
14					
15					
16					
17					
18					
19					
20					
21					
22					
23					
24					
25					
26					
27					
28					
29					
30					
31					

MONTH OF:

MONTHLY PLANNER

SUNDAY	MONDAY	TUESDAY	WEDNESDAY	THURSDAY	FRIDAY	SATURDAY
					1	2
3	4	5	6	7	8	9
10	11	12	13	14	15	16
17	18	19	20	21	22	23
24	25	26	27	28	29	30
31						

MONTH OF,

MONTHLY PLANNER

SUNDAY	MONDAY	TUESDAY	WEDNESDAY	THURSDAY	FRIDAY	SATURDAY
						1
2	3	4	5	6	7	8
9	10	11	12	13	14	15
16	17	18	19	20	21	22
23	24	25	26	27	28	29
30	31					

MONTHLY WORKSHEET

DATE																															DATE
1																															1
2																															2
3																															3
4																															4
5																															5
6																															6
7																															7
8																															8
9																															9
10																															10
11																															11
12																															12
13																															13
14																															14
15																															15
16																															16
17																															17
18																															18
19																															19
20																															20
21																															21
22																															22
23																															23
24																															24
25																															25
26																															26
27																															27
28																															28
29																															29
30																															30
31																															31

FIVE WEEK TRACKING

Monday					
Tuesday					
Wednesday					
Thursday					
Friday					
Monday					
Tuesday					
Wednesday					
Thursday					
Friday					
Monday					
Tuesday					
Wednesday					
Thursday					
Friday					
Monday					
Tuesday					
Wednesday					
Thursday					
Friday					
Monday					
Tuesday					
Wednesday					
Thursday					
Friday					

MONTH BY DAYS

Sunday	
Monday	
Tuesday	
Wednesday	
Thursday	
Friday	
Saturday	
Sunday	
Monday	
Tuesday	
Wednesday	
Thursday	
Friday	
Saturday	
Sunday	
Monday	
Tuesday	
Wednesday	
Thursday	
Friday	
Saturday	
Sunday	
Monday	
Tuesday	
Wednesday	
Thursday	
Friday	
Saturday	
Sunday	
Monday	
Tuesday	
Wednesday	
Thursday	
Friday	
Saturday	

MONTHLY TRACKING

1																			
2																			
3																			
4																			
5																			
6																			
7																			
8																			
9																			
10																			
11																			
12																			
13																			
14																			
15																			
16																			
17																			
18																			
19																			
20																			
21																			
22																			
23																			
24																			
25																			
26																			
27																			
28																			
29																			
30																			
31																			

THIS MONTH'S PLANS

MONTH OF _____, 19___

SUNDAY	MONDAY	TUESDAY	WEDNESDAY	THURSDAY	FRIDAY	SATURDAY

THIS MONTH'S PLANS

MONTH OF _____, 19__

1	
2	
3	
4	
5	
6	
7	
8	
9	
10	
11	
12	
13	
14	
15	
16	
17	
18	
19	
20	
21	
22	
23	
24	
25	
26	
27	
28	
29	
30	
31	

THREE MONTH GOALS

MONTHS OF: _____

	PRIORITY	GOAL	✔
1			
2			
3			
4			
5			
6			
7			
8			
9			
10			

	GOAL #	ACTIVITY	DUE DATE	✔
1				
2				
3				
4				
5				
6				
7				
8				
9				
10				
11				
12				
13				
14				
15				
16				
17				
18				
19				
20				
21				
22				
23				
24				

MONTHLY GOALS

MONTH _____

	PRIORITY	GOAL	✔
1			
2			
3			
4			
5			
6			
7			
8			
9			
10			

	GOAL #	ACTIVITY	DUE DATE	✔
1				
2				
3				
4				
5				
6				
7				
8				
9				
10				
11				
12				
13				
14				
15				
16				
17				
18				
19				
20				
21				
22				
23				
24				

FOUR MONTH PLANNER

MONTH:

SUNDAY	MONDAY	TUESDAY	WEDNESDAY	THURSDAY	FRIDAY	SATURDAY

MONTH:

SUNDAY	MONDAY	TUESDAY	WEDNESDAY	THURSDAY	FRIDAY	SATURDAY

MONTH:

SUNDAY	MONDAY	TUESDAY	WEDNESDAY	THURSDAY	FRIDAY	SATURDAY

MONTH:

SUNDAY	MONDAY	TUESDAY	WEDNESDAY	THURSDAY	FRIDAY	SATURDAY

THREE MONTH PLANNER

SUNDAY	MONDAY	TUESDAY	WEDNESDAY	THURSDAY	FRIDAY	SATURDAY

SUNDAY	MONDAY	TUESDAY	WEDNESDAY	THURSDAY	FRIDAY	SATURDAY

SUNDAY	MONDAY	TUESDAY	WEDNESDAY	THURSDAY	FRIDAY	SATURDAY

TWO MONTH PLANNER

SUNDAY	MONDAY	TUESDAY	WEDNESDAY	THURSDAY	FRIDAY	SATURDAY

SUNDAY	MONDAY	TUESDAY	WEDNESDAY	THURSDAY	FRIDAY	SATURDAY

TWO MONTH PLANNER

SUNDAY	MONDAY	TUESDAY	WEDNESDAY	THURSDAY	FRIDAY	SATURDAY

SUNDAY	MONDAY	TUESDAY	WEDNESDAY	THURSDAY	FRIDAY	SATURDAY

SIX MONTH GOALS

PERIOD OF _____

	PRIORITY	GOAL	✔
1			
2			
3			
4			
5			
6			
7			
8			
9			
10			

	GOAL #	ACTIVITY	DUE DATE	✔
1				
2				
3				
4				
5				
6				
7				
8				
9				
10				
11				
12				
13				
14				
15				
16				
17				
18				
19				
20				
21				
22				
23				
24				

MONTHLY PRIORITIES

DATE _____

DATE DUE:	HIGH PRIORITY		
	ACTIVITY	✔	FOLLOW-UP
	LOW PRIORITY		
	ACTIVITY	✔	FOLLOW-UP
	ON HOLD		
	ACTIVITY	✔	FOLLOW-UP

SIX MONTH PLANNER   19____

JULY	AUGUST	SEPTEMBER

OCTOBER	NOVEMBER	DECEMBER

SIX MONTH PLANNER

19____

JANUARY	FEBRUARY	MARCH

APRIL	MAY	JUNE

THIS YEAR'S DEADLINES

YEAR _____

MONTH NEEDED												DATE NEEDED	CODE	ITEM	FOLLOW-UP	✔
J	F	M	A	M	J	J	A	S	O	N	D					

ANNUAL GOALS

YEAR _____

	PRIORITY	GOAL	✔
1			
2			
3			
4			
5			
6			
7			
8			
9			
10			

	GOAL #	ACTIVITY	DUE DATE	✔
1				
2				
3				
4				
5				
6				
7				
8				
9				
10				
11				
12				
13				
14				
15				
16				
17				
18				
19				
20				
21				
22				
23				
24				

QUARTERLY TRACKING

		1	2	3	4	5	6	7	8	9	10	11	12	13		14	15	16	17	18	19	20	21	22	23	24	25	26		
		27	28	29	30	31	32	33	34	35	36	37	38	39		40	41	42	43	44	45	46	47	48	49	50	51	52		

FOUR QUARTER WORKSHEET

WEEK	1	2	3	4	5	6	7	8	9	10	11	12	13
FIRST QUARTER													

WEEK	14	15	16	17	18	19	20	21	22	23	24	25	26
SECOND QUARTER													

WEEK	27	28	29	30	31	32	33	34	35	36	37	38	39
THIRD QUARTER													

WEEK	40	41	42	43	44	45	46	47	48	49	50	51	52
FOURTH QUARTER													

FOUR QUARTER WORKSHEET

WEEK	
FIRST QUARTER	1
	2
	3
	4
	5
	6
	7
	8
	9
	10
	11
	12
	13
SECOND QUARTER	14
	15
	16
	17
	18
	19
	20
	21
	22
	23
	24
	25
	26
THIRD QUARTER	27
	28
	29
	30
	31
	32
	33
	34
	35
	36
	37
	38
	39
FOURTH QUARTER	40
	41
	42
	43
	44
	45
	46
	47
	48
	49
	50
	51
	52

ONE QUARTER TRACKING

Week											
1											
2											
3											
4											
5											
6											
7											
8											
9											
10											
11											
12											
13											

YEARLY TRACKING

YEAR DIVIDED BY WEEK/QUARTER	SUBJECT
1	
2	
3	
4	
5	
6	
7	
8	
9	
10	
11	
12	
13	
1ST QUARTER	
14	
15	
16	
17	
18	
19	
20	
21	
22	
23	
24	
25	
26	
2ND QUARTER	
6 MONTHS	
27	
28	
29	
30	
31	
32	
33	
34	
35	
36	
37	
38	
39	
3RD QUARTER	
9 MONTHS	
40	
41	
42	
43	
44	
45	
46	
47	
48	
49	
50	
51	
52	
4TH QUARTER	
YEAR TOTAL	

52 WEEK TRACKING

1			
2			
3			
4			
5			
6			
7			
8			
9			
10			
11			
12			
13			
14			
15			
16			
17			
18			
19			
20			
21			
22			
23			
24			
25			
26			
27			
28			
29			
30			
31			
32			
33			
34			
35			
36			
37			
38			
39			
40			
41			
42			
43			
44			
45			
46			
47			
48			
49			
50			
51			
52			

ONE YEAR PROGRESS SHEET

Jan.												Jan.
Feb.												Feb.
Mar.												Mar.
Apr.												Apr.
May												May
Jun.												Jun.
Jul.												Jul.
Aug.												Aug.
Sept.												Sept.
Oct.												Oct.
Nov.												Nov.
Dec.												Dec.

ONE YEAR PROGRESS SHEET

Jan.		Jan.
Feb.		Feb.
Mar.		Mar.
Apr.		Apr.
May		May
Jun.		Jun.
Jul.		Jul.
Aug.		Aug.
Sept.		Sept.
Oct.		Oct.
Nov.		Nov.
Dec.		Dec.

TWELVE MONTH WORKSHEET

19___

DATE	JAN.	FEB.	MAR.	APR.	MAY	JUN.	JUL.	AUG.	SEP.	OCT.	NOV.	DEC.
1												
2												
3												
4												
5												
6												
7												
8												
9												
10												
11												
12												
13												
14												
15												
16												
17												
18												
19												
20												
21												
22												
23												
24												
25												
26												
27												
28												
29												
30												
31												

SIX MONTH WORKSHEET

DATE	MONTH	MONTH	MONTH	MONTH	MONTH	MONTH
1						
2						
3						
4						
5						
6						
7						
8						
9						
10						
11						
12						
13						
14						
15						
16						
17						
18						
19						
20						
21						
22						
23						
24						
25						
26						
27						
28						
29						
30						
31						

ONE YEAR CHECKLIST

Year of ____

Item	J	F	M	A	M	J	J	A	S	O	N	D

52 WEEK CHECKLIST

YEAR _____

	1	2	3	4	5	6	7	8	9	10	11	12	13	14	15	16	17	18	19	20	21	22	23	24	25	26	27	28	29	30	31	32	33	34	35	36	37	38	39	40	41	42	43	44	45	46	47	48	49	50	51	52

52 WEEK WORKSHEET

WEEK	
1	
2	
3	
4	
5	
6	
7	
8	
9	
10	
11	
12	
13	
14	
15	
16	
17	
18	
19	
20	
21	
22	
23	
24	
25	
26	
27	
28	
29	
30	
31	
32	
33	
34	
35	
36	
37	
38	
39	
40	
41	
42	
43	
44	
45	
46	
47	
48	
49	
50	
51	
52	

ONE YEAR CHECKLIST

Year:	J	F	M	A	M	J	J	A	S	O	N	D

52 WEEK CHECKLIST

YEAR _____

ITEM	1	2	3	4	5	6	7	8	9	10	11	12	13	14	15	16	17	18	19	20	21	22	23	24	25	26	27	28	29	30	31	32	33	34	35	36	37	38	39	40	41	42	43	44	45	46	47	48	49	50	51	52

ONE YEAR PROGRESS SHEET

Jan.												Jan.
Feb.												Feb.
Mar.												Mar.
Apr.												Apr.
May												May
Jun.												Jun.
Jul.												Jul.
Aug.												Aug.
Sept.												Sept.
Oct.												Oct.
Nov.												Nov.
Dec.												Dec.

TWO YEARS BY MONTHS

YEAR:	
JAN	
FEB	
MAR	
APR	
MAY	
JUN	
JUL	
AUG	
SEP	
OCT	
NOV	
DEC	
YEAR:	
JAN	
FEB	
MAR	
APR	
MAY	
JUN	
JUL	
AUG	
SEP	
OCT	
NOV	
DEC	

TWO YEAR WORKSHEET

WEEK			WEEK
1			1
2			2
3			3
4			4
5			5
6			6
7			7
8			8
9			9
10			10
11			11
12			12
13			13
14			14
15			15
16			16
17			17
18			18
19			19
20			20
21			21
22			22
23			23
24			24
25			25
26			26
27			27
28			28
29			29
30			30
31			31
32			32
33			33
34			34
35			35
36			36
37			37
38			38
39			39
40			40
41			41
42			42
43			43
44			44
45			45
46			46
47			47
48			48
49			49
50			50
51			51
52			52

TWO YEAR CHECKLIST

ITEM	J	F	M	A	M	J	J	A	S	O	N	D

YEAR ____

ITEM	J	F	M	A	M	J	J	A	S	O	N	D

YEAR ____

TWO YEAR PROGRESS SHEET

Jan.							Jan.
Feb.							Feb.
Mar.							Mar.
Apr.							Apr.
May							May
Jun.							Jun.
Jul.							Jul.
Aug.							Aug.
Sept.							Sept.
Oct.							Oct.
Nov.							Nov.
Dec.							Dec.

Jan.							Jan.
Feb.							Feb.
Mar.							Mar.
Apr.							Apr.
May							May
Jun.							Jun.
Jul.							Jul.
Aug.							Aug.
Sept.							Sept.
Oct.							Oct.
Nov.							Nov.
Dec.							Dec.

TWO YEAR PROGRESS SHEET

Jan.		Jan.
Feb.		Feb.
Mar.		Mar.
Apr.		Apr.
May		May
Jun.		Jun.
Jul.		Jul.
Aug.		Aug.
Sept.		Sept.
Oct.		Oct.
Nov.		Nov.
Dec.		Dec.

Jan.		Jan.
Feb.		Feb.
Mar.		Mar.
Apr.		Apr.
May		May
Jun.		Jun.
Jul.		Jul.
Aug.		Aug.
Sept.		Sept.
Oct.		Oct.
Nov.		Nov.
Dec.		Dec.

THREE YEARS BY MONTHS

YEAR:	
JAN	
FEB	
MAR	
APR	
MAY	
JUN	
JUL	
AUG	
SEP	
OCT	
NOV	
DEC	
YEAR:	
JAN	
FEB	
MAR	
APR	
MAY	
JUN	
JUL	
AUG	
SEP	
OCT	
NOV	
DEC	
YEAR:	
JAN	
FEB	
MAR	
APR	
MAY	
JUN	
JUL	
AUG	
SEP	
OCT	
NOV	
DEC	

FOUR YEARS BY MONTHS

YEAR.													YEAR.												
	JAN	FEB	MAR	APR	MAY	JUN	JUL	AUG	SEP	OCT	NOV	DEC		JAN	FEB	MAR	APR	MAY	JUN	JUL	AUG	SEP	OCT	NOV	DEC
YEAR.													YEAR.												
	JAN	FEB	MAR	APR	MAY	JUN	JUL	AUG	SEP	OCT	NOV	DEC		JAN	FEB	MAR	APR	MAY	JUN	JUL	AUG	SEP	OCT	NOV	DEC

THREE YEAR CHECKLIST

Year:	J	F	M	A	M	J	J	A	S	O	N	D

Year:	J	F	M	A	M	J	J	A	S	O	N	D

Year:	J	F	M	A	M	J	J	A	S	O	N	D

FIVE YEAR TRACKING

Years

	J F M A M J J A S O N D	J F M A M J J A S O N D	J F M A M J J A S O N D
1			
2			
3			
4			
5			
6			
7			
8			
9			
10			
11			
12			
13			
14			
Total		1 2 3 4 5	

Subject List	J F M A M J J A S O N D	J F M A M J J A S O N D	J F M A M J J A S O N D
1			
2			
3			
4			
5			
6			
7			
8			
9			
10			
11			
12			
13			
14			
Total			

FOUR YEAR CHECKLIST

Year:

J F M A M J J A S O N D

Year:

J F M A M J J A S O N D

Year:

J F M A M J J A S O N D

Year:

J F M A M J J A S O N D

LONG RANGE GOALS

DATE _____

	PRIORITY	GOAL	✔
1			
2			
3			
4			
5			
6			
7			
8			
9			
10			

	GOAL #	ACTIVITY	DUE DATE	✔
1				
2				
3				
4				
5				
6				
7				
8				
9				
10				
11				
12				
13				
14				
15				
16				
17				
18				
19				
20				
21				
22				
23				
24				

Alabama 205
Alaska 907
Arizona 602
Arkansas 501

California
Alhambra 818
Anaheim 714
Bakersfield 805
Berkeley 510
Beverly Hills 310
Burbank 818
Burlingame 415
Claremont 714
Covina 818
Downey 310
Eureka 707
Fremont 510
Fresno 209
Long Beach 213
Los Gatos 408
Los Angeles 213
Manhattan Beach 213
Merced 209
Milpitas 408
Monterey 408
Monterey Pk. 818
Novato 415
Ontario 714
Palm Springs 619
Palo Alto 415
Pasadena 818
Redondo Bch. 310
Riverside 714
Sacramento 916
Salinas 408
San Diego 619
San Francisco 415
San Jose 408
San Rafael 415
Santa Clara 408
Santa Rosa 707
Simi Valley 805
S. Whittier 213
Stockton 209
Torrance 310
Vallejo 707
Visalia 209
Whittier 310

CANADA
Alberta 403
British Columbia 604
Manitoba 204
N. Brunswick 506
Newfoundland 709
Nova Scotia 902
Ontario
Ft. William 807
London 519
North Bay 705
Ottawa 613
Thunder Bay 807
Toronto 416
Prince Edward Island 902
Quebec
Montreal 514
Quebec 418
Sherbrooke 819
Saskatchewan 306

CARRIBEAN
All islands 809

Colorado
Aspen 303
Colorado Springs 719
Denver 303
Gd. Junction 303
Pueblo 719
Woodland Pk. 719

Connecticut 203

Delaware 302

District of Columbia 202

Florida
Boca Raton 407
Daytona Bch. 904
Fort Lauderdale 305
Fort Myers 813
Jacksonville 904
Key West 305
Miami 305
Orlando 407
Pensacola 904
Pompano Bch. 305
St. Petersburg 813
Tallahassee 904
West Palm Beach 407

Georgia
Albany 912
Athens 706
Atlanta 404
Augusta 706
La Grange 706
Macon 912
Marietta 404
Savannah 912

Hawaii 808

Idaho 208

Illinois
Aurora 708
Belleville 618
Bloomington 309
Carbondale 618
Chicago 312
Chicago Hgts. 708
Cicero 708
Danville 217
Decatur 217
East St. Louis 618
Elgin 708
Joliet 815
Kankakee 815
Moline 309
Niles 312
Normal 309
North Chicago 708
Park Ridge 708
Peoria 309
Rockford 815
Rock Island 309
Skokie 708
Springfield 217
Urbana 217
Waukegan 708

Indiana
Bloomington 812
Evansville 812
Fort Wayne 219
Gary 219
Indianapolis 317
Kokomo 317
Marion 317
South Bend 219
Terre Haute 812

Iowa
Ames 515
Burlington 319
Cedar Rapids 319
Cncl. Bluffs 712
Des Moines 515
Fort Dodge 515
Ottumwa 515
Sioux City 712
Waterloo 319

Kansas
Emporia 316
Hutchinson 316
Salina 913
Topeka 913
Wichita 316

Kentucky
Covington 606
Frankfort 502
Lexington 606
Louisville 502
Paducah 502

Louisiana
Alexandria 318
Baton Rouge 504
Lafayette 318
Monroe 318
New Orleans 504
Shreveport 318

Maine 207

Maryland
Annapolis 410
Baltimore 410
Cumberland 301
Frederick 301
La Plata 301
Ocean City 410
Rockville 301
Salisbury 410

Massachusetts
Barnstable 508
Beverly 508
Boston 617
Lexington 617
Lowell 508
Lynn 617
Marblehead 617
Nantucket 508
Pittsfield 413
Springfield 413
Taunton 508
Weymouth 617
Worcester 508

Michigan
Ann Arbor 313
Battle Creek 616
Bay City 517
Birmingham 810
Dearborn 313
Detroit 313
East Detroit 810
Ferndale 810
Flint 810
Grand Rapids 616
Highland Park 313
Jackson 517
Kalamazoo 616
Lansing 517
Pontiac 810
Port Huron 810
Saginaw 517
St. Clair Shores 810
Troy 810

Minnesota
Duluth 218
Mankato 507
Minneapolis 612
Moorhead 218
Rochester 507
St. Cloud 612
St. Paul 612
Winona 507

Mississippi 601

Missouri
Afton 314
Columbia 314
Jeff. City 314
Joplin 417
Kansas City 816
St. Louis 314
Sedalia 816
Springfield 417
Suburbs 816

Montana 406

Nebraska
Grand Island 308
Hastings 402
Lincoln 402
North Platte 308
Omaha 402

Nevada 702

New Hampshire
All points 603

New Jersey
Asbury Park 908
Atlantic City 609
Barnegat 609
Bayonne 201
Bound Brook 908
Camden 609
Dover 201
Elizabeth 908
Fort Dix 609
Jersey City 201
Lakewood 908
Long Branch 908
Madison 201
Morristown 201
Mount Holly 609
Newark 201
New Brunswick 908
Newton 201
Paterson 201
Perth Amboy 908
Phillipsburg 908
Princeton 609
Summit 908
Trenton 609

New Mexico 505

New York
Albany & Suburbs 518
Amsterdam 518
Binghamton 607
Bronx 718
Bronxville 914
Brooklyn 718
Buffalo & Suburbs 716
Carmel 914
Cold Spring 914
Cortland 607
Elmira 607
Endicott 607
Fallsburg 914
Fire Island 516
Gloversville 518
Hudson 518
Ithaca 607
Jamestown 716
Kennedy Int'l Airport 718
Kingston 914
Lancaster 716
Livingston Manor 914
Long Island 516
Manhattan 212
Massena 315
Nassau Cty. 516
Newburgh 914
Olean 716
Oneonta 607
Plattsburgh 518
Poughkeepsie 914
Queens 718
Rochester 716
Schenectady 518
Staten Island 718
Suffolk Cty. 516
Syracuse & Suburbs 315
Troy 518
Utica & Suburbs 315
Watertown 315
Westchester County 914
White Plains 914
Yonkers 914

North Carolina
Asheville 704
Camp LeJeune 919
Charlotte 704
Fayetteville 919
Fort Bragg 919
Greensboro 919
High Point 919
Lexington 704
Raleigh 919
Salisbury 704
Wilmington 919
Winston Slm. 919

North Dakota 701

Ohio
Canton 216
Cincinnati 513
Cleveland 216
Columbus 614
Dayton 513
E. Liverpool 216
Elyria 216
Lancaster 614
Lima 419
Mansfield 419
Marion 614
Massillon 216
Portsmouth 614
Sandusky 419
Springfield 513
Steubenville 614
Toledo 419
Youngstown 216

Oklahoma
Bartlesville 918
Oklahoma C. 405
Ponca City 405
Shawnee 405
Tulsa 918

Oregon 503

Pennsylvania
Allentown 215
Altoona 814
Bradford 814
Chambersbrg 717
DuBois 814
Easton 215
Erie 814
Greensburg 412
Harrisburg 717
Hazelton 717
Indiana 412
Johnstown 814
Lancaster 717
McKeesport 412
Philadelphia 215
Pittsburgh 412
Reading 215
Scranton 717
Sharon 412
State College 814
Stroudsburg 717
Uniontown 412
Williamsport 717
York 717

Rhode Island 401

S. Carolina 803

S. Dakota 605

Tennessee
Clarksville 615
Jackson 901
Knoxville 615
Memphis 901
Nashville 615

Texas
Abilene 915
Amarillo 806
Arlington 817
Austin 512
Beaumont 409
Brownsville 512
Bryan 409
Crp. Christi 512
Dallas 214
Denison 903
Denton 817
El Paso 915
Farmers Brch. 903
Fort Hood 817
Fort Worth 817
Galveston 409
Garland 903
Gd. Prairie 903
Houston 713
Irving 214
Killeen 817
Lubbock 806
Mesquite 214
Midland 915
Nacogdoches 409
Paris 903
Richardson 214
San Angelo 915
San Antonio 512
Tyler 903
Victoria 512
Waco 817
Wharton 409
Wichita Falls 817

Utah 801

Vermont 802

Virginia
Alexandria 703
Charlottsvlle 804
Covington 703
Danville 804
Lynchburg 804
Richmond 804
Roanoke 703
Staunton 703
Va. Beach 804

Washington
Fort Lewis 206
Richland 509
Seattle 206
Spokane 509
Vancouver 206
Yakima 509

W. Virginia 304

Wisconsin
Beloit 608
Eau Claire 715
Green Bay 414
Janesville 608
LaCrosse 608
Madison 608
Milwaukee 414
Stevens Pt. 715
Superior 715
Wausau 715

Wyoming 307

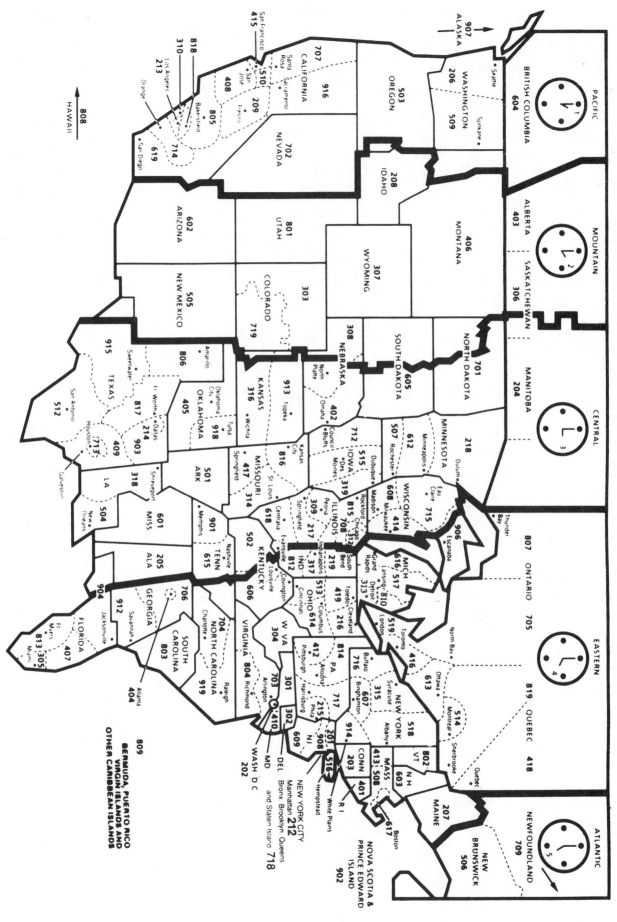

NATIONAL AREA CODE MAP REFERENCE GUIDE

General Planners

1		
2		
3		
4		
5		
6		
7		
8		
9		
10		
11		
12		
13		
14		
15		
16		
17		
18		
19		
20		
21		
22		
23		
24		
25		
26		
27		
28		
29		
30		
31		
32		
33		
34		
35		
36		
37		
38		
39		
40		
41		
42		
43		
44		
45		
46		
47		
48		
49		
50		
51		
52		

1			
2			
3			
4			
5			
6			
7			
8			
9			
10			
11			
12			
13			
14			
15			
16			
17			
18			
19			
20			
21			
22			
23			
24			
25			
26			
27			
28			
29			
30			
31			
32			

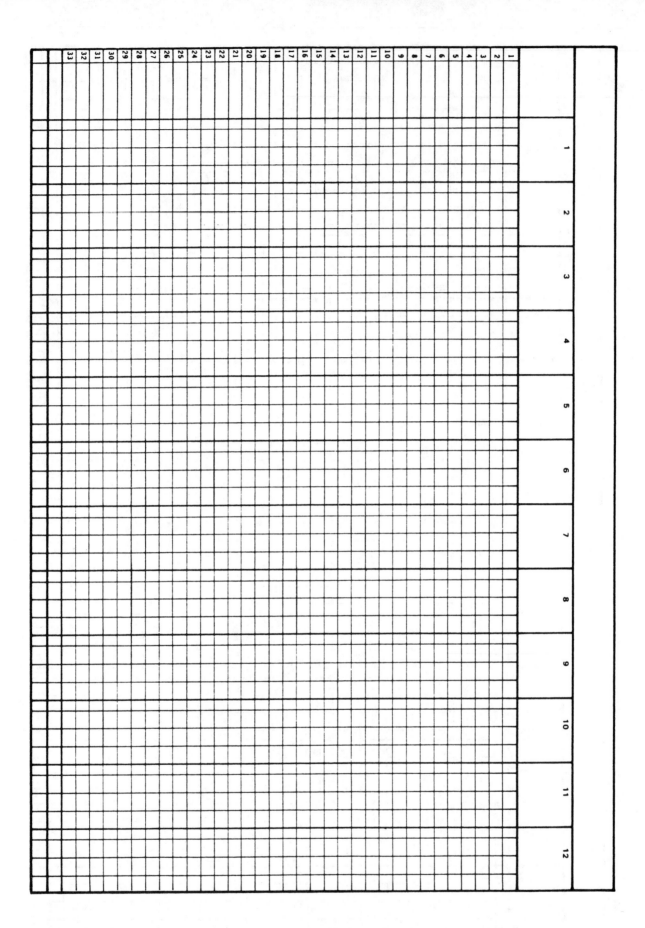

B 114

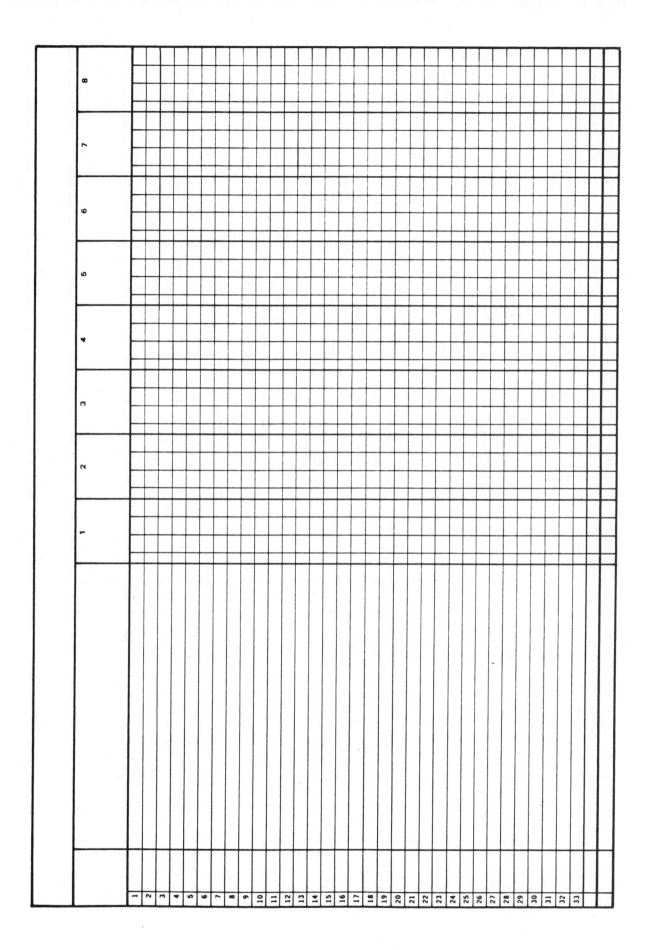

		1	2	3	4	5	6	7	8	9	10
1											
2											
3											
4											
5											
6											
7											
8											
9											
10											
11											
12											
13											
14											
15											
16											
17											
18											
19											
20											
21											
22											
23											
24											
25											
26											
27											
28											
29											
30											
31											
32											
33											

		1	2	3	4	5	6
1							
2							
3							
4							
5							
6							
7							
8							
9							
10							
11							
12							
13							
14							
15							
16							
17							
18							
19							
20							
21							
22							
23							
24							
25							
26							
27							
28							
29							
30							
31							
32							
33							

			1				2				3				4			
1																		
2																		
3																		
4																		
5																		
6																		
7																		
8																		
9																		
10																		
11																		
12																		
13																		
14																		
15																		
16																		
17																		
18																		
19																		
20																		
21																		
22																		
23																		
24																		
25																		
26																		
27																		
28																		
29																		
30																		
31																		
32																		
33																		

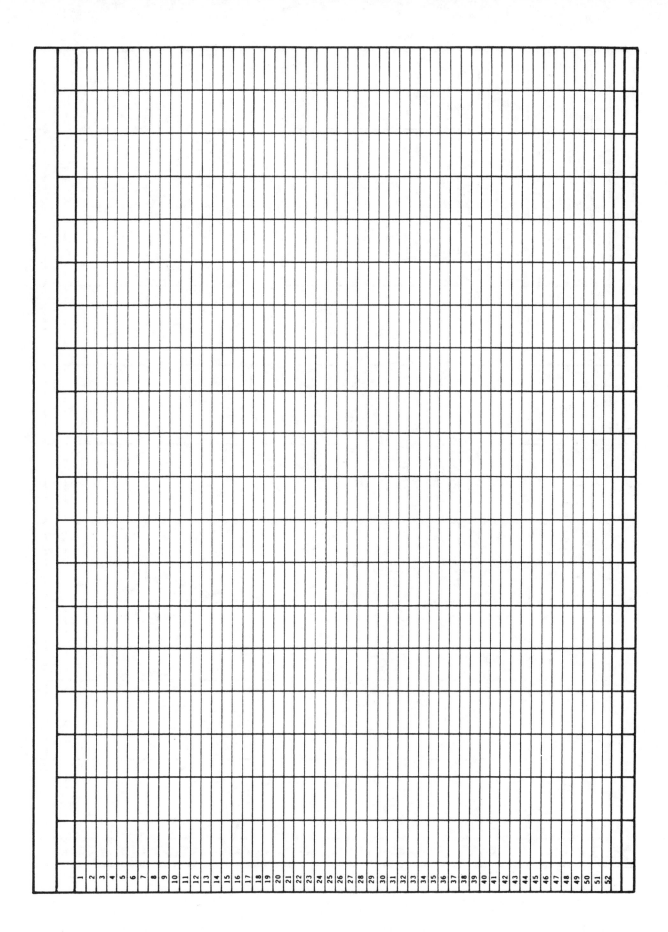

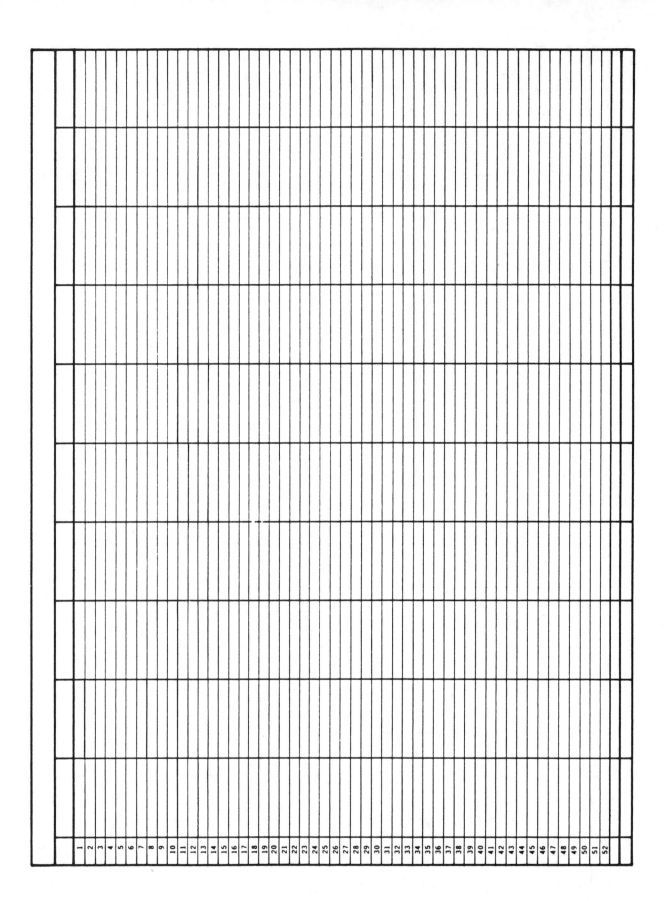

B 120

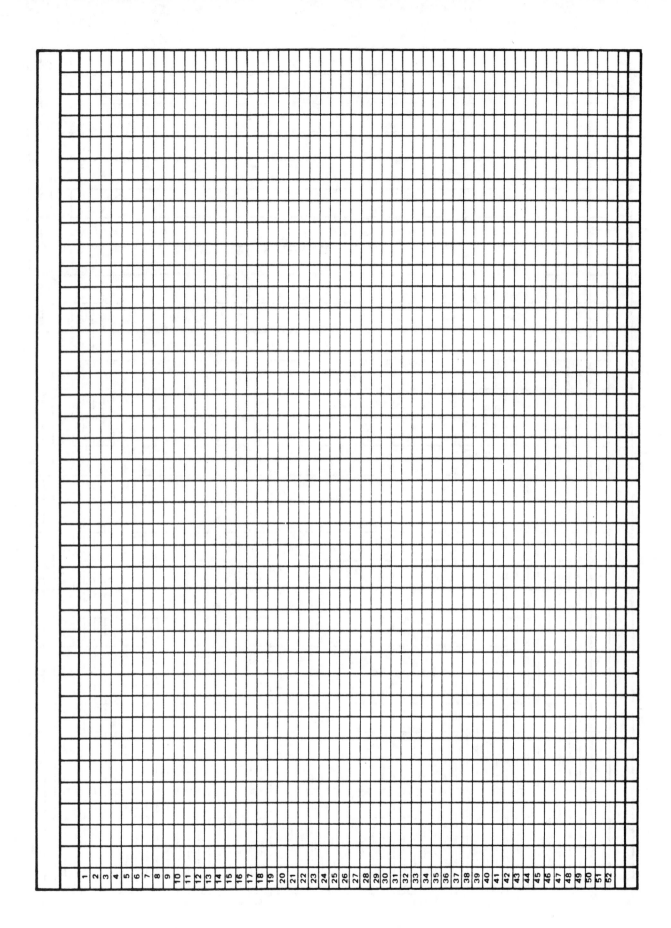

1 2 3 4 5 6 7 8 9 10 11 12 13 14 15 16 17 18 19 20 21 22 23 24 25 26 27 28 29 30 31 32 33 34 35 36 37 38 39 40 41 42 43 44 45 46 47 48 49 50 51 52

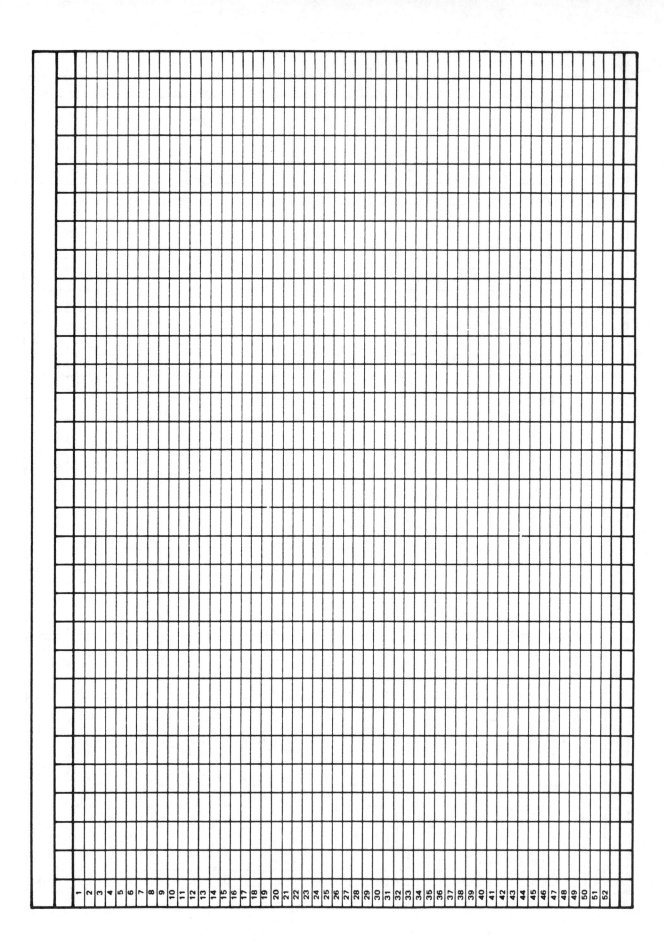

B 122

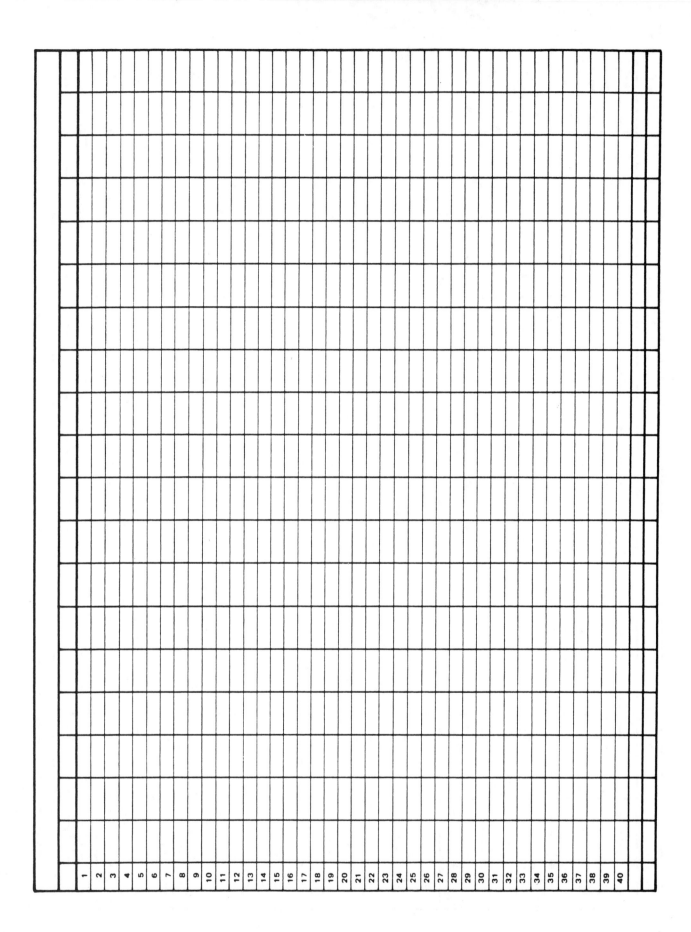

	1	2	3	4	5	6	7	8	9	10	11	12	13	14	15	16	17	18	19	20	21	22	23	24	25	26	27	28	29	30	31	32	33	34	35	36	37	38	39	40

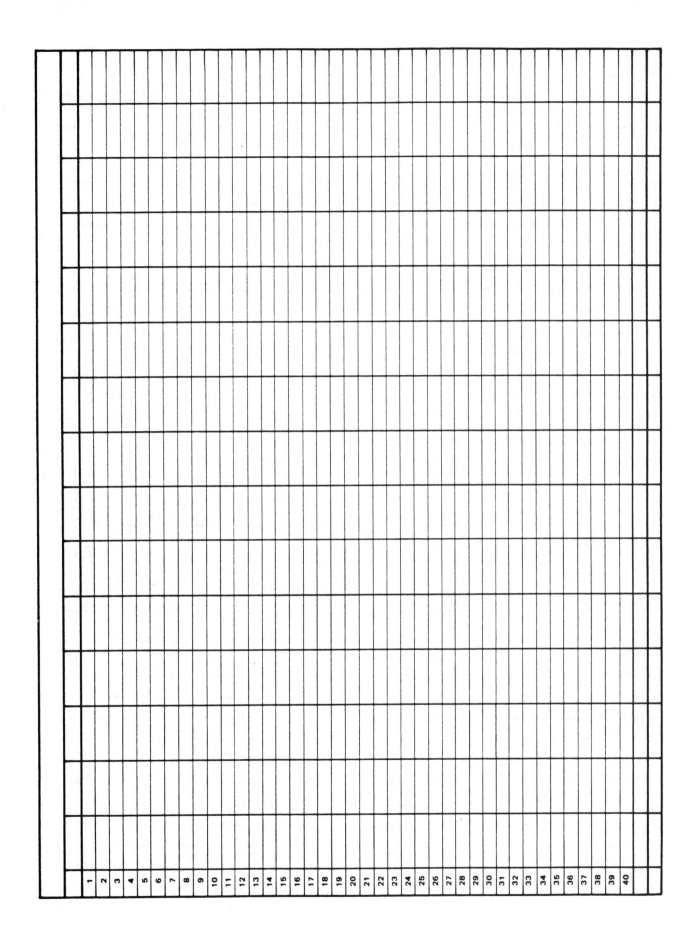

1　2　3　4　5　6　7　8　9　10　11　12　13　14　15　16　17　18　19　20　21　22　23　24　25　26　27　28　29　30　31　32　33　34　35　36　37　38　39　40

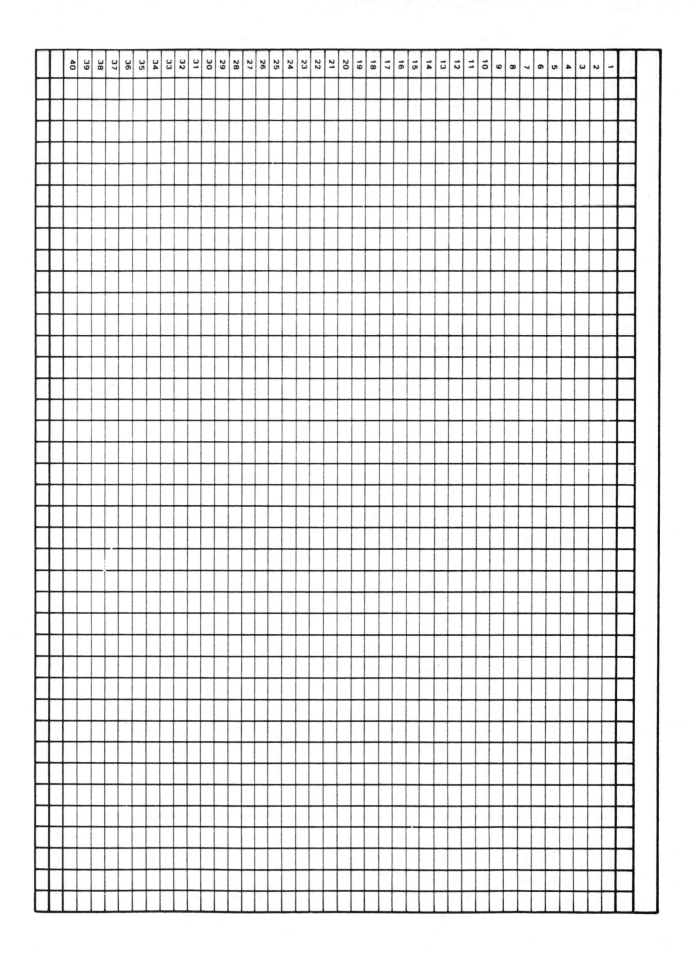

Projects

SEVEN DAY APPOINTMENTS

	SUNDAY	MONDAY	TUESDAY	WEDNESDAY	THURSDAY	FRIDAY	SATURDAY
8:00							
8:30							
9:00							
9:30							
10:00							
10:30							
11:00							
11:30							
12:00							
12:30							
1:00							
1:30							
2:00							
2:30							
3:00							
3:30							
4:00							
4:30							
5:00							
5:30							

WEEKLY PROJECTS

WEEK OF _____

ITEM	DATE NEEDED	FOLLOW-UP	FOLLOW-UP DATE	✔

DAY							
S	M	T	W	T	F	S	

MONTHLY PROJECT REVIEW

DATE _____

DATE	GOAL	ITEM	INITIAL TARGET DATE	NEW TARGET DATE	FOLLOW-UP	✔

LAST REVIEW/UPDATE	NEXT REVIEW/UPDATE

WEEKLY PROJECTS

WEEK OF ———————

	DAY				ITEM	DATE NEEDED	FOLLOW-UP	FOLLOW-UP DATE	✓
	M	T	W	T	F				

3 MONTH GOALS

Period Ending: _____

Priority	Goal	Completed (✔)
_____	_____	_____
_____	_____	_____
_____	_____	_____
_____	_____	_____
_____	_____	_____
_____	_____	_____
_____	_____	_____

ACTIVITY TO COMPLETE GOALS

Activity	Assigned To	Completion Date
_____	_____	_____
_____	_____	_____
_____	_____	_____
_____	_____	_____
_____	_____	_____
_____	_____	_____
_____	_____	_____
_____	_____	_____
_____	_____	_____

KEY PROJECT CONTROL

Project No.	Project/Activity	Assigned To	Completion Date	Last Review Date
———	———	———	———	———
———	———	———	———	———
———	———	———	———	———
———	———	———	———	———
———	———	———	———	———
———	———	———	———	———
———	———	———	———	———
———	———	———	———	———
———	———	———	———	———
———	———	———	———	———
———	———	———	———	———
———	———	———	———	———
———	———	———	———	———
———	———	———	———	———
———	———	———	———	———
———	———	———	———	———
———	———	———	———	———
———	———	———	———	———
———	———	———	———	———
———	———	———	———	———
———	———	———	———	———
———	———	———	———	———

6 MONTH GOALS

Period Ending: _____

Priority	Goal	Completed (✔)
_____	_____	_____
_____	_____	_____
_____	_____	_____
_____	_____	_____
_____	_____	_____
_____	_____	_____
_____	_____	_____

ACTIVITY TO COMPLETE GOALS

Activity	Assigned To	Completion Date
_____	_____	_____
_____	_____	_____
_____	_____	_____
_____	_____	_____
_____	_____	_____
_____	_____	_____
_____	_____	_____
_____	_____	_____
_____	_____	_____
_____	_____	_____

12 MONTH GOALS

Period Ending: _____

Priority	Objective	Completed (✔)
_____	_____	_____
_____	_____	_____
_____	_____	_____
_____	_____	_____
_____	_____	_____
_____	_____	_____
_____	_____	_____

ACTIVITY TO COMPLETE GOALS

Project	Assigned To	Target Date
_____	_____	_____
_____	_____	_____
_____	_____	_____
_____	_____	_____
_____	_____	_____
_____	_____	_____
_____	_____	_____
_____	_____	_____
_____	_____	_____
_____	_____	_____

PROJECT FOLLOW-UP

DATE _____

PRIORITY KEY:
1 - URGENT   2 - HIGH PRIORITY   3 - LOW PRIORITY

PRIORITY	DATE NEEDED	FOLLOW-UP	FOLLOW-UP DATE	✓

PROJECT DELAYS

ACTIVITY	REPORT DATE	REASON FOR DELAY	RESPONSIBLE PERSON	NEW START DATE?	NEW FINISH DATE?	COMMENTS

PROJECT COST SUMMARY

Appropriation Detail

Project Title _____ Purpose of Request _____

Project Number _____ Cost Distribution _____

Date of Request _____ Completion date _____

Requested by _____

Budget/Dept. _____

Approval Date _____

Project Description _____
_____
_____

Project Justification _____
_____
_____

Investment Summary

	Projections				Actual		
	Start-up	1st Full Yr.	5-Yr. Total	10-Yr. Total	Proj. Total	Start-up	1st Full Yr.	5-Yr. Total
Capital Investment								
Working Capital								
Total Investment								
Sales								
Net Income								
Cash Flow								
Discounted ROI								
Payback in Yrs.								

Comments:

Approvals

By _____ By _____

Title _____ Title _____

Date _____ Date _____

B 139

PROJECT EXPENDITURE REVIEW

PROJECT _____ WEEK ENDING _____ SIGNED _____

Item	Original Completion Cost	Actual Cost to Date	% Complete	Over/(Under)			
				This Week	Last Week	Difference	Completion Cost
TOTALS							

ONE YEAR PROJECT PROGRESS

PROJECT:_____   START DATE:_____

PHASE COMPLETED	RESPONSIBLE PERSON	12-Month Progress																

SIX MONTH PROJECT PROGRESS

PROJECT: _____

START DATE _____

TARGET DATE _____

PROGRESS ACTIVITY	PERSON/DEPT.	1	2	3	4	5	6	7	8	9	10	11	12	13	14	15	16	17	18	19	20	21	22	23	24

WEEKS

PROJECT REPORT

Project title: _____

Start date: _____

Estimated completion date: _____

Total estimated project cost: _____

      Budget: 19 _____   **$** _____
                   19 _____   **$** _____

      To complete: **$** _____

Project no.: _____

Priority: _____

Target date: _____

Approved project cost: _____

Review date _____

                                  (year-to-date)

Budget: **$** _____   **$** _____

Actual: **$** _____   **$** _____

Accomplished to date (or since last review): _____

_____

_____

_____

_____

Comments: _____

_____

_____

_____

_____

Signed: _____   Review date: _____

PROJECT ASSIGNMENT RECORD

Date Assigned	Assignment	Assigned To	Due Date	Comments

PROJECT SCHEDULE

DATE _____

PROJECT	START DATE	NEW TARGET DATE	ORIGINAL DUE DATE	PROGRESS TO DATE

PROJECT PLAN

SCHEDULED		ACTUAL		PROJECTS/ITEM	✔
Start	Finish	Start	Finish		

FOR _____

PROJECTS

DATE _____

PROJECT	PRIORITY	ACTIVITY	DUE DATE	✔	FOLLOW-UP

COMMENTS

KEY PROJECT CONTROL

Project	Assigned To	Due Date	Last Review Date

Executive
and
Administrative

MASTER FILE INDEX

*P = Permanent Direct Access   R = Rotational Consecutive

First Name/Title		External Label	Internal Label	Shelf

FILE DESCRIPTION

Group Name

Data Name	Description	Source	Size	Data	Volume	Frequency

FILE SHEET

Date: _____

Project:	Source:	Prepared by:

File name:		File number:

File location:	Storage location:

Access via:

_____

Sequenced by:

_____

Content qualifications:

_____

Age:

_____

Retention period:

_____

Labels:

_____

Notes

Message	Volume		Char. Message	Char. file	
	Avg.	Peak		Avg.	Peak

COMPUTER SOFTWARE RECORD

Software Name			Release Date	Date Received
Modification No.	Date Rec'd.	Date Updated	Notes	

TELEPHONE INDEX

NAME	ADDRESS	AREA CODE	TELEPHONE

TELEPHONE/FAX CALLS

DATE _____

PERSON TO CALL	COMPANY	TELEPHONE	FAX	COM-PLETED ✓	CALL BACK ✓	WILL RETURN CALL ✓	COMMENTS

TELEPHONE/FAX LOG

DATE	CALLER		COMPANY/PERSON			AREA	NUMBER	TEL	FAX	CALLING TIME	CHARGED TO	CHARGES
	NAME	DEPT.	NAME	CITY	STATE	CODE						

TELEPHONE LOG

TIME PERIOD _____

TIME	LENGTH OF CALL	CALLED ✓	RECEIVED ✓	SPOKE TO	PURPOSE	PERSONAL ✓	BUSINESS ✓	RESULT	CHARGE

IN-OUT RECORD

DEPARTMENT _____ DAY _____ DATE _____

NAME	EXT	IN ✓	OUT ✓	IN ✓	OUT ✓	IN ✓	OUT ✓	IN ✓	OUT ✓

MEMO

DATE:
TO:
FROM:
SUBJECT:

PERPETUAL INVENTORY CONTROL

Department: _____

Item: _____ Item number: _____ Page number: _____

Ordered			
Date	Order number	Quantity	Due date

Sold/Disposed of				
Date	Order number	Quantity	Balance	Notes

Received		
Date	Order number	Quantity

INVENTORY

Department/Item category										

Department/Item category

Date	19
Sheet completed (date/time)	Sheet # Folio #
Priced by	Date
Called by Date	Extended by Date
Entered by Date	Examined by Date

ITEM #	DESCRIPTION	✔	QUANTITY	UNIT	PRICE	UNIT	EXTENSION
	Amount forward						

OUT OF STOCK REPORT

Date: _____ Re: Your order no: _____ Order date: _____

To: _____

_____

_____

Item	Description	Quantity

Your order cannot be filled as we are temporarily out of stock on the above. Please complete and return this form to us. We apologize for any inconvenience.

Estimated shipping date: _____ Please return this form to: _____

☐ Ship goods on hand

☐ Ship as soon as possible _____

☐ Substitute (specify) _____

☐ Cancel order _____

Signed: _____ _____

B 163

STOCK BALANCE RECORD

ITEM _____

UNIT OF MEASURE _____ WEIGHT _____

LOCATION: BIN _____ SITE _____

EXPEDITE POINT _____ REVIEW POINT _____

DATE	CODE	ISSUED / REC'D	USED TO DATE	BALANCE	DATE	REFERENCE	ISSUED / REC'D	USED TO DATE	BALANCE

EMPLOYEE PRODUCTIVITY REPORT

(1) EMPLOYEE NAME	HOURS WORKED				HOURS PRODUCED		PRODUCTIVITY PERCENTAGE	
	(2) TOTAL	(3) WAGE INCENTIVE	(4) DAY WORK	(5) DELAYS	(6) WAGE INCENTIVE	(7) DAY WORK	(8) WAGE INCENTIVE (6) ÷ (3)	(9) DAY WORK (7) ÷ (4)
TOTALS								

PRODUCT CONTROL

PRODUCT	DESCRIPTION	PRICE	COST	UNIT/ MEASURE	INVENTORY ON ORDER	INVENTORY ON HAND	COMMITTED INVENTORY

PRODUCTION REPORT

DATE: PERIOD: DEPT:

PRODUCT	NUMBER OF ORDERS	OPEN ORDERS	% TOTAL PRODUCTION	% REJECTS

DAILY PRODUCTION REPORT

DEPARTMENT _____ SHIFT _____ DATE _____

	SCHEDULE			PRODUCTION			
PRODUCTION ORDER NO.	CUSTOMER	PRODUCT	QUOTA QUANTITY	START	STOP	TOTAL HOURS	ACTUAL QUANTITY

NOTES:

PREPARED BY: _____ APPROVED BY: _____

PRODUCTION ORDER

Customer: _____   Production order no.: _____

Customer: _____   Sales order no.: _____

Product description	Cost	Price	On hand

Required materials	Product code no.	Cost	On hand	Out of stock

Scheduled completion date:

Shipping date:

FACTORY ORDER

ORDER NO.	LOT

ITEM	NUMBER	ORDER QTY.

PAGE   OF

DATE SCHEDULED	RELEASE DATE	START DATE	DUE DATE	ORDER MIN.

MATERIAL PER	QUANTITY PER 100	LOT QUANTITY

OPERATOR	DEPT.	OPERATION DESCRIPTION	MACHINE	REPORT DATE		QUANTITY		INSP.
				SCHEDULE	ACTUAL	PASSED	REJECTED	

RECEIVED	BY	DATE	QUANTITY	COMMENTS:

B 170

SHOP ORDER

CODE		MATERIAL		SCHEDULED		SHOP ORDER		PRIORITY	
QUANTITY		QUANTITY		START	FINISH	NUMBER			
NUMBER		SYMBOL		ACTUAL		IN-PROCESS TIME			
				START	FINISH				
MATERIAL						UNIT			
						OTHER			

OPR. NO.	OPERATION	CODE	MACHINE	PRODUCTION		LOAD HOURS		D.W. HRS. PER	TOTAL LOAD HOURS
				GOOD	DEFECT	SET UP	PER		

DEFECTIVE MATERIAL REPORT

VENDOR

SHIPPING INFO

	SHIPPING DATE	BILL OF LADING
PURCHASE ORDER NO.		
RECEIVING NO.	VIA	QUANT.
SHOP JOB NO.	WGT.	CHGS.

MATERIAL DESCRIPTION

PART NO.	QUANT. REC'D	QUANT. REJ.	UNIT PRICE	VALUE

INSPECTION AUTHORIZATION

DISPOSITION	CHARGE VENDOR	OUR EXPENSE	DATE INSPECTED	INSPECTOR
RETURN				

REASONS FOR REJECTIONS

REWORK			
SCRAP			
REWORK			
SCRAP			

OTHER DISPOSAL

REMARKS:

DATE REWORKED	TOTAL PCS.	INITIAL

B 172

REQUEST FOR REPAIR

Dept. _____   Date _____

Machine _____   Number _____

Repair required _____

_____

_____

_____

Signature _____

Mechanic's Report

Name _____

Repairs made _____

_____

_____

_____

_____

Remarks _____

_____

_____

_____

_____

_____

_____

_____

_____

EQUIPMENT SERVICE RECORD

Equipment

Model Number		Serial Number		Code	
Purchase Date		Cost		☐ New ☐ Used	

Purchased From

Leased From		Lease Period		Rate	Remaining Term

Condition of Equipment

Service Contract With				Phone	FAX

Date	Time	Service	Parts	Approved

EQUIPMENT SERVICE RECORD

Dept. _____   Location _____   Machine _____   # _____

DATE	REPAIRS MADE/PARTS REPLACED	PROBLEM	REPAIRED BY	DATE NEXT INSPECTION

QUALITY CONTROL REPORT

DEPT. _____ SHEET # _____

PRODUCT _____ QUANTITY _____

SAMPLE FREQUENCY _____

REMARKS _____

INSPECTOR _____ FROM _____ TO _____

INSPECTOR _____ FROM _____ TO _____

INSPECTOR _____ FROM _____ TO _____

DATE	TIME	SAMPLE NUMBER	No. DEFECTS	+ ✓	− ✓	DATE	TIME	SAMPLE NUMBER	No. DEFECTS	+ ✓	− ✓

QUALITY CONTROL REPORT

ITEM	ORDER	DESCRIPTION		ORDER QUANTITY	QUANTITY REJECTED
EMPLOYEE					

		SHIFT			INSPECTOR	DATE
		1	2	3		

NATURE OF DEFECT	REJECT DUE TO	(√)	DISPOSITION	(X)
	WORKMANSHIP		REWORK	
	MATERIALS		SALVAGE	
	DESIGN		RETURN TO VENDOR	
			SCRAP	
			HOLD FOR INSTRUCTIONS	

COST DEPARTMENT			PRODUCTION DEPARTMENT	
COST	UNIT COST	EXTENSION	REWORK ORDER ISSUED	
			REPLACEMENT ORDER ISSUED	
Material			MATERIAL CONTROL POSTED	DEPT OR SHIFT CHARGED
Labor			INVENTORY POSTED	
Total Cost			BY: _____ CHIEF DIRECTOR	

B 177

CUSTOMER FILE

CUSTOMER NAME	BILL TO	SHIP TO	INVOICE NO.	CUSTOMER TRADE CLASS	DISCOUNT CLASSIFICATION	CREDIT RATING	CREDIT LIMIT

MATERIAL REQUISITION REPORT

PROJECT: _____   LOCATION: _____   DATE: _____

HOW DELIVERED	INVOICE NO.	DESCRIPTION	DELIVERED BY	COST PER UNIT	QUANTITY	COMMENTS

BALANCE-OF-STORES RECORD

ITEM

<table>
<tr><td colspan="12">REQUIRED</td><td colspan="3">USED ON</td><td>PART NO.</td></tr>
<tr><td>MO.</td><td>QTY.</td><td>MO.</td><td>QTY.</td><td>MO.</td><td>QTY.</td><td>MO.</td><td>QTY.</td><td>MO.</td><td>QTY.</td><td>MO.</td><td>QTY.</td><td></td><td></td><td></td><td></td></tr>
<tr><td>1</td><td></td><td>2</td><td></td><td>3</td><td></td><td>4</td><td></td><td>5</td><td></td><td>6</td><td></td><td></td><td></td><td></td><td>UNIT</td></tr>
<tr><td>7</td><td></td><td>8</td><td></td><td>9</td><td></td><td>10</td><td></td><td>11</td><td></td><td>12</td><td></td><td></td><td></td><td></td><td>CLASSIFICATION</td></tr>
</table>

<table>
<tr><td>DATE</td><td>ORDER NUMBER</td><td>QUANTITY</td><td>RECEIVED</td><td>BALANCE ON ORDER</td><td colspan="2">ISSUED</td><td>STOCK BALANCE</td><td>ALLOCATED</td><td>AVAILABLE BALANCE</td></tr>
<tr><td></td><td></td><td></td><td></td><td></td><td></td><td></td><td></td><td></td><td></td></tr>
<tr><td></td><td></td><td></td><td></td><td></td><td></td><td></td><td></td><td></td><td></td></tr>
<tr><td></td><td></td><td></td><td></td><td></td><td></td><td></td><td></td><td></td><td></td></tr>
<tr><td></td><td></td><td></td><td></td><td></td><td></td><td></td><td></td><td></td><td></td></tr>
<tr><td></td><td></td><td></td><td></td><td></td><td></td><td></td><td></td><td></td><td></td></tr>
<tr><td></td><td></td><td></td><td></td><td></td><td></td><td></td><td></td><td></td><td></td></tr>
<tr><td></td><td></td><td></td><td></td><td></td><td></td><td></td><td></td><td></td><td></td></tr>
<tr><td></td><td></td><td></td><td></td><td></td><td></td><td></td><td></td><td></td><td></td></tr>
<tr><td></td><td></td><td></td><td></td><td></td><td></td><td></td><td></td><td></td><td></td></tr>
<tr><td></td><td></td><td></td><td></td><td></td><td></td><td></td><td></td><td></td><td></td></tr>
<tr><td></td><td></td><td></td><td></td><td></td><td></td><td></td><td></td><td></td><td></td></tr>
<tr><td></td><td></td><td></td><td></td><td></td><td></td><td></td><td></td><td></td><td></td></tr>
<tr><td></td><td></td><td></td><td></td><td></td><td></td><td></td><td></td><td></td><td></td></tr>
<tr><td></td><td></td><td></td><td></td><td></td><td></td><td></td><td></td><td></td><td></td></tr>
<tr><td></td><td></td><td></td><td></td><td></td><td></td><td></td><td></td><td></td><td></td></tr>
<tr><td></td><td></td><td></td><td></td><td></td><td></td><td></td><td></td><td></td><td></td></tr>
<tr><td></td><td></td><td></td><td></td><td></td><td></td><td></td><td></td><td></td><td></td></tr>
<tr><td></td><td></td><td></td><td></td><td></td><td></td><td></td><td></td><td></td><td></td></tr>
<tr><td></td><td></td><td></td><td></td><td></td><td></td><td></td><td></td><td></td><td></td></tr>
</table>

PARTS INVENTORY

Date _____

Bin Number _____

Sheet _____ Of _____

Part	Quan.	Unit Price	Extension		Part	Quan.	Unit Price	Extension	
								SUB-TOTAL		
								TOTAL		

B 181

DAILY TIME REPORT

DATE: _____

JOB ARRIVAL	JOB DEPART.	DATE	JOB COMP. %	JOB NAME	WORK PERFORMED	HOURS

_____
Employee

B 182

DAILY SCHEDULE

DATE: _____

TIME	CUSTOMER	ADDRESS	PHONE	SERVICE	C	CHARGE	REMARKS	CO.

B 183

INVENTORY CONTROL

USAGE FOR _____ DATE_____

DEPARTMENT_____ LOCATION _____

ITEM	RETAIL	SOLD LAST SEASON	ON HAND	ON ORDER	TO ORDER	TOTAL	UNITS LEFT	UNITS SOLD	FOR NEXT YEAR

DAILY TIME REPORT

CLOCK No.

NAME _____ DATE _____

ORDER No.	CUSTOMER	PART	OPERATION OR MACHINE No.	TIME STARTED	TIME STOPPED	TOTAL TIME	RATE	FOR OFFICE USE		✔
								CHG.	NON-CHG.	
DEDUCTIONS										

APPROVED BY: _____

RUN RECORD

Date _____

Machine			Machine No.	Operator

Time Run Started	Time Run Stopped	Comments	By

WORK ASSIGNMENT SCHEDULE

Department:			Date	
Employee	Job	Machine	From	To

MACHINE TIME RECORD

Date _____

Machine	Employee	Operation Machine No.	Time Started	Time Stopped	Total Time	✓

Name & Address: _____

CUSTOMER LEDGER

PURCHASE ORDER NO.	SALES ORDER NUMBER	DATE	ACCT. NO.	QTY.	DESCRIPTION		SHIPPED		DATE BILLED
					PART	PART NO.	BY	DATE	

CUSTOMER ORDER FILE

CUSTOMER	CUSTOMER ORDER NO.	ORDER DATE	AVAILABLE INVENTORY	INVENTORY FOR ORDER	SPECIAL INSTRUCTIONS	SHIP DATE	SHIP FROM	PAYMENT TERMS	INVOICE AMOUNT	CUSTOMER DISCOUNT	NET INVOICE

INVENTORY LEDGER

Unit: _____

Minimum quantity: _____

Location: _____

Date	Item	Received			Disbursed		Balance On Hand	
		Quantity	Amount	Unit Cost	Quantity	Amount	Quantity	Amount

INVENTORY DISCOUNT SCHEDULE

Discount to apply from: _____ To:_____

Item	Retail Price	Quantity	% – Amount Of Discount	Net Unit Price

SPEED MEMO

From _____

_____

_____

To _____

_____

_____

REFER TO			
❑ Your	❑ My	❑ Below	❑ Attached
❑ Letter	❑ Phone call	❑ Order	
❑ Inquiry	❑ Memo	❑ Telegram	

Date _____

Message

Signature	Title	Location	Phone	Date

Reply

Signature	Title	Location	Phone	Date

INTEROFFICE MEMO

Date _____

To _____

From _____

Subject _____

Message

| Signature | Title | Location | Phone | Date |

Reply

| Signature | Title | Location | Phone | Date |

INTEROFFICE MEMO

Date _____

To _____

From _____

Subject _____

Message

| Signature | Title | Location | Phone | Date |

ROUTING INSTRUCTIONS

DATE	
ATTENTION	
RE:	

TO

☐ REVIEW & FILE
☐ REVIEW & RETURN
☐ REVIEW & RETURN WITH COMMENTS
☐ FOR YOUR APPROVAL
☐ FOR YOUR USE
☐ FOR YOUR SIGNATURE
☐ PREPARE FOR MY SIGNATURE
☐ PREPARE FOR _____
    SIGNATURE

☐ INVESTIGATE AND REPORT TO ME
☐ INVESTIGATE AND REPORT TO _____
☐ REWORK PER COMMENTS & DIRECTION

☐ ATTACHED IS ☐ APPROVED ☐ REJECTED
☐ _____

☐ SEE ME ABOUT ☐ ATTACHED ☐ ABOVE ON
_____ AT _____ AM/PM

COMMENTS

PREPARED BY		PREPARED FOR/APPROVED BY	
TITLE		TITLE	
LOCATION		LOCATION	
PHONE	FAX	PHONE	FAX

TRANSMITTAL LETTER

	DATE
	ATTENTION
TO	**RE**

WE ARE SENDING ☐ ATTACHED ☐ UNDER SEPARATE COVER VIA _____:

☐ SAMPLES	☐ SHOP DRAWINGS	☐ CONTRACTS
☐ LITERATURE	☐ ENGINEERING DRAWINGS	☐ OTHER _____
☐ PLANS	☐ CHANGE ORDERS	_____
☐ PRINTS	☐ LETTERS	_____
☐ COPIES	☐ PAYMENT	

DESCRIPTION

THESE ARE BEING SENT:

☐ FOR YOUR APPROVAL	☐ APPROVED AS NOTED	☐ RESUBMIT _____ COPIES FOR APPROVAL
☐ FOR YOUR USE	☐ APPROVED AS SUBMITTED	☐ SUBMIT _____ COPIES FOR DISTRIBUTION
☐ FOR YOUR REVIEW	☐ APPROVED AS CHANGED	☐ RENEW _____ COPIES FOR
☐ FOR YOUR COMMENTS	☐ REJECTED AS NOTED	☐ _____
☐ FOR YOUR SIGNATURE	☐ REJECTED AS CHANGED	_____
☐ FOR YOUR _____	☐ RETURNED FOR CORRECTIONS	_____

COMMENTS _____

COPY TO	**BY**
	PHONE | **FAX**

EXPENSE RECORD

NAME: _____ FOR WEEK ENDING:_____ DEPT._____

	SUNDAY	MONDAY	TUESDAY	WEDNESDAY	THURSDAY	FRIDAY	SATURDAY	TOTAL FOR WEEK
FROM								
TO								
TO								
TOTAL AUTO MILES								
MILEAGE MI.								
GAS—OIL—LUBE								
PARKING & TOLLS								
AUTO RENTAL								
LOCAL—CAB/LIMO								
AIR—RAIL—BUS								
LODGING								
BREAKFAST								
LUNCH								
DINNER								
LAUNDRY								
PHONE & FAX								
TIPS								
OTHER								
ENTERTAINMENT*								
TOTAL PER DAY								

*DETAILED ENTERTAINMENT RECORD

DATE	PERSONS ENTERTAINED / BUSINESS RELATIONSHIP	PLACE NAME & LOCATION	PURPOSE	AMOUNT

PURPOSE OF TRIP:_____

_____

REMARKS:_____

_____

DATE:_____SIGNATURE:_____

SUMMARY

TOTAL EXPENSES	
LESS CASH ADVANCED	
LESS CHARGES TO CO.	
AMOUNT DUE ☐ ME ☐ CO.	

TURNOVER REPORT

DEPARTMENT				YEAR		

MONTH	THIS MONTH			YEAR TO DATE		
	No. Employees	Terminations	Turnover	No. Employees	Terminations	Turnover
TOTALS						

NOTES

PREPARED BY

APPROVED BY

Accounting
and
Finance

COMMERCIAL CREDIT APPLICATION

T **NAME** _____

O **ADDRESS** _____

CITY/STATE/ZIP _____

CREDIT MANAGER _____

PHONE NUMBER _____ FAX _____

F **NAME** _____

R **ADDRESS** _____

O **CITY/STATE/ZIP** _____

M _____

PHONE NUMBER _____ FAX _____

BUSINESS TYPE: ☐ Sole Proprietorship ☐ Partnership ☐ Corporation - State of _____

Number of years in business _____ D and B Reference _____

NAME AND ADDRESS OF OWNERS/PARTNERS/CORPORATE OFFICERS

_____

_____

_____

PERSON TO CONTACT ON PURCHASE ORDERS AND PAYMENTS

_____ _____

_____ _____

_____ _____

_____ _____

_____ _____

BANK REFERENCE

_____

_____

_____

_____

_____

BANK ACCOUNT NUMBER, CONTACT, TITLE AND PHONE NUMBER

_____

_____

_____

_____

_____

TRADE REFERENCES: COMPANY NAME, ADDRESS, CONTACT, TITLE, AND PHONE NUMBER.

_____ _____ _____

_____ _____ _____

_____ _____ _____

_____ _____ _____

_____ _____ _____

THE ABOVE INFORMATION IS SUBMITTED FOR OPENING AN ACCOUNT AND I CERTIFY THIS INFORMATION TO BE TRUE.

SIGNED _____

TITLE _____

DATE _____

CREDIT INQUIRY

To:

Date _____

_____

Re:

_____

Address

_____

City/State/Zip

_____

Contact

_____

Phone

To enable us to process a credit application that we have received on the above account, could you please provide us with the information requested below. We will keep your response strictly confidential.

Sales volume from _____ to _____ Totaled $_____

Total sales in year 19 _____ = $ _____ in year 19 _____ = $ _____

Terms _____ Special terms _____

Total amount now owed $ _____ Current: ☐ Yes ☐ No Amount past due $ _____

Largest amount owed $ _____ When _____ Current: ☐ Yes ☐ No

Recent trends: ☐ Prompt ☐ Full-term ☐ Slightly slow ☐ Very slow

Makes unjust claims _____

_____

Credit: ☐ Honored ☐ Refused

Explain: _____

_____

☑ Check manner of payment

☐ Excellent account - best recommendation ☐ Asks for additional time ☐ In hands of an attorney

☐ Prompt and takes discounts ☐ Slow but collectable ☐ Extending credit to this account

☐ Prompt to _____ days slow ☐ Accepts C.O.D.s promptly   not recommended

☐ Makes partial payments ☐ Collected by an attorney

Other comments:

Thank you for your assistance.

_____   _____

Name   Title

CREDIT CONTROL LIST

Period From: _____ To: _____

Number	Name	Date Opened	Credit Limit	Credit Available	Credit Used	Current	30	60	90+
TOTALS ___									

OVERDUE ACCOUNT FILE

Account _____ Tel. _____ FAX _____

Address _____

_____

Employer _____ Telephone _____

Address _____

_____

Guarantor _____ Telephone _____ FAX _____

Address _____

_____

Date account opened _____   Original balance due _____

Date delinquent file started _____   Turned over to _____

Date	Amount Paid	Balance	Date	Amount Paid	Balance

Date	Collection History

CREDIT HISTORY

Name: _____

Address: _____

_____

_____

Telephone: _____ Fax: _____

Business Name: _____

Business Address: _____

_____ _____

Business Telephone: _____ Business Telephone: _____

Date Approved	Credit Limit	Payment Due Amount	Payment Due Date	Payment Received Amount	Payment Received Date	Balance	Notice Date	Date 2nd Notice

Collection Call: _____ Date To Attorney: _____

Comments: _____

_____

ACCOUNTS RECEIVABLE RECAP REPORT

CUSTOMER	TOTAL BALANCE	MONTH	MONTH	MONTH	MONTH	PREVIOUS ITEMS	
						DATE	AMOUNT
BALANCE BROUGHT FORWARD							

EXPENSE BUDGET

Month Of:_____

_____

	Estimate	Actual	Variance $	%
PERSONNEL:				
	_____	_____	_____	_____
	_____	_____	_____	_____
	_____	_____	_____	_____
Others (List):	_____	_____	_____	_____
	_____	_____	_____	_____
OPERATING: Advertising:	_____	_____	_____	_____
Bad Debts:	_____	_____	_____	_____
Cash Discounts:	_____	_____	_____	_____
Delivery:	_____	_____	_____	_____
Depreciation:	_____	_____	_____	_____
Dues and Subscriptions:	_____	_____	_____	_____
Employee Benefits:	_____	_____	_____	_____
Insurance:	_____	_____	_____	_____
Interest:	_____	_____	_____	_____
Legal and Auditing:	_____	_____	_____	_____
Maintenance and Repairs:	_____	_____	_____	_____
Office Supplies:	_____	_____	_____	_____
Postage:	_____	_____	_____	_____
Rent or Mortgage:	_____	_____	_____	_____
Sales Expenses:	_____	_____	_____	_____
Shipping and Storage:	_____	_____	_____	_____
Supplies:	_____	_____	_____	_____
Taxes:	_____	_____	_____	_____
Telephone:	_____	_____	_____	_____
Utilities:	_____	_____	_____	_____
	_____	_____	_____	_____
	_____	_____	_____	_____
TOTAL:	_____	_____	_____	_____

GENERAL AND ADMINISTRATIVE EXPENSE BUDGET

	Month Ending _____ 19 _____			Year to Date		
	Budget	Actual	+ or –	Budget	Actual	+ or –
Fixed						
Exec. salaries						
Office salaries						
Employee benefits						
Payroll taxes						
Pensions						
Travel and entertainment						
Directors' fees & expenses						
Insurance						
Rent						
Depreciation						
Taxes						
Legal						
Audit						
Telephone and telegraph						
Utilities						
Contributions						
Postage						
Dues						
Other						
Variable						
Office salaries						
Employee benefits						
Payroll taxes						
Travel and entertainment						
Telephone and telegraph						
Stationery and office supplies						
Bad debts						
Postage						
Contributions						
Other						
TOTAL						

EXPENSE DISTRIBUTION ANALYSIS

Month of _____ 19 _____   Item _____   Sheet _____ of _____

Date

B 211

MONTHLY CASH FLOW PROJECTIONS

Year:	Month:												
		Estimate		Actual		Estimate		Actual		Estimate		Actual	
		$	% of total	$	% of total	$	% of total	$	% of total	$	% of total	$	% of total
Cash on hand, first of month:													
Cash receipts, total:													
Cash sales:													
Collections:													
Loans:													
Total cash available													
Cash paid out Salaries and wages:													
Payroll taxes:													
Rent/Mortgage:													
Health insurance:													
Insurance:													
Supplies:													
Utilities:													
Telephone:													
Repairs and maintenance:													
Purchases:													
Taxes, licenses:													
Professional fees:													
Commissions:													
Travel:													
Entertainment:													
Purchases:													
Advertising:													
Transportation:													
Subtotal													
Loan payment with interest:													
Capital purchases:													
Owner's withdrawal:													
Total cash paid out													
Cash position													

CASH FLOW BUDGET

	Jan.	Feb.	Mar.	April	May	June	July	Aug.	Se
Cash balance - beginning									
Cash from operations									
Total Available Cash									
Less:									
Capital expenditures									
Interest									
Dividends									
Debt									
Other									
Total Cash Disbursements									
Cash Balance (deficit)									
Add:									
Short-term loans									
Long-term loans									
Capital stock issues									
Cash Balance - end									

Y

Net Inc
Taxes
Net Income a

Extraordinary Gain
Income tax on extra

NET INCOME (NET PROFI

---
company name

INCOME STATEMENT

For _____ (month) and year to date ended _____ , 19_____

	Current Month		Year to Date	
	Amount	% of Sales	Amount	% of Sales
REVENUE				
Gross Sales	_____		_____	
Less sales returns and allowances	_____		_____	
Net Sales	_____	100	_____	100
Cost of Sales	_____	_____	_____	_____
Beginning inventory	_____	_____	_____	_____
Plus purchases or cost of goods	_____	_____	_____	_____
Total Goods Available	_____	_____	_____	_____
Less ending inventory	_____	_____	_____	_____
Total Cost of Goods Sold	_____	_____	_____	_____
Gross Profit (Gross Margin)	_____		_____	
OPERATING EXPENSES				
Selling				
Salaries and wages	_____	_____	_____	_____
Commissions	_____	_____	_____	_____
Advertising	_____	_____	_____	_____
Depreciation	_____	_____	_____	_____
Others (detail)	_____	_____	_____	_____
Total Selling Expenses	_____	_____	_____	_____
General/Administrative				
Salaries and wages	_____	_____	_____	_____
Employee benefits	_____	_____	_____	_____
Insurance	_____	_____	_____	_____
Depreciation	_____	_____	_____	_____
Total General/Administrative Expenses	_____	_____	_____	_____
Total Operating Expenses	_____	_____	_____	_____
Other Operating Income	_____	_____	_____	_____
Other Revenue and Expenses	_____	_____	_____	_____
...come before Taxes	_____	_____	_____	_____
...n Income	_____	_____	_____	_____
...fter Taxes	_____	_____	_____	_____
...or Loss	_____	_____	_____	_____
...ordinary gain	_____	_____	_____	_____
...)	_____	_____	_____	_____

B 214

BALANCE SHEET

Year Ending _____ , 19 _____

ASSETS
Current Assets
Cash _____

Accounts receivable_____
   less allowance
   doubtful accounts_____
     Net _____

Inventory _____
Temporary investment _____
Prepaid expenses _____
   Total Current Assets _____

Long-Term Investments _____

Fixed Assets
Land _____

Buildings _____ at
   cost, less accumulated
   depreciation of _____
   Net book value _____

Equipment _____ at
   cost, less accumulated
   depreciation of _____
   Net book value _____

Furniture/Fixtures _____ at
   cost, less accumulated
   depreciation of _____
   Net book value _____

Total Net Fixed Assets _____

Other Assets _____

TOTAL ASSETS _____

LIABILITIES
Current Liabilities
Accounts payable _____
Short-term notes _____
Current portion
   of long-term notes _____
Interest payable _____
Taxes payable _____
Accrued payroll _____
Total Current Liabilities _____

Equity _____
   Total owner's equity _____

or

   Total Partner's equity _____

Shareholder's equity
   (corporation)
Capital stock _____
Capital paid-in in
   excess of par _____
Retained earnings _____
   Total shareholder's
   equity _____

TOTAL LIABILITIES AND EQUITY _____

CHART OF MONTHLY SALES

———, 19 —— to ——, 19 ———

PRO-FORMA BALANCE SHEET

	19 ___	19 ___	19 ___	19 ___
Current Assets				
Cash				
Accounts receivable less allowance for bad debts				
Net accounts receivable				
Notes receivable				
Inventory				
Prepaid expenses				
Other				
Total Current Assets				
Fixed Assets				
Land				
Buildings				
Equipment				
Total Net Fixed Assets				
Other assets				
Total Assets				
Current Liabilities				
Accounts payable				
Notes payable				
Accrued expenses				
Taxes payable				
Other				
Total Current Liabilities				
Long-term liabilities				
Equity				
Withdrawals				
Net equity				
Total Liability & Equity				

PRO-FORMA INCOME STATEMENTS

Period _____

Revenues				
Sales allowances				
Net Revenues				
Cost of goods sold				
Gross Margin				
Expenses				
Selling				
Salaries				
Advertising				
Other				
General/Administrative				
Salaries				
Employee benefits				
Professional services				
Rent				
Insurance				
Depreciation				
Amortization				
Office supplies				
Interest				
Utilities				
Bad debt				
Other				
TOTAL EXPENSES				
Net Income before Taxes				
Provision for taxes				
Net Income after Taxes				
Prior period adjustments				
Net Increase/(Decrease) to Retained Earnings				

FINANCIAL PERFORMANCE TRENDS

Key Indicators	19 _____	19 _____	19 _____	19 _____
Income data				
Net sales				
Cost of goods sold				
Gross profit				
Net profit before taxes				
Net profit after taxes				
Asset/liability data				
Accounts receivable				
Inventory				
Total assets				
Accounts payable				
Short term debt				
Long term debt				
Total liabilities				
Net worth				
Ratios				
Current				
Total debt to total assets				
Collection period				
Net sales to inventory				
Net profit margin after taxes				
Return on net worth				

Comments:

FINANCIAL COMPARISON ANALYSIS

		Industry			Company	
	19 ____	19 ____	19 ____	19 ____	19 ____	19 ____
Assets:						
Accts & notes receivable						
Inventory						
Total current						
Fixed assets (net)						
TOTAL ASSETS						
Liabilities						
Accts & note payable						
Total current						
Long-term debt						
Net worth						
TOTAL LIABILITIES						
& NET WORTH						
Income Data						
Net sales						
Cost of goods sold						
Gross profit						
Operating expenses						
Operating profit						
Other expenses (net)						
PROFIT BEFORE TAXES						
Ratios						
Current						
Total debt/total Assets						
Total debt/tangible net worth						
Collection period days						
Net sales/inventory						
Total assets turnover						
Gross profit margin						
Operating profit margin						
Return on net worth						

MONTHLY SALES RECORD

Month Of			Month Of			Month Of		
Receipts			Receipts			Receipts		
Day	Amount		Day	Amount		Day	Amount	
1			1			1		
2			2			2		
3			3			3		
4			4			4		
5			5			5		
6			6			6		
7			7			7		
8			8			8		
9			9			9		
10			10			10		
11			11			11		
12			12			12		
13			13			13		
14			14			14		
15			15			15		
16			16			16		
17			17			17		
18			18			18		
19			19			19		
20			20			20		
21			21			21		
22			22			22		
23			23			23		
24			24			24		
25			25			25		
26			26			26		
27			27			27		
28			28			28		
29			29			29		
30			30			30		
31			31			31		
Total Month			Total Month			Total Month		
Total Year to Date			Total Year to Date			Total Year to Date		
Comments:			Comments:			Comments:		

PAYMENT RECORD

Period From: _____ To: _____

Date	Paid to	For	Charge Account	Amount

_____
Approved By

_____
Date

B 222

VENDOR PAYMENT RECORD

Period From: _____ To: _____

Month of: _____

Vendor Number	Invoice Number	Vendor	Description	30 Days	60 Days	Over 90 Days	Total

TOTAL _____ _____ _____ _____

INVOICE CONTROL

Month of _____

Page _____ of _____

Invoice Date	Invoice Number	Credit Accounts Payable	Description	General Accounts		Date Paid	Check Number
				Account	Amount		
			Amount Forwarded				

DAILY CASH REPORT

CHECKS PAID TO:		
Total		

REPORT DATE _____		
Receipts from Name Title Company		
Receipts from Name Title Company		
Receipts from Name Title Company		
Total receipts		
Cash paid out −		
Cash working fund +		
Balance		
Over or short		

CASH PAID TO:		
Total		

BANK DEPOSIT
Deposit #
Deposit date
Deposit made by
Signature

PETTY CASH REPORT

DATE _____ BEGINNING PETTY CASH AMOUNT $ _____

MANAGER _____

DATE	PAID TO	PURPOSE	AMOUNT		BALANCE	

TOTAL _____

Amount to be reimbursed $ _____

Approved by _____

PETTY CASH RECONCILIATION

Department _____   Supervisor _____

Petty cash check # _____   To _____

Previous audit date _____   Auditor _____

DATE	PAID TO/ RECEIVED FROM	PURPOSE	CASH RECEIVED (+)/ CASH DISBURSED (−)	BALANCE
	Balance from preceding page			

CURRENT AUDIT:

Date _____ by _____

Reimbursement: date _____ amount _____

by _____ check # _____

_____
Audited/reconciled by

_____
Approved by

SUMMARY:

Cash on hand _____

Petty cash slips _____

Total _____

☐ Over _____   ☐ Short _____

Disposition _____   Disposition _____

_____   _____

B   227

DAILY CASH BALANCE

Date _____

CASH ON HAND . . . . $ _____

CASH SALES . . . . $ _____

C.O.D. SALES . . . . $ _____

COLLECTIONS . . . . $ _____

LESS: Deposits . . . . $ _____

_____ . . . . $ _____

      BALANCE . . . . $ _____

CASH . . . . $ _____

CHECKS . . . . $ _____

CASH PAYOUTS. . . . . $ _____

OUT TICKETS . . . . $ _____

_____ . . . . $ _____

      BALANCE . . . . $ _____

REMARKS: _____

_____

_____

CASH REGISTER RECONCILIATION

NAME _____ DAY _____

SHIFT _____ DATE _____

OPENING - CASH		
OPENING - F/S		
REGISTER READING		
EXTRA CASH		
REBATES		
TOTAL		
	TWENTIES	
	TENS	
	FIVES	
	ONES	
	HALVES	
	QUARTERS	
	DIMES	
	NICKELS	
	PENNIES	
	CHECKS	
	ENDING - CASH	
	ENDING - F/S	
	PAYOUTS	
	DEPOSITS	
	REFUND	
	TOTAL	_____

OVER _____   SHORT _____

BANK RECONCILIATION

Account _____ Month of _____ 19____

Bank _____ Prepared by _____

	$		BALANCE PER BANK STATEMENT	$	
GENERAL LEDGER ACCOUNT BALANCE			AS OF .... 19......		
ADD DEBITS	$		ADD DEPOSITS IN PROCESS	$	
....			....		
....			....		
....			....		
....			....		
Total Dr	$		Total in Transit	$	
Total	$		Total		
LESS CREDITS:	$		LESS CHECKS OUTSTANDING:	$	
....			(See list below)		
....			....		
....			....		
....			....		
Total Cr	$		Total	$	
BANK BALANCE – Per General Ledger	$		BANK BALANCE – Per Reconciliation	$	

CHECKS OUTSTANDING

NUMBER	AMOUNT	NUMBER	AMOUNT	NUMBER	AMOUNT	NUMBER	AMOUNT
						TOTAL	$

GENERAL LEDGER

Account Number ——————— Tel. Number ——————— Page ——— of ———

Account Name ——————— Address ———————

Date	Description	Charges	Credits	Balance Charges	Credits
Amount Forwarded					

B 231

JOURNAL

Name/Number: _____   Month of: _____ _____ 19____

		Charges					

Accounts Receivable	Accounts Payable	General Ledger		Date	Description	Credits	
		Acct. No.	Amount			General Ledger	
						Acct. No.	Amount
					Amount Forwarded		

				Accounts Payable	Accounts Receivable

B 232

EMPLOYER TAX DEPOSIT RECORD

	January	February	March	
Number Employees:	_____	_____	_____	
Total Wages:	_____	_____	_____	
Withholding Tax:	_____	_____	_____	
Employer's Social Security Contribution:	_____	_____	_____	TOTAL FOR
Employee's Social Security Contribution:	_____	_____	_____	QUARTER
TOTAL DEPOSIT:	_____	_____	_____	_____

	April	May	June	
Number Employees:	_____	_____	_____	
Total Wages:	_____	_____	_____	
Withholding Tax:	_____	_____	_____	
Employer's Social Security Contribution:	_____	_____	_____	TOTAL FOR
Employee's Social Security Contribution:	_____	_____	_____	QUARTER
TOTAL DEPOSIT:	_____	_____	_____	_____

	July	August	September	
Number Employees:	_____	_____	_____	
Total Wages:	_____	_____	_____	
Withholding Tax:	_____	_____	_____	
Employer's Social Security Contribution:	_____	_____	_____	TOTAL FOR
Employee's Social Security Contribution:	_____	_____	_____	QUARTER
TOTAL DEPOSIT:	_____	_____	_____	_____

	October	November	December	
Number Employees:	_____	_____	_____	
Total Wages:	_____	_____	_____	
Withholding Tax:	_____	_____	_____	
Employer's Social Security Contribution:	_____	_____	_____	TOTAL FOR
Employee's Social Security Contribution:	_____	_____	_____	QUARTER
TOTAL DEPOSIT:	_____	_____	_____	_____

TOTAL FOR YEAR _____

EXPENSE RECORD

EMPLOYEE _____   WEEK/MONTH OF _____

TERRITORY NO.	DEPARTMENT	PRODUCT LINE/SALES GROUP	COMPANY CHARGE CARD NO.
			☐ TELEPHONE _____
			☐ OTHER _____

DATE	TRANS.	PARKING/ TOLLS	HOTEL	MEALS	ENTERTAINMENT PURPOSE	ENTERTAINMENT AMOUNT	MISC.	COMPANY CHARGE	EMPLOYEE CHARGE	CASH	DAILY TOTALS
TOTALS											

MONTHLY AUTO EXPENSE RECORD	
LESS CASH ADVANCE	
LESS CHARGES TO COMPANY	
BALANCE DUE ☐ COMPANY ☐ EMPLOYEE	

IF SUBMITTED AS AN EXPENSE REPORT - SIGN BELOW	
SIGNATURE/TITLE	DATE
APPROVAL SIGNATURE/TITLE	DATE

B 234

MONTHLY EXPENSE RECORD

MONTH OF _____

SALES _____

ADDRESS _____

CITY _____

STATE _____ ZIP _____

TERRITORY NO.	BRANCH/REGION OR ZONE	PRODUCT LINE/SALES GROUP	COMPANY CHARGE CARD NO.
			☐ TELEPHONE _____
			☐ OTHER _____

DATE	TRANS.	PARKING/ TOLLS	HOTEL	MEALS	ENTERTAINMENT		MISC.	PAYMENT METHOD			DAILY TOTALS
					PURPOSE	AMOUNT		COMPANY CHARGE	EMPLOYEE CHARGE	CASH	
TOTALS											

	MONTHLY AUTO EXPENSE RECORD	
	LESS CASH ADVANCE	
	LESS CHARGES TO COMPANY	
	☐ COMPANY	
	BALANCE DUE ☐ EMPLOYEE	

IF SUBMITTED AS AN EXPENSE REPORT - SIGN BELOW	
PREPARER SIGNATURE/TITLE	DATE
APPROVAL SIGNATURE/TITLE	DATE

AUTO EXPENSE RECORD

EMPLOYEE _____   WEEK/MONTH OF _____

TERRITORY NO.	DEPARTMENT	PRODUCT LINE/SALES GROUP	COMPANY CHARGE CARD NO.
			☐ _____ # _____ ☐ _____ # _____

DATE	ODOMETER READING		MILEAGE	GAS/OIL	PARKING TOLLS	MISC	PAYMENT METHOD			DAILY TOTALS
	START	STOP					COMPANY CHARGE	EMPLOYEE CHARGE	CASH	
TOTALS										

MONTHLY AUTO EXPENSE RECORD	
LESS CASH ADVANCE	
LESS CHARGES TO COMPANY	
BALANCE DUE ☐ COMPANY ☐ EMPLOYEE	

IF SUBMITTED AS AN EXPENSE REPORT - SIGN BELOW	
SIGNATURE/TITLE	DATE
APPROVAL SIGNATURE/TITLE	DATE

B 236

ASSET DEPRECIATION SCHEDULE

Company: _____   Date: _____

	Item	Date Purchased	Total Cost	No. Yrs. Useful Life	Salvage Value	Total Depreciation	Annual Depreciation	Depreciation Years	
								From	To
1									
2									
3									
4									
5									
6									
7									
8									
9									
10									
11									
12									
13									
14									
15									
16									
17									
18									
19									
20									

TOTAL
ANNUAL FIXED ASSETS
DEPRECIATION: _____

ANNUAL EXPENSE SUMMARY

FOR YEAR _____

EMPLOYEE _____

DEPARTMENT _____

MONTH	PHONE	MEALS	TRAVEL	HOTELS	ENTERTAINMENT	MISC.	MONTHLY TOTAL
JANUARY							
FEBRUARY							
MARCH							
1st QUARTER TOTAL							
APRIL							
MAY							
JUNE							
2nd QUARTER TOTAL							
JULY							
AUGUST							
SEPTEMBER							
3rd QUARTER TOTAL							
OCTOBER							
NOVEMBER							
DECEMBER							
4th QUARTER TOTAL							
ANNUAL TOTAL							

MONTHLY FINANCIALS

			1	2
1				
2				
3				
4				
5				
6				
7				
8				
9				
10				
11				
12				
13				
14				
15				
16				
17				
18				
19				
20				
21				
22				
23				
24				
25				
26				
27				
28				
29				
30				
31				
32				
33				

Purchasing
and
Shipping

VENDOR MASTER FILE

Vendor _____   Address _____

Contact _____   Phone _____ FAX _____

Title _____   Credit Rating _____   Our Rating _____

Delivery time:
   Freight _____   Express _____   Other _____

Date	Purchase Order No.	Items	Catalog #	Quantity	Notes

STOCK RECORD CARD

ITEM						SIZE		BIN		MINIMUM			STOCK NO.
ITEM NUMBER						UNIT		SHELF		MAXIMUM			

RECEIVED			RELEASED			BALANCE	RECEIVED			RELEASED			BALANCE
DATE	ORDER	QUANTITY	DATE	ORDER	QUANTITY	ON HAND	DATE	ORDER	QUANTITY	DATE	ORDER	QUANTITY	ON HAND

PURCHASE ORDER REQUISITION

Date: _____   Requisition No.: _____

For: _____   Department: _____

Purpose Or Use: _____   Charge To: _____

Source: _____   Ship Via: _____

Remarks: _____

Quantity	Unit	Item Number	Description	Date Needed	Estimated Cost

Requested By: _____   For Purchasing Department Use:

Departmental Approval: _____   Approved: _____

Ordered From: _____

P.O. No.: _____ Date: _____

MATERIAL REQUISITION

DATE	REQUESTED BY	MUST HAVE BY	CHARGE TO	DELIVER TO

ITEM	QTY.	UNIT	DESCRIPTION	ESTIMATED COST	PURCHASING USE ONLY	
					UNIT PRICE	EXTENDED

CERTIFICATION ☐ YES ☐ NO | SHIP VIA | APPROVED BY | DATE | TOTAL | TOTAL

RECOMMENDED VENDORS

1

2

3

PURCHASING USE ONLY

VENDOR		VENDORS AGREED SHIP DATE
ADDRESS		☐ RESALE ☐ TAXABLE
		TERMS	P.O. NUMBER
CONTACT	TELEPHONE	BUYER	P.A. APPROVAL

PURCHASE REQUISITION INDEX

Requisition No.	Date Received	Item	Symbol/ Code	Quantity	Buyer	Bids Re- quired	Purchase Order No.	Order Date	Vendor	Invoice Received	Invoice Paid

REQUEST FOR QUOTATION

NUMBER
THIS IS NOT AN ORDER!

DATE	DATE DELIVERY REQUIRED	REPLY NOT LATER THAN	REQUISITION NO.	JOB NO.

VENDOR

-
-
-
-
-
-

SUMMARY OF QUOTATIONS

ITEM	QUANTITY	VENDOR 1	VENDOR 2
TERMS			
F.O.B.			
DELIVERY			

1. TERMS	2. F.O.B.	3. SHIPMENT VIA	4. SHIPPING WEIGHT	5. DATE SHIPMENT CAN BE MADE

ITEM	QUANTITY	DESCRIPTION	6. UNIT PRICE	7. AMOUNT

REASON ORDER PLACED WITH SUCCESSFUL VENDOR

BUYER _____

B 248

REQUEST FOR QUOTATION

To:

DATE	
DELIVERY	

PLEASE QUOTE YOUR BEST PRICE AND DELIVERY ON THE ITEMS BELOW:

PRICES QUOTED F.O.B.	TERMS	TO BE SHIPPED VIA	EARLIEST SHIPPING DATE

QUANTITY	DESCRIPTION	PRICE	AMOUNT

BY _____

B 249

QUOTATION RECORD

Item _____

Description _____

Specification No. _____

Unit _____

Date	Purchase Order No.	Quantity Purchased	List	Discount	Net Price	Freight	Total Price	Unit Price	Vendor	Comments

B 250

Date: _____

For: _____

Job Number: _____

Description: _____

Vendor	Contact	Item	Quantity	Delivery Schedule	Terms	Total Price	Unit Price	Delivery Charge	Net Price	Remarks

Notes:

VENDOR PRICE ANALYSIS

Product:

	Vendor	Price/Quantity					Lead time	Est. del. $	Other	Terms
		25 ea.	50 ea.	75 ea.	100 ea.					
1										
2										
3										
4										
5										
6										
7										
8										
9										
10										
11										
12										
13										
14										

Department: By: Date:

REQUEST FOR SAMPLE

Date:_____

To: _____ Title:_____ Address: _____

Company: _____ City: _____

Telephone: _____ Fax: _____ State: _____ Zip:_____

☐ New Account ☐ Previous Customer ☐ Inquiry Only ☐ Charge ☐ No Charge

Quantity	Description	Total

Print Name: _____

Ship Via: _____ Company: _____

Signed: _____ Address: _____

B 253

PURCHASE REQUISITION

☐ Please Confirm
  Verbal Order Placed

Purchased From _____ Purchase Order No. _____

_____ Date _____ 19 _____

For _____ To Be Used For _____

Shop Order No. _____ Needed By _____ Classification _____

F. O. B. Point _____ Terms _____ Ship Via _____

QUANTITY	DESCRIPTION	PRICE		UNIT

Signed _____ Approved _____

　　　　　DEPT. HEAD　　　　　　　　　　　　　　　　　　　　　PURCHASING AGENT

PURCHASE ORDER

P.O. NUMBER	
DATE	DATE REQUIRED
TERMS	
SHIP VIA	
F.O.B.	

TO

SHIP TO

QTY.	UNIT	PLEASE SHIP ITEMS BELOW	UNIT PRICE	AMOUNT

IMPORTANT

This Purchase Order Number must appear on all invoices, acknowledgments, bills of lading, correspondence and shipping cartons.

Please notify us immediately if you cannot ship complete order by date specified.

STATE RESALE NUMBER

☐ RESALE   ☐ USE

OTHER:

AUTHORIZED SIGNATURE

B 255

PURCHASE ORDER

DATE _____ 19 ____

SHIP TO

TO

SHIP VIA	F.O.B.	TERMS	DELIVERY REQUIRED BY

QUANTITY		DESCRIPTION	PRICE	UNIT	AMOUNT
ORDERED	RECEIVED				

IMPORTANT

Above Order Number must appear on all correspondence, invoices, packages and shipping papers. Notify us
immediately if you are unable to ship complete order by date specified.

BY _____

B 256

PURCHASE ORDER

P.O. NUMBER	
DATE	DATE REQUIRED
TERMS	
SHIP VIA	
F.O.B.	

TO

_____

_____

_____

SHIP TO

_____

_____

_____

QTY.	UNIT	PLEASE SUPPLY ITEMS BELOW	UNIT PRICE	AMOUNT

IMPORTANT
This Purchase Order Number must appear on all invoices, acknowledgments, bills of lading, correspondence and shipping cartons.

Please notify us immediately if you are unable to ship complete order by date specified.

STATE RESALE NUMBER

_____

☐ RESALE ☐ USE

Please send _____ copies of your invoice

_____

AUTHORIZED SIGNATURE

B 257

PURCHASE ORDER FOLLOW-UP

DATE _____ 19 _____

THIS IS OUR _____ REQUEST
PLEASE ANSWER IMMEDIATELY

REPLY TO ITEMS
CHECKED BELOW BY

	THIS FORM	FAX	PHONE
	☐	☐	☐

OUR PURCHASE ORDER NO.	REQUEST FOR QUOTATION NO.	YOUR INVOICE NO.	DATE	AMOUNT	YOUR REFERENCE

☐ 1. Rush shipment. Advise earliest date.
☐ 2. When will shipment be made? If shipped, advise method.
☐ 3. Please trace shipment.
☐ 4. If shipment has been made, mail invoice, today.
☐ 5. Please mail receipted freight bill.
☐ 6. Why did you not ship as promised? Advise when you will ship?
☐ 7. Will you ship on date shown on purchase order?
☐ 8. Release shipments as shown under remarks.
☐ 9. Please mail us acceptance copy of our purchase order.
☐ 10. Please acknowledge our order.
☐ 11. Please make your date more specific.
☐ 12. When will balance of order be shipped?
☐ 13. When will price be submitted? Please rush.

☐ 14. Please mail shipping notice.
☐ 15. Please indicate our purchase order number on papers referred to, or attached.
☐ 16. We have no record of transaction covered by your invoice. Advise date of shipment, name of person placing order and furnish signed delivery receipt copy.
☐ 17. Invoice returned herewith.
☐ 18. Invoice is required in _____ copies.
☐ 19. Price or discount is not in accordance with quotation.
☐ 20. Terms on invoice are not in accordance with the purchase order.
☐ 21. Enclosed invoice sent to us in error.
☐ 22. Difference in quantity.

REPLY

DATE _____ 19 _____

VENDOR _____

BY _____   BY _____

DAILY RECEIVING REPORT

Reporting period: from _____ to _____

Date _____   Shift _____   Page _____ of _____ pgs

TIME	REC'D FROM	DESCRIPTION OF CONTENTS	OUR ORDER #	COMPLETE/ PARTIAL	CARRIER & FREIGHT BILL #	PREPAID OR COLLECT	NUMBER OF CARTONS	WEIGHT	REC'D BY

Receiving staff this shift

Supervisor this shift

FOR OFFICE USE ONLY

Print name: _____   Reviewed by: _____ Approved by: _____

Sign name: _____

Title _____   Title _____   Date _____   Title _____   Date _____

RECEIVING REPORT

Received from _____

Address _____

City/state/zip _____

Shipped from _____

_____

Date: _____

Carrier name: _____

❑ UPS   ❑ Rail   ❑ Express Mail

❑ Parcel post   ❑ Shipper's truck   ❑ Other:

❑ Truck   ❑ Air express   _____

❑ Pre-paid   ❑ Collect $ _____

OUR ORDER #	DATE SHIPPED	SHIPPED TO	LOCATION	TELEPHONE

QUANTITY	DESCRIPTION	# OF CARTONS	WEIGHT EACH	WEIGHT TOTAL	CARTON CONDITION	REC'D BY (INITIALS)

Shipment:	Total # cartons	Total weight	# of items rec'd OK _____
❑ Complete ❑ Partial			# of items rec'd damaged _____

Rec'd by	Date	Rec'd in office by	Date

Checked by	Date	Audited by	Date

B 260

INSPECTION REPORT

Received from _____

Address _____

City/state/zip _____

Shipped from _____

_____

Our purchase order _____

Quantity received _____

Date: _____

Carrier name: _____

❑ UPS ❑ Rail ❑ Express Mail
❑ Parcel post ❑ Shipper's truck ❑ Other:
❑ Truck ❑ Air express _____

Inspected: ❑ On dock ❑ In quality control

Quantity accepted _____

Quantity rejected _____

| ITEM | DESCRIPTION | INSPECTION | | | |
		APPROVED	REJECTED	REASON	ACTION RECOMMENDED
1					
2					
3					
4					
5					
6					
7					
8					
9					
10					
11					
12					
13					
14					
15					
16					
17					
18					
19					
20					

Rec'd by	Date	Rec'd in office by	Date
Checked by	Date	Audited by	Date
Approved by	Date	Accounting disposition by	Date

BACKORDER CONTROL

Period From:_____ To:_____

Item	Description	Qty. Ordered	Qty. On B.O.	TOTAL	Date Ordered	Date Due	Date Received

Signed: _____

B 262

INVOICE CHECK

Date received _____ Purchase order no. _____

Discount date _____ Invoice no. _____

Date paid _____ Voucher no. _____

Terms OK _____

F.O.B. point OK _____

Unit price OK _____

Discounts OK _____

Extensions OK _____

Quantity OK _____

Amount of invoice ....$ _____

Deductions:

  Cash discount ....$ _____

  Rejections ....$ _____

  Other deductions ....$ _____

  Total deductions ....$ _____

Net due ....$ _____

Comments: _____

_____

_____

_____

Payment approved _____

INVOICE RECORD

Company _____

Address _____

Order No.	Invoice No.	Invoice Date	Date Received	Amount	Deduc-tions	Net	Discount Date	Date Paid	By	Comments

PROPOSAL

Proposal No.

Sheet No.

Date

FROM

Proposal Submitted To	Work To Be Performed At
Name_____	Street _____
Street_____	City_____ State _____
City_____	Date of Plans_____
State _____ Zip _____	Architect _____
Telephone Number_____ Fax_____	

We hereby propose to furnish all the materials and perform all the labor necessary for the completion of

_____

_____

_____

_____

_____

_____

_____

_____

_____

_____

_____

All material is guaranteed to be as specified, and the above work to be performed in accordance with the drawings and specifications submitted for above work and completed in a substantial workmanlike manner for the sum of_____ _____ Dollars ($_____), with payments to be made as follows: _____

_____

_____

Any alteration or deviation from above specifications involving extra costs, will be executed only upon written orders, and will become an extra charge over and above the estimate. All agreements contingent upon strikes, accidents or delays beyond our control. Owner to carry fire, tornado and other necessary insurance upon above work. Workmen's Compensation and Public Liability Insurance on above work to be taken out by _____

Submitted By _____

NOTE — This proposal may be withdrawn by us if not accepted within _____ days.

ACCEPTANCE OF PROPOSAL

The above prices, specifications and conditions are satisfactory and are hereby accepted. Payment will be made as outlined above.

_____

Accepted _____ Signature _____

Date _____ Signature _____

B 265

QUOTATION

TO

DATE:

F.O.B.

TERMS:

DELIVERY:

THANK YOU FOR YOUR INQUIRY OF _____ NO. _____

WE ARE PLEASED TO QUOTE YOU AS FOLLOWS:

QUANTITY	DESCRIPTION	PRICE

SALES ORDER

DATE REQUIRED _____

SHIP VIA _____

DATE _____ 19 _____

Charge to _____ ☐ WILL CONFIRM

_____

Ship to _____

_____

Customer Order No. _____ Order received by _____ OPEN ☐

Ordered by _____ Ship via _____ COMPLETE ☐

PREPAID ☐   COLLECT ☐   C.O.D. ☐   SALESPERSON _____

TELEPHONE SALES ORDER

Sold to _____

_____

Sold by _____

_____

Ship to _____

_____

Customer # _____

Terms _____

Ship week of _____

Ship via _____

FOB _____

Routing _____

Interest rate
   % per month _____

   % annual rate _____

	YOUR ORDER NO.		ORDER DATE		OUR ORDER NO.	
ITEM	QUANTITY ORDERED	DESCRIPTION	DATE NEEDED	UNIT COUNT	UNIT PRICE	COST
1						
2						
3						
4						
5						
6						
7						
8						
9						
10						
11						
12						
13						
14						
15						
16						

Order # _____ Total _____

Telephone sales representative _____ Date _____

TELEPHONE ORDER

Date: _____

Sold To:

Company: _____ Order no: _____

Address: _____ Attention: _____

City: _____ State: _____ Zip code: _____

Ship To:

Company: _____ Order no: _____

Address: _____ Attention: _____

City: _____ State: _____ Zip code: _____

Called in or placed by: _____

Taken by: _____ Time: _____

Item	Quantity	Description	Unit Price	Total

Special instructions: _____

_____

_____

_____

LAYAWAY ORDER

_____

Sold To: _____   Date: _____

_____   Salesperson: _____

_____   ☐ To be picked up   ☐ Delivered   ☐ _____

Item/description	Quantity	Unit price	Amount

Total _____

Sales tax _____

Total due _____

Deposit _____

Date: _____   Amount due: _____   Payment: _____   Balance _____

JOB ESTIMATE

To:

Estimate # _____

Date _____

Prepared by _____

RE: ☐ Day work   ☐ Contract

Explanation _____

Job name _____

Job # _____

Job location _____

Job phone _____ Ext _____

Start date _____ End date _____

From:

ITEM #	MATERIALS	QUANTITY	UNIT PRICE	TOTAL COST
1				
2				
3				
4				
5				
6				
7				
8				
9				
10				
11				
12				
13				
14				
15				
16				
17				
18				
19				
20				
21				

ITEM #	LABOR	RATE	HOURS	TOTAL COST
1				
2				
3				
4				
5				
6				
7				

	MISCELLANEOUS OTHER ITEMS	COST
1		
2		
3		
4		
5		

SUMMARY	COST
Materials	
Labor	
Miscellaneous	
Overhead	
Total costs	

Estimate approved by _____

Total bid _____

Less total cost _____

Total profit _____

WORK ORDER

DATE _____   CUST. ORDER NO. _____

CUSTOMER _____

PART DESCRIPTION _____

_____

QUANTITY _____ DEL. DATE _____

_____

_____

_____

MATERIAL	COST	OUTSIDE WORK	AMOUNT

TOTALS

MATERIAL COST		
DIRECT LABOR		
OUTSIDE WORK		
OVERHEAD		
TOTAL COST		
SELLING PRICE		
PROFIT		

B 272

JOB ORDER

CUSTOMER		DATE	
NAME		JOB NAME	
STREET		JOB LOCATION	
CITY			
STATE, ZIP		JOB PHONE	FAX
PHONE	FAX		

Location	Stock No.	Description	Size	Area	FOR OFFICE USE ONLY:
					Material in stock ☐
					Material to be ordered ☐
					Date ordered:
					_____
					Date received:
					_____

Job assigned to _____ Estimated time _____

Date to start _____ A.M. ☐   P.M. ☐

Date started _____

Date completed _____

Job completed by _____
                        Signature

Remarks if any:

JOB INSPECTED AND APPROVED

_____
Customer's Signature

B 273

JOB ORDER CHANGE

To:

Estimate # _____

Date _____

Prepared by _____

Re: ☐ Day work   ☐ Contract   ☐ Extra

Explanation _____

From:

Job name _____

Job # _____

Job location _____

Job phone _____ Ext _____

Start date _____ End date _____

ADDITIONAL WORK AUTHORIZATION

#	MATERIAL	QTY	UNIT PRICE	TOTAL COST
1				
2				
3				
4				
5				
6				
7				
8				
9				
10				
11				
12				
13				
14				
15				
16				

#	LABOR	RATE	HRS	TOTAL COST
1				
2				
3				
4				
5				
6				
7				
8				
9				

#	MISCELLANEOUS OTHER ITEMS	TOTAL COST
1		
2		
3		
4		
5		

Your order # _____ Date _____

Work ordered by _____

Explanation _____

_____

_____

_____

Estimate approved by _____

_____

Signature approval for quotation release

Additional work summary

Total materials _____

Total labor _____

Total miscellaneous _____

Total tax/permit/insur _____

Total cost _____

Tax _____

Total billing _____

CHANGE ORDER

NO.

PROJECT _____ DATE _____

SUB-CONTRACTOR:

⌐   ⌐

Our Job No._____

L   ⌐

Type of Work_____

YOU ARE AUTHORIZED TO MAKE THE FOLLOWING CHANGES IN YOUR WORK ON THE ABOVE NAMED PROJECT.

		Original Contract Price	$
		This Change Order	$

DESCRIPTION OF ADDED OR DELETED ITEMS	INCREASE	DECREASE	
	$	$	
	$	$	
Revised Contract Price Through Change Order			$

ACCEPTED:

FOR _____

BY _____

DATE _____

BY _____

TITLE _____

B 275

CHANGE ORDER

CHANGE ORDER
NO.

ADDRESSEE:	JOB:

REFERENCE:

THE ABOVE AGREEMENT IS HEREBY CHANGED AS FOLLOWS:

ITEM	DESCRIPTION OF CHANGE	ADD	DEDUCT

PREVIOUS AMOUNT	THIS CHANGE ORDER		REVISED AMOUNT
	ADD	DEDUCT	

EXCEPT AS MODIFIED BY THIS CHANGE ORDER (AND PREVIOUS CHANGE ORDERS, IF ANY) THE AGREEMENT
REMAINS UNCHANGED AND CONTINUES IN FULL FORCE AND EFFECT.

PLEASE SIGN AND RETURN THE ORIGINAL OF THIS CHANGE ORDER.

BY: _____   BY: _____

TITLE: _____   DATE: _____

DATE: _____

SERVICE INVOICE

Sold To: _____ Service At: _____

_____ _____

_____ _____

_____ _____

Equipment	Model	Serial No.	Date Repaired

PARTS

Quantity	Item	Price		Amount

Date	No. Hours	Rate/Hour	Amount	Total	
				Tax	
				Total Labor	
				TOTAL BILL	
		TOTAL			

Comments:

_____

_____

_____

_____

Service Personnel _____ Signed: _____

TIME AND MATERIAL REPORT

JOB NO. _____

EMPLOYEE _____ DATE _____

SCALE: Straight Time_____   Overtime _____

No. Hours   _____   _____

WAGES   _____   _____   TOTAL WAGES _____

MATERIAL

QUANTITY	DESCRIPTION	PRICE PER UNIT	TOTAL PRICE		QUANTITY	DESCRIPTION	PRICE PER UNIT	TOTAL PRICE
	TOTAL						TOTAL	

SUMMARY		
MATERIAL		
PERMIT		
LABOR		
JOB COST		
PROFIT		
OVERHEAD		
PRICE OF JOB		
+		
−		

REMARKS

WORK AUTHORIZATION

NAME		DATE	PHONE
ADDRESS		DATE PROMISED	DATE COMPLETED
CITY		ITEM	

COMPLAINT/PROBLEM:

AMT.	PART & NUMBER	AMOUNT		DESCRIPTION OF WORK	AMOUNT
				LABOR ONLY	
				PARTS	
	PARTS			TOTAL	
	TAX			TAX	
	TOTAL AMOUNT			TOTAL AMOUNT	

CUSTOMER'S SIGNATURE

RETURN AUTHORIZATION

Sold and shipped to: _____

_____

_____

_____

Authorization to return to: _____

_____

_____

_____

Customer # _____

Terms _____

COMPLETE FOR RETURN SHIPMENT
INCLUDE THIS FORM AS PACKING LIST

Date shipped _____

FOB _____

Routing _____

YOUR ORDER NO.		DATE OF ORDER			OUR ORDER NO.	

ITEM	QUANTITY ORDERED	DESCRIPTION	QUANTITY RECEIVED	UNIT PRICE	TOTAL
1					
2					
3					
4					
5					
6					
7					
8					
9					
10					
11					
12					

DATE	TOTAL ITEMS RETURNED	$ AMOUNT

Approved by	Date	Items rec'd at our plant by

STATEMENT

DATE _____

NUMBER _____ TERMS _____

AMOUNT PAID

$ _____

DATE	INVOICE/DESCRIPTION	CHARGE	CREDIT	BALANCE
PREVIOUS BALANCE BROUGHT FORWARD				

THANK YOU   PLEASE PAY THIS AMOUNT ►

CREDIT MEMO

Sold to _____

_____

_____

_____

Shipped to _____

_____

_____

_____

Customer # _____

Terms _____

Received at our plant _____

REASON FOR CREDIT
Approved by _____
Date _____

		YOUR ORDER NO.	DATE OF ORDER	OUR ORDER NO.	
ITEM	QUANTITY ORDERED	INVOICE NUMBER/DESCRIPTION		UNIT PRICE	TOTAL
1					
2					
3					
4					
5					
6					
7					
8					
9					
10					
11					
12					
13					
14					

Issue date	Total credit memo amount $

B 282

DEBIT MEMO

B

Sold to _____

_____

_____

_____

Shipped to _____

_____

_____

_____

Customer # _____

Terms _____

Received at our plant _____

REASON FOR DEBIT
Approved by _____
Date _____

YOUR ORDER NO		DATE OF ORDER		OUR ORDER NO.	
ITEM	**QUANTITY ORDERED**	**INVOICE NUMBER/DESCRIPTION**		**UNIT PRICE**	**TOTAL**
1					
2					
3					
4					
5					
6					
7					
8					
9					
10					
11					
12					
13					
14					

Issue date	Total debit memo amount $

ESTIMATE OF REPAIR COSTS

NAME	ADDRESS	PHONE NO.	PHONE EXT.	DATE

MAKE OF CAR	TYPE	STATE	LICENSE NUMBER	JOB NO.	INSPECTOR

YEAR	MILEAGE	MOTOR NO.	SERIAL NO.	INSURANCE	ASSURED	ADJUSTER

QUAN.	WORK TO BE DONE	PARTS NO.	PARTS	LABOR

The above is an estimate based on our inspection and does not cover any additional parts or labor which may be required after the work has been opened up. Occasionally after the work has started, worn or damaged parts are discovered which are not evident on the first inspection. Because of this the above prices are not guaranteed, and are for immediate acceptance only.

	PARTS	LABOR
TOTAL LABOR		
TOTAL PARTS		
TAX ON PARTS		
TOTAL OF ESTIMATE		

B 284

CONTRACTOR'S INVOICE

DATE	
CUSTOMER ORDER NO.	
ORDER TAKEN BY	

CUSTOMER

JOB ADDRESS — STARTING DATE

JOB PHONE — COMPLETE DATE

BILL TO — ☐ DAY WORK

ADDRESS — ☐ CONTRACT

PHONE — ☐ EXTRA

DESCRIPTION OF WORK — INSPECTION

☐ PERMIT

☐ FINAL

☐ COVER

BUILDING PERMIT

SIGNATURE

☐ I AUTHORIZE THE ABOVE DESCRIBED WORK

☐ AT OUR REGULAR RATES   ☐ C.O.D.

☐ FOR THE AMOUNT OF   ☐ INVOICE

WORK ORDERED BY   TIME STARTED

☐ COMPLETE   TIME FINISHED

☐ JOB INCOMPLETE   TRAVEL TIME

DATE	HOURS	TOTAL MATERIAL		
EMPLOYEE(S)		TOTAL LABOR		
		PERMIT		
		OTHER		
		TOTAL AMOUNT		

B 285

SERVICE CONTRACT

Customer's Name _____

Address _____

Phone _____

Date _____

ADDRESS(ES) OF WORK TO BE PERFORMED	JOB ESTIMATE	MAINTAINING PRICE(S)

Services to Be Performed _____

_____

_____

_____

_____

_____

Terms _____

_____

Contractor: Approved by:

_____   _____

                                     CUSTOMER'S SIGNATURE

                          _____

                                  DATE

INVOICE

SOLD TO _____

_____

SHIP TO _____

_____

_____

DATE _____ 19 _____

TERMS _____

ORDER NO. _____

DEPT. _____

SHIP VIA _____

SALESPERSON _____

QUANTITY	NO.	DESCRIPTION	PRICE		TOTAL	

INVOICE

	INVOICE DATE	
	OUR ORDER NO.	
	YOUR ORDER NO.	
	TERMS	F.O.B.
	SALESPERSON	

SHIPPED TO

SHIPPED VIA	PPD. or COLL.

QUANTITY	DESCRIPTION	PRICE	AMOUNT

B 288

INVOICE

SHIPPED TO

SOLD
TO

OUR ORDER NO.	YOUR ORDER NO.	DATE	TERMS	SHIPPED BY	PPD. or COLL.

QUANTITY	DESCRIPTION	PRICE	AMOUNT

SERVICE INVOICE

QUAN.	DESCRIPTION	PRICE

PERSON CALLING/AUTHORIZED BY

PHONE NUMBER:
FAX NUMBER:
☐ OFFICE　　☐ HOME

NAME:

STREET:

CITY:　　STATE　　ZIP

WORK TO BE COMPLETED:

MODEL	SERIAL NUMBER

☐ WARRANTY - REASON -

☐ REGULAR　　☐ SERVICE CONTRACT　　☐ TIME & MATERIAL ☐

DATE　　WORK PERFORMED

UPON INSPECTION, WE RECOMMEND THE FOLLOWING:

I HAVE AUTHORITY TO ORDER THE ABOVE WORK WHICH HAS BEEN SATISFACTORILY PERFORMED. IT IS AGREED THAT THE SELLER WILL RETAIN TITLE TO ANY EQUIPMENT OR MATERIAL THAT MAY BE FURNISHED UNTIL FINAL PAYMENT IS MADE.

CUSTOMER

SERVICE CHARGE	
MATERIAL	
TAX	
TOTAL DUE	**$**

SERVICE WORK STRICTLY CASH

RECEIPT FOR GOODS

DATE_____ 19_____

OUR P. O. NO. _____

CHARGES
PREPAID $_____

CHARGES
COLLECT $_____

RECEIVED FROM _____

ADDRESS _____

DELIVERED BY _____

DEPT _____

JOB _____ REQ. NO. _____

B/L NUMBER	FREIGHT BILL NO.

FOR OFFICE USE

☐ FREIGHT ☐ AIR FREIGHT ☐ EXPRESS ☐ AIR EXPRESS ☐ LOCAL DELIVERY
☐ P. P. ☐ AIR P. P. ☐ PICK-UP ☐ MESSENGER ☐

INVOICE NO. _____

CASES	CARTONS	PACKAGES	CRATES	BUNDLES	DRUMS	

INVOICE DATE_____

TOTAL PACKAGES	WEIGHT	PARTIAL	

	QUANTITY	DESCRIPTION	CONDITION	WEIGHT	ENTERED
1					
2					
3					
4					
5					
6					
7					
8					
9					
10					
11					
12					
13					
14					
15					
16					
17					
18					
19					
20					
21					
22					
23					
24					

REMARKS:

RECEIVED BY	CHECKED BY

B 291

STATEMENT

_____ 19 _____

_____

_____

_____

_____

_B 292_

TAX EXEMPT RESALE CERTIFICATE

To: _____

_____

_____

_____

The undersigned hereby certifies that all tangible personal property hereafter purchased is for the purpose of resale. Purchaser assumes liability for payment of Retailers Occupation Tax, Service Occupation Tax, or Use Tax with respect to receipts from resale of this property.

This certificate shall be a part of each transaction between Vendor and Purchaser unless otherwise specified.

Purchaser: _____ Date: _____

Address: _____ Signature of Purchaser or Authorizing Agent: _____

City: _____ Certificate of Registration No. of Vendor: _____

To: _____

_____

_____

_____

The undersigned certifies that all tangible personal property hereafter purchased is for the purpose of resale and assumes assumes liability for payment of Retailers Occupation Tax, Service Occupation Tax, or Use Tax with respect to receipts from resale of this property.

This certificate shall be a part of each transaction between Vendor and Purchaser unless otherwise specified.

Purchaser: _____ Date: _____

Address: _____ Signature of Purchaser or Authorizing Agent: _____

City: _____ Certificate of Registration No. of Vendor: _____

SHIPPING ORDER

SOLD TO

SHIP TO

CUSTOMER _____

TERMS _____

SALES _____

APP. SHIP WEEK _____

DATE SHIPPED _____

FOB _____

ROUTING _____

INTEREST WILL BE CHARGED AT _____ % PER MONTH
OR _____ % ANNUAL RATE

YOUR ORDER NO.	ORDER DATE	OUR ORDER NO.

ITEM	QUANTITY	DESCRIPTION

QUANTITY SHIPPED	NO. CARTONS	WEIGHT	PACKED BY

TOTALS	QUANTITY	CARTONS	TOTAL WEIGHT
PACKED BY		DATE	
CHECKED BY		DATE	

B 294

SHIPPING ORDER

Deliver to: Date

                                                   Cust. Order No.

                                                   Our Order No.

QUANTITY ORDERED	QUANTITY SHIPPED	ITEMS

Sales
and
Marketing

SALES PROSPECT FILE

New ☐   Update ☐   Follow-up date: _____

Company: _____

Contact: _____ Title: _____

Address: _____

_____

Telephone: _____ Fax: _____

Market segment: _____ Classification: _____

Call-in ☐   Referral ☐   Referred by: _____

Current supplier: _____

Approximate volume (monthly): _____

Letters sent: _____

Material sent: _____

Sales calls (date/summary): _____

_____

_____

_____

_____

_____

Potential: Very high ☐   High ☐   Medium ☐   Low ☐

Possibility of closing   100% ☐   90% ☐   70% ☐   50% ☐   30% ☐   None ☐

General comments/follow-up: _____

_____

_____

SALES LEAD

APPOINTMENT DATE

Day _____ Date _____ Time _____ ☐ a.m. ☐ p.m.

Source _____ Date _____

Name _____

Address _____

Phone No. _____ Fax No. _____

Interested in _____

_____

_____

_____

Remarks: _____

_____

_____

_____

SALES LEAD

APPOINTMENT DATE

Day _____ Date _____ Time _____ ☐ a.m. ☐ p.m.

Source _____ Date _____

Name _____

Address _____

Phone No. _____ Fax No. _____

Interested in _____

_____

_____

_____

Remarks: _____

_____

_____

_____

SALES PROJECTIONS WORKSHEET

PREPARED BY _____ DEPT. _____ DATE _____

	NEW BUSINESS			REORDERS			TOTAL		
	GOAL	ACTUAL	+ OR –	GOAL	ACTUAL	+ OR –	GOAL	ACTUAL	+ OR –

MONTHLY SALES PROJECTIONS

SALESPERSON/DEPARTMENT _____ DATE _____

	NEW BUSINESS			REORDERS			TOTAL		
	GOAL	ACTUAL	+ OR –	GOAL	ACTUAL	+ OR –	GOAL	ACTUAL	+ OR –
JAN									
FEB									
MAR									
APR									
MAY									
JUN									
JUL									
AUG									
SEP									
OCT									
NOV									
DEC									
YEAR									

CHART OF MONTHLY SALES

_____, 19___ to _____, 19___

1st	2nd	3rd	4th	5th	6th	7th	8th	9th	10th	11th	12th

SALES FORECAST

SALESPERSON _____ TERRITORY _____ DATE _____

ACCOUNT NAME & ADDRESS	STATUS			PURCHASES ($)	
	PAST ✓	PRESENT ✓	POTEN. ✓	PAST YEAR	FORECAST THIS YEAR

THREE YEAR SALES FORECAST

SALESPERSON/DEPARTMENT _____

		NEW SALES			REORDERS			TOTAL		
		GOAL	ACTUAL	VARIANCE	GOAL	ACTUAL	VARIANCE	GOAL	ACTUAL	VARIANCE
19	1									
	2									
	3									
	4									
19	1									
	2									
	3									
	4									
19	1									
	2									
	3									
	4									
TOTAL										

BY _____

SALES/PROFIT PROJECTIONS

DATE _____

		MONTH			YTD			ESTIMATED YR. END	
		FORECAST	ACTUAL	VARIANCE	FORECAST	ACTUAL	VARIANCE	FORECAST	ACTUAL	VARIANCE
TOTAL										
PROFIT										

B 306

SALES ACTIVITY ANALYSIS

SALESPERSON_____ TERRITORY_____ DATE_____

		FORECAST	ACTUAL
SALES & PROFIT	Gross Sales		
	Gross Profit		
	% Gross Profit to Gross Sales		
	Net Profit		
	% Net Profit to Gross Sales		
SELLING COST	Salary		
	Commission		
	Expense: Auto		
	Travel		
	Telephone		
	Entertainment		
	Other		
ACTIVITY	Total Days Worked		
	Number of Calls Made		
	Avg. No. Calls per Day		
ACCT. INFO.	No. New Accounts		
	No. Lost Accts.		
	Active Accts. at Period End		
	% Selling Costs to Total Sales		

BY _____

MONTHLY SALES ACTIVITY ANALYSIS

SALESPERSON _____ TERRITORY _____ BY _____ DATE _____

		JAN	FEB	MAR	APR	MAY	JUN	JUL	AUG	SEP	OCT	NOV	DEC	YEAR
PROFIT	Gross Sales													
	Gross Profit													
	% Gross Profit to Gross Sales													
	Net Profit													
	% Net Profit to Gross Sales													
SALES COST	Salary													
	Commission													
	Expense: Auto													
	Travel													
	Telephone													
	Entertainment													
	Other													
ACCT. INFO.	Total Days Worked													
	No. Calls Made													
	Avg. No. Calls per Day													
ACTIVITY	No. New Accounts													
	No. Lost Accts.													
	Active Accts. at Month End													

B 308

MONTHLY RECORD OF AD RECEIPTS

Product		Selling Price		Key	
Publication		Circulation		Issue	On Sale
Ad Cost		Size of Ad		Monthly Profit	Monthly Loss

Projection: Total Number of Orders   Total Income

Month _____ Day of Month	Daily Number of Orders	Total Number of Orders	Daily Income	Total Income	
1					
2					
3					
4					
5					
6					
7					
8					
9					
10					
11					
12					
13					
14					
15					
16					
17					
18					
19					
20					
21					
22					
23					
24					
25					
26					
27					
28					
29					
30					
31					
Total					

QUARTERLY SALES ACTIVITY ANALYSIS

SALESPERSON_____ TERRITORY_____ DATE_____

		1		2		3		4		YEAR	
		Forecast	Actual	Forecast	Actual	Forecast	Actual	Forecast	Actual	Forecast	Actual
SALES & PROFIT	Gross Sales										
	Gross Profit										
	% Gross Profit to Gross Sales										
	Net Profit										
	% Net Profit to Gross Sales										
SELLING COST	Salary										
	Commission										
	Expense: Auto										
	Travel										
	Telephone										
	Entertainment										
	Other										
ACTIVITY	Total Days Worked										
	Number of Calls Made										
	Avg. No. Calls per Day										
ACCT. INFO.	No. New Accounts										
	No. Lost Accts.										
	Active Accts. at Qtr. End										

BY _____

B 310

MONTHLY SALES TREND ANALYSIS

	$ LAST YEAR	$ GOAL THIS YR	$ ACTUAL THIS YR	% DIFF	$ LAST YEAR	$ GOAL THIS YR	$ ACTUAL THIS YR	% DIFF	TOTAL $ LAST YEAR	$ GOAL THIS YR	$ ACTUAL THIS YR	% DIFF
JAN												
FEB												
MAR												
APR												
MAY												
JUN												
JUL												
AUG												
SEP												
OCT												
NOV												
DEC												
YEAR												

BY _____

PRODUCT SALES TREND ANALYSIS 19___

	LAST YEAR $	GOAL THIS YR $	% CHANGE	LAST YEAR $	GOAL THIS YR $	% CHANGE	LAST YEAR $	GOAL THIS YR $	% CHANGE	LAST YEAR $	GOAL THIS YR $	% CHANGE	LAST YEAR $	GOAL THIS YR $	% CHANGE	TOTAL LAST YEAR $	GOAL THIS YR $	% CHANGE
JAN																		
FEB																		
MAR																		
APR																		
MAY																		
JUN																		
JUL																		
AUG																		
SEP																		
OCT																		
NOV																		
DEC																		
TOTAL																		

BY _____

DATE _____

MEDIA FORECAST

19___

PRODUCT:

MEDIA

	TELEVISION		RADIO		MAGAZINE		NEWSPAPER		DIRECT MAIL		OTHER		TOTAL	
	FORECAST	ACTUAL	FORECAST	ACTUAL	FORECAST	ACTUAL	FORECAST	ACTUAL	FORECAST	ACTUAL	FORECAST	ACTUAL	FORECAST	ACTUAL
JANUARY														
FEBRUARY														
MARCH														
APRIL														
MAY														
JUNE														
JULY														
AUGUST														
SEPTEMBER														
OCTOBER														
NOVEMBER														
DECEMBER														
YEAR														

ADVERTISING ANALYSIS

MEDIA

19___

PRODUCT:

			COST	SALES		COST	SALES		COST	SALES		COST	SALES		COST	SALES		COST	SALES		COST	SALES		COST	SALES
JANUARY																									
FEBRUARY																									
MARCH																									
APRIL																									
MAY																									
JUNE																									
JULY																									
AUGUST																									
SEPTEMBER																									
OCTOBER																									
NOVEMBER																									
DECEMBER																									
YEAR																									

PROFITABILITY ANALYSIS

	SALES				COSTS				PROFITS			
	FORECAST		ACTUAL		FORECAST		ACTUAL		FORECAST		ACTUAL	
	MO.	YTD	MO.	YTD	MO.	YTD	MO.	YTD	MO.	YTD	MO.	YTD
JANUARY												
FEBRUARY												
MARCH												
APRIL												
MAY												
JUNE												
JULY												
AUGUST												
SEPTEMBER												
OCTOBER												
NOVEMBER												
DECEMBER												

BY _____   DATE _____

B 315

DIRECT MAIL ANALYSIS

PRODUCT/PROMOTION _____ DATE _____

PRODUCT		PROMOTION	
1. SELLING PRICE		16. CIRCULARS	
2. ADD: SERVICE CHARGE		17. INSERTS	
3. **TOTAL SELLING PRICE**		18. LETTERS	
4. LESS: PRODUCT COST		19. ENVELOPES	
5. SHIPPING/DELIVERY		20. ORDER FORMS	
6. ORDER PROCESSING		21. LIST RENTAL	
7. COST OF RETURNS		22. INSERTING	
8. BAD DEBT		23. ADDRESSING–LABELS	
9.		24. MAILING	
10.		25. POSTAGE	
11.		26. MISCELLANEOUS	
12.		27. **TOTAL CIRCULATION COST**	
13.			
14. **TOTAL COST**		28. TOTAL COST(C)	
15. **UNIT PROFIT(P)**		29. BREAK EVEN SALES PER M (C ÷ P)	

NET PROFIT

FORECASTED NET SALES PER M (In Units)	
LESS: BREAK EVEN SALES-LINE 30 (In Units)	—
UNIT SALES PER M EARNING TOTAL PROFIT	
UNIT PROFIT - LINE 15	X
NET PROFIT PER M	$
M CIRCULARS MAILED	X
TOTAL NET PROFIT	

BY _____

PROMOTION BUDGET

DATE_____

FIXED COSTS

ITEMS	NEEDED BY	COST
	TOTAL (A)	

VARIABLE COSTS

ITEMS	NEEDED BY	COST
	TOTAL (B)	

TOTAL DIRECT COST (A + B)	
INDIRECT COSTS	
OTHER COSTS	
TOTAL PROMOTIONAL COSTS	

COMPARATIVE ADVERTISING PLAN

DATE _____

MEDIA

	TELEVISION		RADIO		MAGAZINE		NEWSPAPER		DIRECT MAIL		OTHER		TOTAL	
	LAST YEAR	THIS YEAR	LAST YEAR	THIS YEAR	LAST YEAR	THIS YEAR	LAST YEAR	THIS YEAR	LAST YEAR	THIS YEAR	LAST YEAR	THIS YEAR	LAST YEAR	THIS YEAR
JANUARY														
FEBRUARY														
MARCH														
APRIL														
MAY														
JUNE														
JULY														
AUGUST														
SEPTEMBER														
OCTOBER														
NOVEMBER														
DECEMBER														
YEAR														

ANNUAL ADVERTISING FORECAST 19___

MEDIA

	FORECAST	ACTUAL	FORECAST	ACTUAL	FORECAST	ACTUAL	FORECAST	ACTUAL	FORECAST	ACTUAL	FORECAST	ACTUAL	FORECAST	ACTUAL
JANUARY														
FEBRUARY														
MARCH														
APRIL														
MAY														
JUNE														
JULY														
AUGUST														
SEPTEMBER														
OCTOBER														
NOVEMBER														
DECEMBER														
TOTAL														

MAILING LIST UPDATE

	Date Added To List	Name	Address	Mailing Sent	Keep On List	Drop
1						
2						
3						
4						
5						
6						
7						
8						
9						
10						
11						
12						
13						
14						
15						
16						
17						
18						
19						
20						
21						
22						
23						
24						
25						
26						

COMMISSION REPORT

Salesperson: _____   Period From: _____ To: _____

Order Date	Order Number	Account	Invoice Amount	Commission Rate	Due Salesperson

Total Sales _____

Total Commission Earned _____

Less Advance/Credit _____

Commission Due _____

_____   _____
              Signed   Date

B 321

DAILY TELEPHONE SALES REPORT

To:

Date _____

Reporting period:

from _____ to _____

Sales representative _____

Address _____

City/state/zip _____

Telephone # _____

Product line _____

Territory # _____

Branch/region or zone _____

Date submitted _____

Report # _____

Page _____ of _____ pgs

NAME AND ADDRESS OF FIRM	CONTACT AND TITLE	PRODUCTS PRESENTED OR SOLD

Signature _____

Title _____

COMMISSION INCOME JOURNAL

MONTH _____
YEAR _____

ORDER NO.	CUSTOMER	ORDER NO/DATE	ORDER AMOUNT	COMMISSION DUE			SHIPPING/INVOICE INFORMATION			COMMISSIONS PAID			NOTES
				%	AMOUNT	DATE	REQ. SHIP DT.	ACTUAL SHIP DT.	ACTUAL INV. AMT.	DATE	CK. #	AMOUNT	
PAGE TOTALS →			$		$				$			$	

TELEMARKETING PROSPECT SHEET

Date: _____ Time: _____ Client: _____ Product: _____

Prospect: _____

Individual spoken to: _____ Title: _____

Address: _____

Business telephone: _____ Fax: _____

Preferred contact:

   Time: _____

   Place: _____

·   ·   ·

Reason for call: _____

Previous purchase (if any): _____

Current sale: _____

Future potential: _____

Potential reference: _____

·   ·   ·

Comments: _____

_____

_____

_____

_____

_____

Follow up: _____

_____

Caller: _____

TELEMARKETING CALLBACK WORKSHEET

Telemarketer: _____ Date: _____

Call frequency: _____

Account/prospect: _____

Contact: _____ Title: _____

Mailing address: _____

Delivery address: _____

Delivery instructions: _____

Business telephone: _____ Fax: _____

Contact: _____

   Time: _____

   Place: _____

Objective(s) of this call: _____

Objective(s) of last call: _____

Last purchase: _____

SUMMARY:

_____

_____

_____

_____

_____

_____

_____

_____

_____

Next follow-up date: _____

B 325

TELEMARKETING REPORT

REPORT FOR WEEK OF: _____ FROM: _____

	NUMBER OF CALLS COMPLETED			NUMBER OF ORDERS RECEIVED	
	TO CLIENTS	TO PROSPECTS		FROM CLIENTS	FROM PROSPECTS
MONDAY					
TUESDAY					
WEDNESDAY					
THURSDAY					
FRIDAY					
THIS WEEK'S TOTAL					
LAST WEEK'S TOTAL					
NEXT WEEK'S TOTAL					

Notes: _____

_____

_____

_____

_____

_____

_____

_____

_____

_____

TELEPHONE SALES ANALYSIS

Date: _____   Product: _____   By: _____

PROSPECT NAME	TELEPHONE NO.	RESULTS/OBJECTIONS/COMMENTS	FOLLOW-UP

Personnel

PERSONNEL ACTIVITY REPORT

Month _____ Year _____ Dept. _____

Date prepared _____ by _____

	Salaried	Hourly	P/T
# employees at start			
# employees at end			
# positions open			
# applicants interviewed			
# applicants hired			
% hires to interviews			
# employees terminated			
# employees resigned			
# vacancies at start			
# vacancies at end			
Total positions to fill			
Employee requisitions received			
Employee requisitions filled			
Employee requisitions unfilled			
Employee turnover rate			

Comments:

AFFIRMATIVE ACTION SUMMARY

Date	Applicants for Hire		New Hires		Applicants for Promotion		Promotions		Terminations	
	Male	Female	Male	Female	Male	Female	Male	Female	Male	Female
White										
Black										
Hispanic										
Asian										
American Indian										

NOTES

REQUEST FOR APPROVAL
TO HIRE

Requisition No._____Date_____

Applicant_____ S.S.N. _____

Title/Job Classification/Rank _____

_____

_____

P/T_____ F/T_____ Perm._____ Temp._____

Starting Salary $_____

Reports To_____

Replacement_____New Position_____

Department_____Budget_____

Description of Duties_____

_____

_____

_____

Other: _____

_____

_____

_____

_____

_____

_____

Starting Date_____

_____

Requested By

EMPLOYMENT REQUISITION

JOB TITLE _____

DEPARTMENT _____ LOCATION _____ SUPERVISOR _____ EXT. _____

Date to start	Shift	Addition ☐ Replacement ☐	If Replacement, For whom?	Desired Starting Rate: _____

DUTIES: _____

EXPERIENCE REQUIRED: _____

SPECIAL SKILLS: _____

SIGNED _____ DATE _____ APPROVED _____ DATE _____

FOR OFFICE USE ONLY

DATE RECEIVED _____

DATE	INSTRUCTIONS	DATE	INSTRUCTIONS

Person Hired	Starting Date	Starting Pay	Remarks

Job Code _____ Rate Range _____

Signed _____ Date _____

B 334

EMPLOYMENT APPLICATION

PERSONAL INFORMATION:

Date _____ Social Security Number _____

Name _____

| Last | First | Middle |

Present Address _____

| Street | City | State | Zip |

Permanent Address _____

| Sreet | City | State | Zip |

Phone No. _____ Fax: _____

Are Any Relatives, Other Than Spouse, Already Employed By This Company? _____

Referred by _____

(Right margin vertical labels: Last, First, Middle)

EMPLOYMENT DESIRED:

Position _____ Date You Can Start _____ Salary Desired _____

Are You Employed Now? _____ If So—May We Inquire of Your Present Employer? _____

Ever Applied to this Company Before? _____ Where _____ When _____

EDUCATION:

	Name and Location of School	Circle Last Year Completed	Did You Graduate?	Subjects Studied and Degree(s) Received
Grammar School		1 2 3 4	☐ Yes ☐ No	
High School		1 2 3 4	☐ Yes ☐ No	
College		1 2 3 4	☐ Yes ☐ No	
Trade, Business or Correspondence School		1 2 3 4	☐ Yes ☐ No	

Subjects of Special Study or Research Work: _____

What Foreign Languages Do You Speak Fluently? _____

Read? _____ Write? _____

List Activities Other Than Religious (Civic, Athletic, etc.) _____

EXCLUDE ORGANIZATIONS—THE NAME OR CHARACTER OF WHICH INDICATES THE RACE, CREED, COLOR OR NATIONAL ORIGIN OF ITS MEMBERS.

(Continued on Reverse Side)

_B 335_

FORMER EMPLOYERS: *List Below the Last Four Employers—Starting with Last One First*

Date Month and Year	Name and Address of Employer	Salary	Position	Reason for Leaving
From				
To				
From				
To				
From				
To				
From				
To				

REFERENCES: *List Below the Names of Three Persons, Not Related To You, Whom You Have Known At Least One Year.*

	Name	Address	Business	Years Acquainted
1				
2				
3				

PHYSICAL RECORD: *Do you have any physical condition which may limit your ability to perform the job applied for?*

In Case of Emergency Notify

Name   Address   Phone No.

I authorize investigation of all statements contained in this application. I understand that misrepresentation or omission of facts called for is cause for dismissal. Further, I understand and agree that my employment is for no definite period and may, regardless of the date of payment of my wages and salary, be terminated at any time without any previous notice.

Date   Signature

DO NOT WRITE BELOW THIS LINE

Interviewed By   Date

REMARKS:

Neatness		Attitude	
Personality		Ability	

Hired	Dept.	Position		Will Report	Salary Wages

Approved: 1.   2.   3.

Personnel   Department Head

EMPLOYMENT ELIGIBILITY VERIFICATION

1 **EMPLOYEE INFORMATION AND VERIFICATION:** (To be completed and signed by employee.)				
Name: (Print or Type) Last	First	Middle	Maiden
Address: Street Name and Number	City	State	ZIP Code
Date of Birth (Month/Day/Year)		Social Security Number	

I attest, under penalty of perjury, that I am (check a box):

☐ A citizen or national of the United States.

☐ An alien lawfully admitted for permanent residence (Alien Number A_____).

☐ An alien authorized by the Immigration and Naturalization Service to work in the United States (Alien Number A_____,

or Admission Number _____, expiration of employment authorization, if any _____).

I attest, under penalty of perjury, the documents that I have presented as evidence of identity and employment eligibility are genuine and relate to me. I am aware that federal law provides for imprisonment and/or fine for any false statements or use of false documents in connection with this certificate.

Signature	Date (Month/Day/Year)

PREPARER TRANSLATOR CERTIFICATION (If prepared by other than the individual). I attest, under penalty of perjury, that the above was prepared by me at the request of the named individual and is based on all information of which I have any knowledge.

Signature	Name (Print or Type)		
Address (Street Name and Number)	City	State	Zip Code

2 **EMPLOYER REVIEW AND VERIFICATION:** (To be completed and signed by employer.)

Examine one document from those in List A and check the correct box, _or_ examine one document from List B **and** one from List C and check the correct boxes. Provide the **_Document Identification Number_** and **_Expiration Date_**, for the document checked in that column.

List A Identity and Employment Eligibility	List B Identity	**and**	List C Employment Eligibility
☐ United States Passport ☐ Certificate of United States Citizenship ☐ Certificate of Naturalization ☐ Unexpired foreign passport with attached Employment Authorization ☐ Alien Registration Card with photograph	☐ A State issued driver's license or I.D. card with a photograph, or information, including name, sex, date of birth, height, weight, and color of eyes. (Specify State_____) ☐ U.S. Military Card ☐ Other (Specify document and issuing authority) _____		☐ Original Social Security Number Card (other than a card stating it is not valid for employment) ☐ A birth certificate issued by State, county, or municipal authority bearing a seal or other certification. ☐ Unexpired INS Employment Authorization Specify form #_____
Document Identification #_____	**_Document Identification_** #_____		**_Document Identification_** #_____
Expiration Date (if any) _____	**_Expiration Date (if any)_** _____		**_Expiration Date (if any)_** _____

CERTIFICATION: I attest, under penalty of perjury, that I have examined the documents presented by the above individual, that they appear to be genuine, relate to the individual named, and that the individual, to the best of my knowledge, is authorized to work in the United States.

Signature	Name (Print or Type)	Title
Employer Name	Address	Date

Form 1-9 (03/20/87)
OMB No. 1115-0136

U.S. Department of Justice
Immigration and Naturalization Service

Employment Eligibility Verification

Section 1.   Employee's/Preparer's instructions for completing this form.

Instructions for the employee.

All employees, upon being hired, must complete Section 1 of this form. Any person hired after November 6, 1986 must complete this form. (For the purpose of completion of this form the term "hired" applies to those employed, recruited or referred for a fee.)

All employees must print or type their complete name, address, date of birth, and Social Security Number. The block which correctly indicates the employee's immigration status must be checked. If the second block is checked, the employee's Alien Registration Number must be provided. If the third block is checked, the employee's Alien Registration Number *or* Admission Number must be provided, as well as the date of expiration of that status, if it expires.

All employees must sign and date the form.

Instructions for the preparer of the form, if not the employee.

If the employee is assisted with completing this form, the person assisting must certify the form by signing it, and printing or typing his or her complete name and address.

Section 2.   Employer's instructions for completing this form.

(For the purpose of completion of this form, the term "employer" applies to employers and those who recruit or refer for a fee.)

Employers must complete this section by examining evidence of identity and employment authorization, and:
- checking the appropriate box in List A *or* boxes in both Lists B and C;
- recording the document identification number and expiration date (if any);
- recording the type of form if not specifically identified in the list;
- signing the certification section.

NOTE: Employers are responsible for reverifying employment eligibility of aliens upon expiration of any employment authorization documents, should they desire to continue the alien's employment.

Copies of documentation presented by an individual for the purpose of establishing identity and employment eligibility may be copied and retained for the purpose of complying with the requirements of this form and no other purpose. Any copies of documentation made for this purpose should be maintained with this form.

Employers may photocopy or reprint this form, as necessary, for their use.

RETENTION OF RECORDS.

After completion of this form, it must be retained by the employer during the period beginning on the date of hiring and ending:
- three years after the date of such hiring, or;
- one year after the date the individual's employment is terminated, whichever is later.

U.S. Department of Justice
Immigration and Naturalization Service

OMB #1115-0136
Form 1-9 (03 20 87)

TEMPORARY
EMPLOYMENT REQUISITION

Date:_____

Position/Duties_____

Department_____ Location _____

Supervisor/Dept. Head _____

Dates Required:_____ To_____

Shift Required:_____ To_____

Reasons for Hiring _____

_____

_____

_____

_____

Estimated Cost: _____

Budget No:_____

Are Funds Budgeted? _____yes   _____no

_____
Requested By

Date:_____   _____
Approved By

INTERVIEW SCHEDULE

Time	Date	Applicant	Position	Tests	Comments	Follow-up

INTERVIEW SUMMARY

Date:

Applicant_____

Position_____ Dept. _____

Date/Time Interviewed _____

Date Available to Start Employment_____

Salary Requested_____

EVALUATION

	Excellent	Good	Fair	Poor
Appearance	____	____	____	____
Experience	____	____	____	____
Education	____	____	____	____
Skills	____	____	____	____
Enthusiasm	____	____	____	____
Attitude	____	____	____	____
Other:	____	____	____	____
	____	____	____	____
	____	____	____	____

Comments:

_____

_____

Recommendations:

_____

_____

_____
Interviewer

TELEPHONE REFERENCE REPORT

Applicant		Position	
Address:		Telephone No.	Fax. No.
Reference Name	Company	Title	
Relationship to Applicant		Years Known	
Employment Dates From To		Starting Salary	Ending Salary
Position		Reason for Leaving	
Duties			

	Excellent	Good	Fair	Poor	Comments
Overall Performance					
Productivity					
Work Quality					
Attitude					
Ability to work with others					
Ability to work with little supervision					

Strengths
Weaknesses
Supervisory Experience
Overall Evaluation
Follow-up

By	Date

NEW EMPLOYEE RECORD CHART

Employee_____ Date _____

Department_____ Starting Date _____

The above new employee must have
checked item(s) in file *before* starting work.

Document	(√) Required	(√) Completed
Employment Application	_____	_____
Personal Data Sheet	_____	_____
Employee Verification Checklist	_____	_____
W-4	_____	_____
Fidelity Bond	_____	_____
Physical/Medical Report	_____	_____
Employment Contract	_____	_____
Non-Compete Agreement	_____	_____
Trade Secret Agreement	_____	_____
Conflict of Interest Declaration	_____	_____
Indemnity Agreement	_____	_____
Security Form	_____	_____

Other:

_____	_____	_____
_____	_____	_____
_____	_____	_____
_____	_____	_____

By: _____

EMPLOYEE PERSONNEL FILE

EMPLOYEE _____

ADDRESS _____

	City	State	Zip	Telephone
	City	State	Zip	Telephone
	City	State	Zip	Telephone

SOCIAL SECURITY NO. _____ DATE OF BIRTH _____ SEX: ☐ M ☐ F

MARITAL STATUS: ☐ SINGLE ☐ MARRIED ☐ SEPARATED ☐ DIVORCED

SPOUSE _____ NO. DEPENDENTS _____

IN EMERGENCY NOTIFY _____ RELATIONSHIP _____

ADDRESS _____ TELEPHONE _____

EDUCATION: ELEMENTARY _____ HIGH _____ COLLEGE _____ GRADUATE _____

OTHER _____

HISTORY

DATE		POSITION/DEPARTMENT	PAY	
FROM	TO		AMOUNT	PER

UNION MEMBER: ☐ YES ☐ NO   UNION (Local) NAME _____

NAME	DATES		NAME	DATES	
	Eligible	Enrolled		Eligible	Enrolled
PENSION PLAN			GROUP INSURANCE		
PROFIT SHARING					
CREDIT UNION					

SPECIAL SKILLS _____

SECURITY CLEARANCE _____

TERMINATION DATA

DATE TERMINATED _____ WOULD WE REHIRE? YES ☐ NO ☐

REASON FOR TERMINATION: _____

CONFIDENTIAL EMPLOYEE HISTORY

EMPLOYEE		EMPLOYED SINCE	STATUS
			☐ REGULAR ☐ PART TIME ☐ TEMPORARY

YEARS OF SERVICE	1	2	3	4	5	6	7	8	9	10	11	12	13	14	15	16	17	18	19	20	21	22	23	24	25	26		SECURITY CLEARANCE	LEVEL

BIRTHDATE	SEX	SOCIAL SECURITY NO.	MARITAL STATUS	SPOUSE	NO. CHILDREN

FEDERAL WITHHOLDING:	EXEMPTIONS CLAIMED												
	ADDITIONAL AMOUNT WITHHELD												

	DATE ELIGIBLE	DATE JOINED	DATE WITHDRAWN	INSURANCE	DATE ELIGIBLE	DATE JOINED	DATE WITHDRAWN
UNION STATUS				LIFE			
PENSION PLAN				MEDICAL			
CREDIT UNION							

ADDRESS	CITY	STATE	ZIP	PHONE
ADDRESS	CITY	STATE	ZIP	PHONE
ADDRESS	CITY	STATE	ZIP	PHONE
ADDRESS	CITY	STATE	ZIP	PHONE

NOTIFY IN EMERGENCY	RELATION	CITY	STATE	ZIP	PHONE
	RELATION	CITY	STATE	ZIP	PHONE

RELATIVES OR FRIENDS EMPLOYED BY THIS CO.	NAMES	RELATION	NAMES	RELATION

EDUCATION	GRADE_____ J H S _____ S H S _____	SPECIAL SKILLS/ TRAINING	
	COLLEGE 1 2 3 4 MAJOR _____		
	OTHER _____		

TERMINATION RECORD

☐ RESIGNATION DATE_____	REASON
☐ DISMISSAL DATE_____	REASON

RECOMMENDED FOR RE-EMPLOYMENT ☐ YES ☐ NO

EMPLOYEE HEALTH RECORD

NAME		ADDRESS		PHONE

SEX	AGE		PHYSICIAN		PHONE

DATE EMPLOYED	POSITION		DEPARTMENT	SUPERVISOR	

DATE OF PRE-EMPLOYMENT EXAM					

IN EMERGENCY, NOTIFY:		RELATION	ADDRESS		PHONE

MEDICAL HISTORY

DATE	TIME	REASON FOR VISIT	TREATMENT	TREATED BY

SUPERVISORS ORIENTATION CHECKLIST

Employee_____Department_____

Employment Date_____

Position_____

	Items Reviewed	(√)
Duties		_____
Work Hours		_____
Co-Employee Introduction		_____
Locker/Desk/Office		_____
Supplies & Storage		_____
Safety Procedures		_____
Equipment & Tools		_____
Recordkeeping Procedures		_____
Job Training		_____
Overtime Policy		_____
Other Policies		
_____		_____
_____		_____
_____		_____

Date:

    I acknowledge the above checked information has been reviewed with me to my satisfaction and understanding.

_____   _____
          Employee   **Supervisor**

B 347

RECEIPT FOR COMPANY PROPERTY

Employee_____

ID No._____

Department/Section_____

    I acknowledge receipt of the below company-owned equipment. I agree to maintain the equipment in good condition and to return it when I terminate employment with the company, or upon request. I shall immediately report any loss or damage, and use said property only for work-related purposes.

Receipt			*Return*	
Item	*Quantity*	*No.*	*Returned to*	*Date*
_____	____	_____	_____	_____
_____	____	_____	_____	_____
_____	____	_____	_____	_____
_____	____	_____	_____	_____
_____	____	_____	_____	_____
_____	____	_____	_____	_____
_____	____	_____	_____	_____
_____	____	_____	_____	_____

_____
Signature

_____
Date

Issued By:_____

PAYROLL SUMMARY

For week/month ending ———

Employee	Salary Rate	Total Hours	Regular Hours	Straight Overtime	Premium Overtime	Sick Leave	Vacation	Earnings

DEPARTMENT OVERTIME LIST

Department			Period	
Employee	Date	Overtime hrs.	Overtime amount	% payroll

Prepared by: Approved by:

OVERTIME PERMIT

Employee _____ Date_____

Department _____

    Is authorized to work overtime a maximum of   hours between the dates of

    and

    The overtime rate shall be in accordance with company policy.

                  Other Comments/Conditions

_____

_____

_____

_____

_____

_____

_____

Requested By _____

Approved By _____

OVERTIME SUMMARY

Department		Date

Payroll Period	Total O.T. hours	Total O.T. amount	% of total payroll

Prepared by: Approved by:

EMPLOYEE STATUS CHANGE

Employee_____ Date_____

Department_____ I.D. No._____

Effective Date_____

1.   Change Pay

      From_____ To_____

2.   Change Job Title

      From_____ To_____

3.   Change Job Classification

      From_____ To_____

4.   Change Shift

      From_____ To_____

5.   Temporary/Permanent Change:

      From_____ To_____

6.   Other: (Describe)

      _____

      _____

      _____

      _____

_____   _____
      Prepared By   Approved By

CONSENT TO RELEASE OF INFORMATION

Date:_____

To:_____(Employee)

Verification of employment information concerning you has been received from: _____

_____

Please check (√) those items for which information may be released:

_____ **Salary**

_____ Position/title/duties

_____ **Department.**

_____ Supervisor/Department head

_____ **Dates of employment.**

_____ Hours worked

_____ **Whether you worked under a maiden name.**

_____ Garnishes or wage attachments

_____ **Reason for separation.**

_____ Health/Medical information

_____ Other.

_____   _____
Employee Signature   **Date**

PLEASE RETURN THIS FORM AS SOON AS POSSIBLE SO WE MAY
RESPOND TO THE REQUEST FOR INFORMATION.
YOUR CONSENT ON THIS OCCASION WILL NOT CONSTITUTE A CON-
SENT TO RELEASE OF INFORMATION ON FUTURE OCCASIONS.

DAILY ATTENDANCE REPORT

	1	2	3	4	5	6	7	8	9	10	11	12	13	14	15	16	17	18	19	20	21	22	23	24	25	26	27	28	29	30	31	LATE HRS	LATE MIN	SICK	DAYS ABSENT EXC	INEXC
19 JAN																																				
FEB																																				
MARCH																																				
APRIL																																				
MAY																																				
JUNE																																				
JULY																																				
AUG.																																				
SEPT.																																				
OCT.																																				
NOV.																																				
DEC.																																				
TOTAL																																				

	1	2	3	4	5	6	7	8	9	10	11	12	13	14	15	16	17	18	19	20	21	22	23	24	25	26	27	28	29	30	31					
19 JAN.																																				
FEB.																																				
MARCH																																				
APRIL																																				
MAY																																				
JUNE																																				
JULY																																				
AUG.																																				
SEPT.																																				
OCT.																																				
NOV.																																				
DEC.																																				
																																TOTAL				

CODE:

I – INEXCUSED ABSENCE   V – VACATION   L – LATE (SHOW NO. OF MINUTES LATE)

E – EXCUSED ABSENCE   S – SICK

NOTES:

JOB TIME RECORD

Employee			Employee Number	
Date	Department	Title	Salary	Comments

EMPLOYEE TIME SHEET

Employee_____   Period ending_____

Department_____   Supervisor _____

Date	Time started	Time finished	Overtime	Total hours
Authorized Signature		Title		Date

DAILY TIME SHEET

Day: _____ Date: _____ Dept: _____ Location: _____

Employee	Began Work	End Work	Over Time Hours	Comments

Supervisor _____

B 358

WEEKLY SCHEDULE

WEEK ENDING _____

EMPLOYEE	DEPT	HOURS						
		SUN	MON	TUE	WED	THU	FRI	SAT

B 359

WEEKLY TIME SHEETS

For week ending _____   Department _____   Location _____

Employee	Mon	Tues	Wed	Thurs	Fri	Sat	Sun	Total	Gross Pay	Ded	Net Pay
Totals											

PAYROLL REGISTER

DATE _____ DEPT. _____ LOCATION _____

YEAR-TO-DATE		EMPLOYEE		NAME OF EMPLOYEE	HOURS WORKED	BASE RATE	EARNINGS				DEDUCTIONS			NET PAY
EARNINGS	WITH TAX	DEPT	NUMBER				REGULAR	OT	OTHER	TOTAL	FICA	WITH TAX	MISC.	

B 361

WEEKLY PAYROLL SUMMARY

DEPARTMENT

LOCATION

WEEK ENDING

EMPLOYEE NAME	HOURS WORK'D	RATE	TOTALS			DEDUCTIONS						NET PAY	CHECK NO.
			REG. WAGES	O.T. WAGES	GROSS WAGES	FED. TAXES	STATE TAXES	FICA	INS.	DUES			

EMPLOYEE EARNINGS RECORD

EMPLOYEE		EMP. No.		SOCIAL SECURITY No.	DEPENDENTS	SALARY/WAGES

FIRST QUARTER

WEEK ENDING	HOURS		DEDUCTIONS				NET PAY
	Reg.	O.T.	Fed. W.H.	St. W.H.	FICA		
TOTAL 1st QUARTER							
TOTAL 3 MONTHS							

THIRD QUARTER

WEEK ENDING	HOURS		DEDUCTIONS				NET PAY
	Reg.	O.T.	Fed. W.H.	St. W.H.	FICA		
TOTAL 3rd QUARTER							
TOTAL 9 MONTHS							

SECOND QUARTER

WEEK ENDING	HOURS		DEDUCTIONS				NET PAY
	Reg.	O.T.	Fed. W.H.	St. W.H.	FICA		
TOTAL 2nd QUARTER							
TOTAL 6 MONTHS							

FOURTH QUARTER

WEEK ENDING	HOURS		DEDUCTIONS				NET PAY
	Reg.	O.T.	Fed. W.H.	St. W.H.	FICA		
TOTAL 4th QUARTER							
TOTAL 12 MONTHS							

EMPLOYEE FLEXTIME SCHEDULE

Employee

Week of:

Department:

Supervisor:

Day	Time In	Meals		Time Out	Other Absences		Hours for Day	Cumulative Total
		Out	In					
Monday								
Tuesday								
Wednesday								
Thursday								
Friday								
Saturday								
Sunday								

VACATION SCHEDULE

Department _____

Dept. Head _____

EMPLOYEE ON VACATION	ALTERNATE TO COVER DUTIES	WEEK BEGINNING:						OTHER WEEKS
		APRIL	MAY	JUNE	JULY	AUGUST		

INJURY REPORT

Employee: _____ Social Security No.: _____

Home address: _____ Tel. No. _____

Next of Kin: _____

Age: _____ ☐ Male

Shift _____ ☐ Female

Dept.: _____ Supervisor: _____

Is injury or illness related to employment?   Yes ☐   No ☐

Date of injury or initial diagnosis: _____ Time of injury: _____ Place: _____

Describe the illness or injury in detail and indicate the part of body affected.

_____

_____

_____

Use reverse side if necessary.
Attach my medical records.   Did employee return to work?   Yes ☐   No ☐

If employee did not return to work, indicate last day worked: _____

Name and address of physician: _____

_____

If hospitalized, name and address of hospital: _____

_____

Witnesses: _____

_____

Comments: _____

_____

Employee Signature: _____

Signature of attending nurse or first aid person: _____

Date: _____

PHYSICIAN'S REPORT

Doctor_____ Date_____

Address_____

Re:_____

Dear Doctor:

Our above employee was absent from work on the days noted on the reverse side of this letter. We have been advised that our employee has been under your care. It is our policy to verify protracted medical absences, so we would appreciate your completing this form and returning it for our records. Our employee (your patient) consents to this disclosure.

Sincerely,

_____

I authorize my above physician to furnish this information.

_____
Employee

Physicians Report

I certify that _____ has been under my medical care and that the absences listed were medically advisable.

Dated:_____   _____
                                              Physician's Signature

B 367

VACATION/LEAVE
REQUEST

Employee_____ Request date: _____

Department_____ Position_____

This is for vacation (√) _____ leave of absence (√) _____.

1. Date(s) Requested:

From_____To_____

2. Alternate Dates Acceptable:

From_____ To_____, or
From_____ To_____

3. Reasons (For Leave of Absence):

_____
_____
_____
_____

4. Non-Vacation Leave Time To Be:

____With Pay ____Without Pay ____Made-Up ____At Partial Pay Rate

5. Comments

_____
Employee

Approved By   Date

_____   _____

ABSENCE REQUEST

EMPLOYEE	DATE	DEPARTMENT

DATE(S) REQUESTED	HOUR(S) REQUESTED
FROM TO	FROM TO

___WITH PAY   ___WITHOUT PAY   ___MAKEUP

REMARKS/REASONS/EXPLANATIONS

EMPLOYEE SIGNATURE

APPROVED BY	DATE(S) APPROVED

ABSENCE REPORT

Employee	Date	Department

Date(s) absent	Date returned to work	Day(s) missed

Did employee notify company

_____Yes   _____No

Person Notified _____ Title _____

Reason for absence

Was absence approved ?

_____yes   _____no

If not, why not?

Verification

ACTION TAKEN

___   NONE

___   DEDUCT PAY

___   MAKE-UP

___   WARNING

___   OTHER

Comments

SIGNED	TITLE	DATE

LATE REPORT

EMPLOYEE	DATE	DEPARTMENT

TIME DUE AT WORK	ACTUAL ARRIVAL TIME	TIME MISSED

DID EMPLOYEE NOTIFY COMPANY?

_____YES   _____NO

PERSON NOTIFIED _____ TITLE _____

HOW AND WHEN NOTIFIED? _____

_____

_____

_____

_____

_____

COMMENTS

ACTION TAKEN

____   NONE

____   DEDUCT PAY

____   MAKE-UP

____   WARNING

____   OTHER

SIGNED	TITLE	DATE

MEDICAL SUMMARY

Date _____

For period ending _____

Dept. _____

Employee	medically treated by	Time	Injury/Illness	Treatment

Comments:

SALARY REVIEW FORM

NAME _____ | EFFECTIVE DATE

POSITION _____

DEPT. _____

SUPERVISOR _____ | EMPLOYMENT DATE _____

TIME IN PRESENT POSITION _____ | AGE _____ | ☐ MALE ☐ FEMALE

PRESENT SALARY _____

RECOMMENDED INCREASE _____

RECOMMENDED NEW SALARY _____

ATTENDANCE PAST 12 MONTHS

PAID ABSENCES	NON-PAID ABSENCES	TARDY

EXPLAIN ANY PERIOD OF ABSENCE BELOW.

☐ PROMOTION – SHOW QUALIFICATIONS UNDER REASON

DATE PROMOTED _____ | FORMER POSITION AND DEPT. _____

FORMER SALARY _____

☐ MERIT –   ☐ OTHER

REASON

FOR INCENTIVE JOBS: RECOMMENDING DEPARTMENT HEAD MUST NOTIFY HUMAN RESOURCES THAT THERE HAS BEEN A CHANGE IN RATE FOR THE EMPLOYEE.

SALARY ACTION

FOR SAL. ADMIN. AND PAYROLL USE				NON-EXEMPT
PRESENT RATE ANNUAL	NEW RATE ANNUAL	INCREASE	ANNUAL INCREASE	HRLY. RATE

REQUEST FOR TRANSFER

EMPLOYEE		EMPLOYEE NO.	SHIFT
DEPARTMENT		DEPT.	
PRESENT POSITION		YEARS AT POSITION	
POSITION REQUESTED			
EXPERIENCE FOR NEW POSITION			
REASON FOR TRANSFER REQUEST			
EMPLOYEE'S SIGNATURE		DATE	EXTENSION

SUPERVISOR'S COMMENTS

EVALUATION IN PRESENT POSITION

RECOMMENDATION:

SUPERVISOR'S SIGNATURE		DATE	EXTENSION

HUMAN RESOURCES

DATE RECEIVED	DATE INTERVIEWED	INTERVIEWED BY IEWED

COMMENTS

ACTION

DATE EMPLOYEE NOTIFIED	INTERVIEWER'S SIGNATURE	DATE

EMPLOYEE PERFORMANCE
CHECKFORM

Employee_____ Date_____

Department_____ Review Period _____

Reviewer_____

Checklist

	Excellent	Good	Fair	Poor	Comments
Honest y	____	____	____	____	____
Productivity	____	____	____	____	____
Work Quality	____	____	____	____	____
Skills	____	____	____	____	____
Work Consistency	____	____	____	____	____
Enthusiasm	____	____	____	____	____
Cooperativeness	____	____	____	____	____
Attitude	____	____	____	____	____
Initiative	____	____	____	____	____
Working Relations	____	____	____	____	____
Originality	____	____	____	____	____
Punctuality	____	____	____	____	____
Attendance	____	____	____	____	____
Dependability	____	____	____	____	____
Appearance	____	____	____	____	____
Other:					
_____	____	____	____	____	____
_____	____	____	____	____	____

_____
Reviewer

EMPLOYEE SELF-EVALUATION
(CONFIDENTIAL)

Date	Name of employee	Dept.	Period

My most successful job accomplishments in this period are:

A._____

B._____

C._____

D._____

My least successful accomplishments in this period are:

A._____

B._____

C._____

My key strengths are:

A._____

B._____

C._____

The following areas need improvement:

A._____

B._____

I will take this action to improve:

_____

_____

_____

_____

INCIDENT/GRIEVANCE
REPORT

Date:_____

Employee_____ Department _____

1.   Nature of Incident/Grievance _____

_____

_____

_____

_____

_____

_____

_____

_____

2.   Witnesses:

Name	Address
_____	_____
_____	_____
_____	_____
_____	_____

3.   Reported To:

Person	Date
_____	_____
_____	_____
_____	_____
_____	_____

_____

Completed By

**USE REVERSE SIDE FOR
ADDITIONAL REMARKS**

B 377

FIRST WARNING NOTICE

Employee _____ Dept. _____

Supervisor _____ Date of
                                             Warning _____

Date of violation _____ Time of violation _____

Nature of Violation

___ Unsatisfactory   ___ Conduct   ___ Tardiness

___ Carelessness   ___ Disobedient   ___ Absenteeism

___ Ringing out ahead of time   ___ Ringing out wrong time card   ___ Intoxication or drinking

___ Other _____

_____

_____

_____

_____

Additional Remarks

_____

_____

_____

_____

_____

_____

Employee Comments

_____

_____

_____

_____

Signatures

_____   _____   _____
Employee   Supervisor   Personnel Manager

B 378

DISCIPLINARY REPORT

Employee	Date	Department

Nature of offense

Date of offense	Location	Time

Reported by	Title	Department

Witnesses

Details

Supervisor's Signature	Employee's Signature

Offense Number	Date and type of last Offense

Action Taken

Recommendations

The above offense(s) have been noted and have been recorded as
part of the above employee's personnel file.

Human Resources _____ **Date**_____

B 379

NOTICE OF DISMISSAL

Date:

To:

    We must advise you that we are terminating your employment on   , 19   , for the following reasons:

_____

_____

_____

_____

_____

_____

    You shall receive severance pay in accordance with company policy, and within 30 days of termination you shall receive a statement of accrued benefits. Your insurance benefits shall continue in accordance with applicable law and/or the provisions of our personnel policy. Please contact   , at your earliest convenience, who will explain each of these items and arrange with you for the return of any company property in your possession.

    We sincerely regret this action is necessary and wish you well in your future endeavors.

                               Very truly,

Copies to:

B 380

SEPARATION REPORT

Employee_____Date_____

Department_____ Position _____

Supervisor_____ Length of Employment_____

1.   Termination Date:_____ Pay Through:_____

2.   Reason for Termination:_____

_____

_____

3.   Unemployment Compensation Eligible? _____

_____

_____

4.   Continued Benefits Eligible? _____

_____

_____

5.   Assessment of Employee? _____

_____

_____

6.   Would Company Rehire?_____

_____

_____

7.   Comments?_____

_____

_____

_____

Supervisor

CHECKOUT RECORD

Employee_____ Department_____

Termination Date_____ This date _____

Each of the below items (as applicable)
must be returned or completed upon
termination and before issuance of
final pay check.

Return	(√)	(√)	Complete		
Company Equipment	_____	_____	Exit Interview	_____	_____
ID Badge	_____	_____	Expense Reports	_____	_____
Security Statement	_____	_____	Terminations Form	_____	_____
Air Travel Cards	_____	_____	Confidentiality Report	_____	_____
Credit Cards	_____	_____	Other:		
Petty Cash Advances	_____	_____	_____	_____	_____
Expense Accounts	_____	_____	_____	_____	_____
Keys	_____	_____	_____	_____	_____
Sales Items	_____	_____			
Sample Products	_____	_____			
Automobile	_____	_____			
Company Documents	_____	_____			
Customer Lists	_____	_____			
Other:					

_____ _____ _____

_____ _____ _____

_____ _____ _____

_____
Supervisor

TELEPHONE LOG

Period From _____ to _____

DATE	CALLER		PARTY CALLED			AREA	TELEPHONE	COL-LECT	PER. TO PER.	CALLING	CHARGED	CHARGE
	NAME	DEPT.	NAME	CITY	STATE	CODE	NUMBER	✓	✓	TIME	TO	

B 383

EMPLOYEE PROFIT-SHARING RECORD

NAME_____ ☐ MALE ☐ SINGLE

ADDRESS_____ ☐ FEMALE ☐ MARRIED

_____

DATE OF BIRTH_____ DEPARTMENT _____

DATE ENTERED PLAN_____ SUPERVISOR _____

AGE AT ENTRY_____ POSITION _____

DATE EMPLOYED_____ _____

NORMAL RETIREMENT DATE_____ _____

PARTICIPATION TERMINATION: DATE_____

☐ RETIREMENT ☐ DEATH ☐ DISABILITY ☐ SEVERANCE ☐ OTHER _____

NEW ADDRESS:

DATE	NEW ADDRESS	DATE	NEW ADDRESS

BENEFICIARIES:

NAME	ADDRESS	RELATIONSHIP	DATE DESIGNATED

OTHER NOTES:

Date: _____

PROFIT-SHARING PLAN RECORD

EMPLOYEE	ANNIVERSARY DATE	SHARE OF INCREASE (OR DECREASE) IN VALUE OF FUND	SHARE OF FORFEITURES	SHARE OF CONTRIBUTIONS	WITHDRAWALS	PRESENT BALANCE	PERCENT VESTING	VESTED AMOUNT

STATEMENT OF
ACCRUED BENEFITS

Date of Issue:_____

Employee_____ Department_____

Benefits Accrued As Of:_____

Vacation Days   _____

Vacation Pay $_____

Sick Days   _____

Sick Pay $_____

Profit-Sharing - Non-Vested $_____

Profit-Sharing Vested $_____

Stock Dividends $_____

Company Shares   _____

Vested Pension $_____

Non-Vested Pension $_____

Cash Value Life Insurance $_____

Credit Union Balance $_____

Severance Pay $_____

Expenses $_____

Other Accrued Benefits

_____   _____

_____   _____

_____   _____

THIS STATEMENT IS
SUBJECT TO CORRECTION

by_____

B 386

EXIT INTERVIEW REPORT

Employee _____ S.S.N. _____

Department_____Position_____

Employed From _____ To_____

Supervisor_____

Reason For Termination   _____

Return of:

    _____ keys   _____ company documents   _____ uniform

    _____ ID card   _____ safety equipment   _____ tools

    _____credit card   _____ other company property   _____ company auto

Employee informed of restrictions concerning:

    _____ trade secrets   _____ employment with competitor (if applicable)

    _____ patents   _____ removing company documents

    _____ other data   _____ other_____

Employee exit questions:

1.   Did management adequately recognize your contributions as an employee?_____
_____

2.   Do you feel that you have had the full support of management? _____
_____

3.   Were you adequately trained for your job?_____
_____

4.   Did you find your work rewarding?_____
_____

5.   Do you feel you were fairly treated by the company?_____
_____

6.   Was your salary adequate for the work you did? _____

_____

7.   Were you satisfied with your working conditions? _____

_____

8.   Do you feel you were properly supervised? _____

_____

9.   Did you fully understand the company policies and the reasons for them? _____

_____

10.   Have you observed incidences of theft of company property?_____

_____

11.   How can the company improve security?_____

_____

12.   How can the company improve working conditions?_____

_____

13.   What are the company's strengths?_____

_____

14.   What are the company's weaknesses?_____

_____

15.   Other comments:_____

_____

_____

_____

USE ADDITIONAL SHEETS FOR FURTHER COMMENTS.

ALL ANSWERS ARE FULLY CONFIDENTIAL.

TELEPHONE REFERENCE LOG

Date:_____ Time:_____

Reference requested on employee: _____ Department: _____

Person inquiring:_____

Company:_____

Address:_____

Tel. No. _____ Fax: _____

Reason for inquiry:_____

_____

Reference Summary:

_____

_____

_____

_____

_____

_____

_____

_____

Specific Questions/Replies:

_____

By

Graphs and Charts

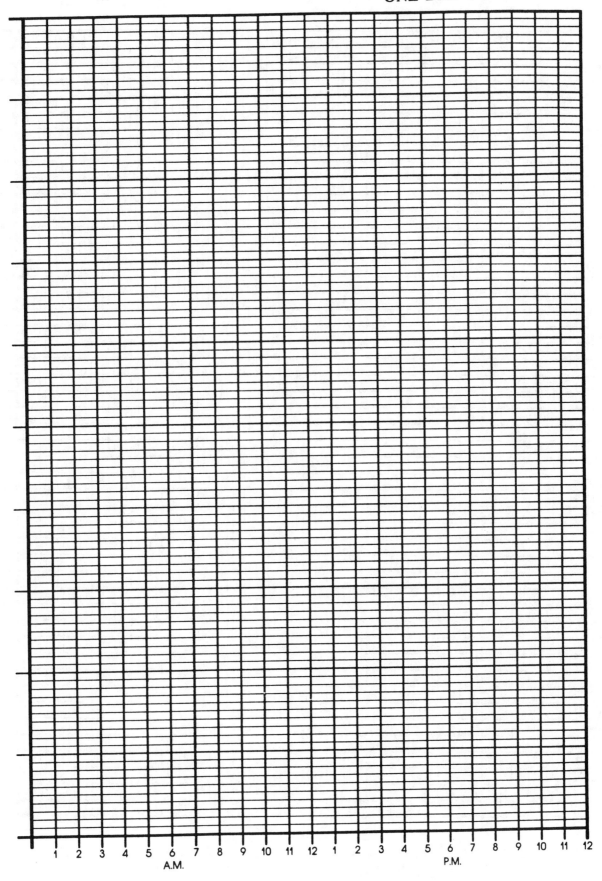

A.M.   P.M.

1 2 3 4 5 6 7 8 9 10 11 12 1 2 3 4 5 6 7 8 9 10 11 12

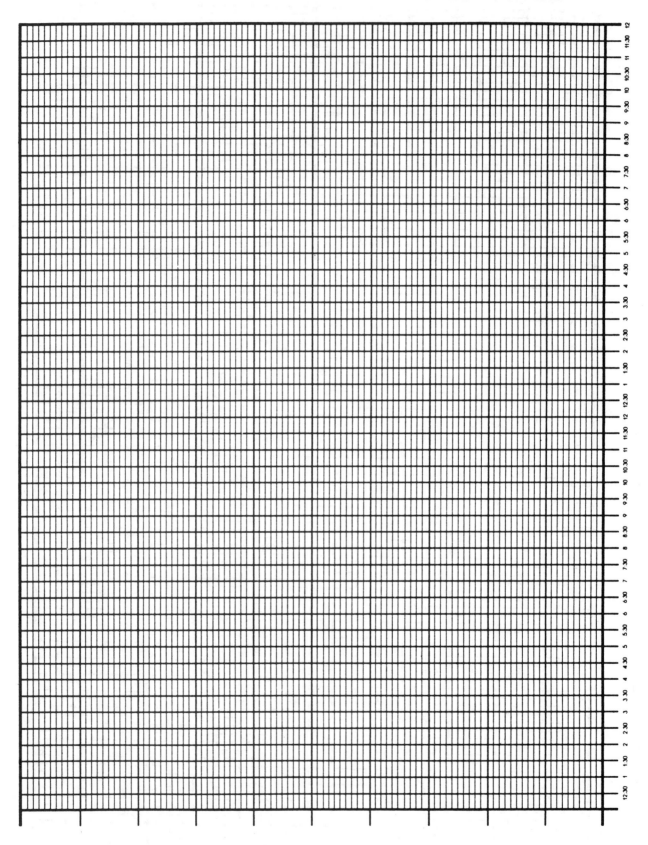

SEVEN DAY GRAPH

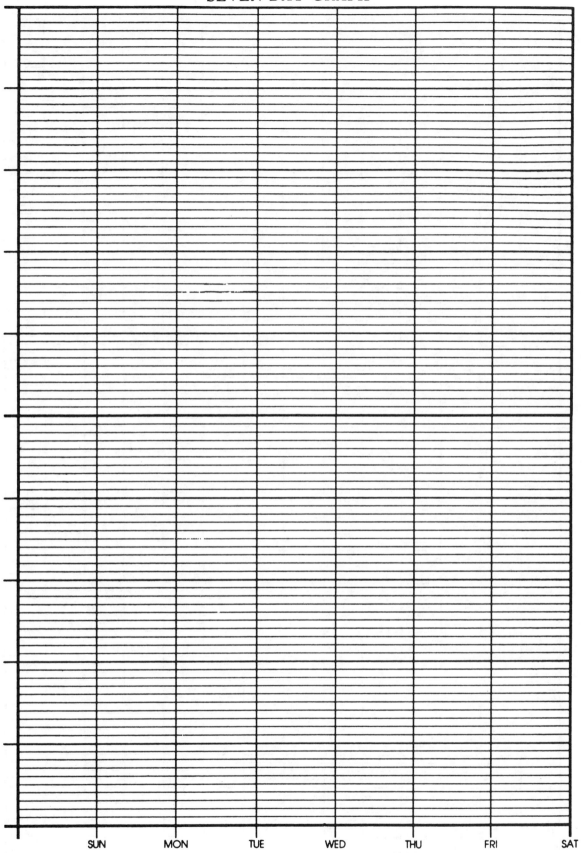

SUN   MON   TUE   WED   THU   FRI   SAT

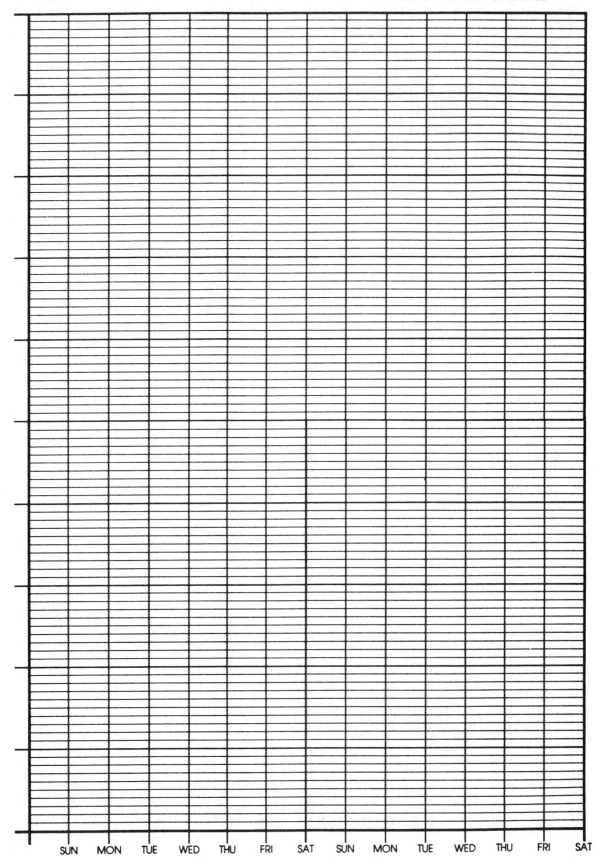

SUN MON TUE WED THU FRI SAT SUN MON TUE WED THU FRI SAT

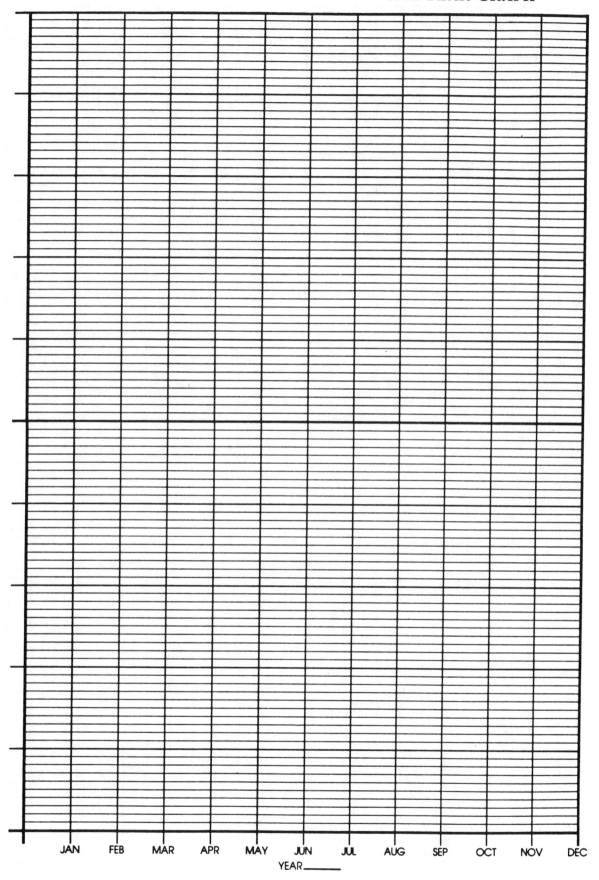

JAN   FEB   MAR   APR   MAY   JUN   JUL   AUG   SEP   OCT   NOV   DEC

YEAR_____

24 MONTH GRAPH

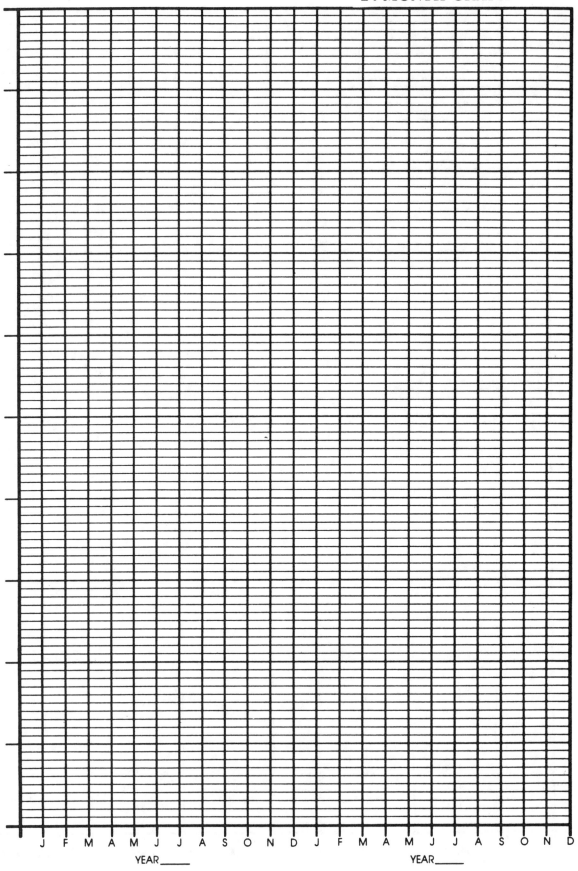

J F M A M J J A S O N D J F M A M J J A S O N D

YEAR_____   YEAR_____

TWO YEAR GRAPH

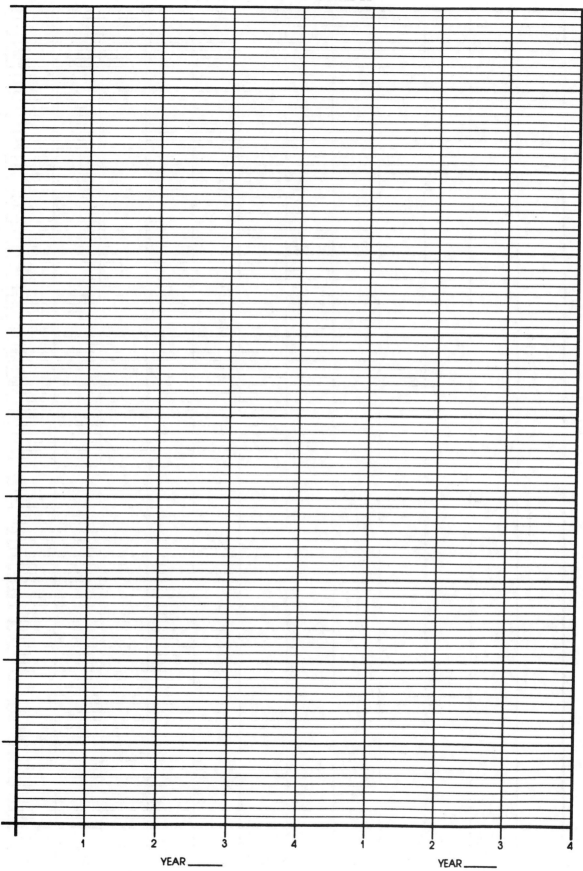

THREE YEAR GRAPH

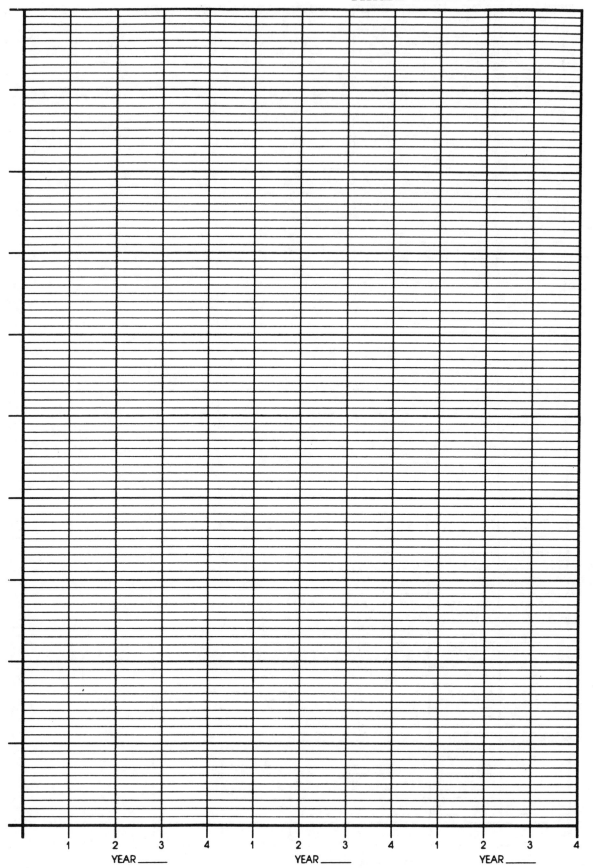

1 2 3 4 1 2 3 4 1 2 3 4

YEAR _____ YEAR _____ YEAR _____

FOUR YEAR GRAPH

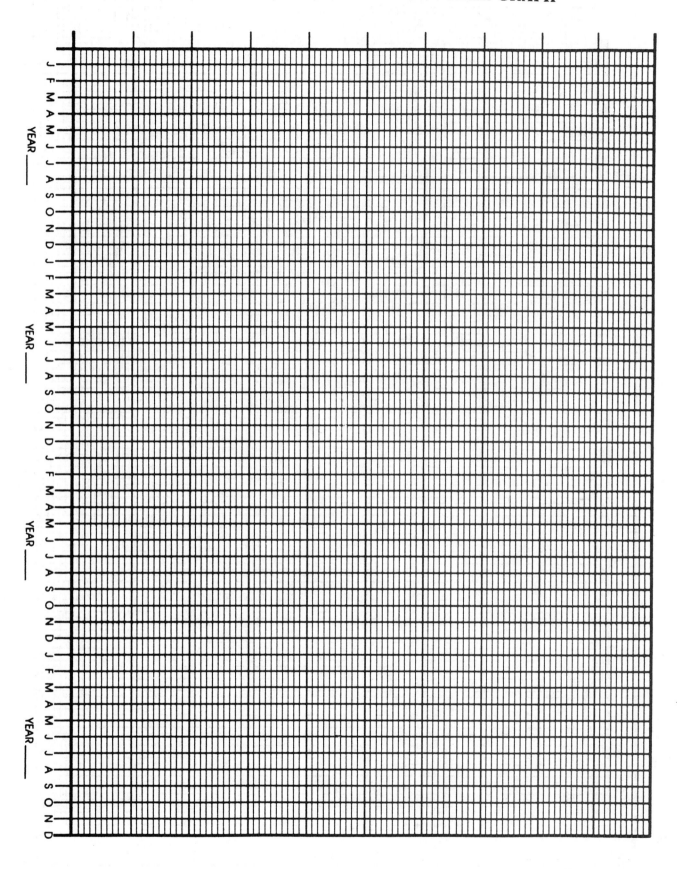

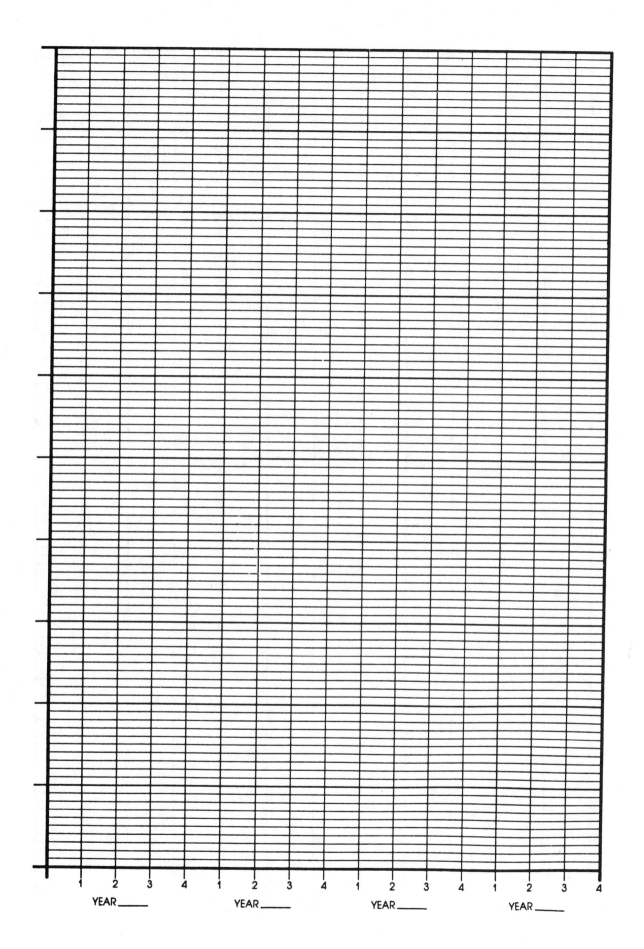

YEAR_____   YEAR_____   YEAR_____   YEAR_____

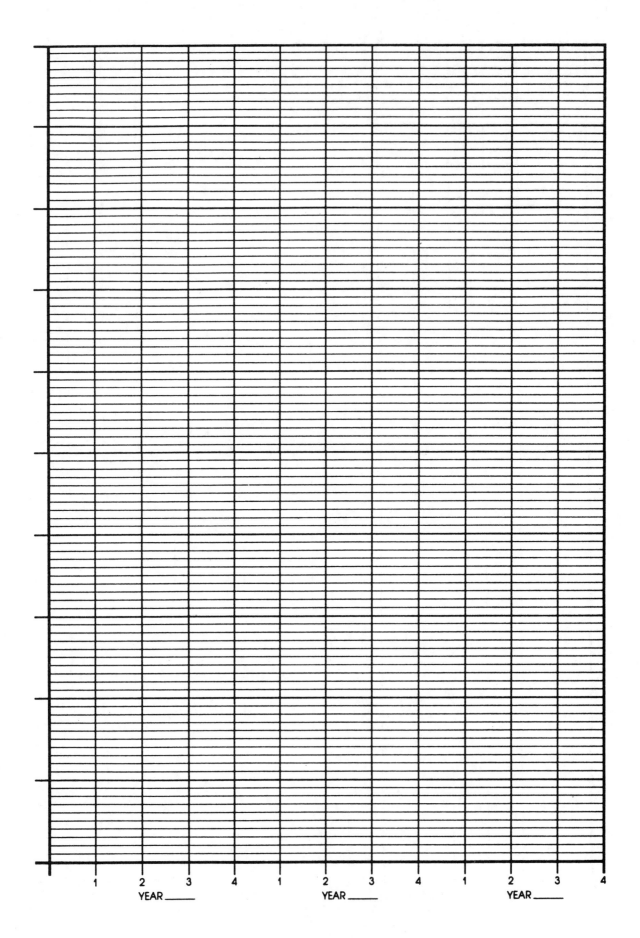

1 2 3 4 1 2 3 4 1 2 3 4

YEAR _____ YEAR _____ YEAR _____

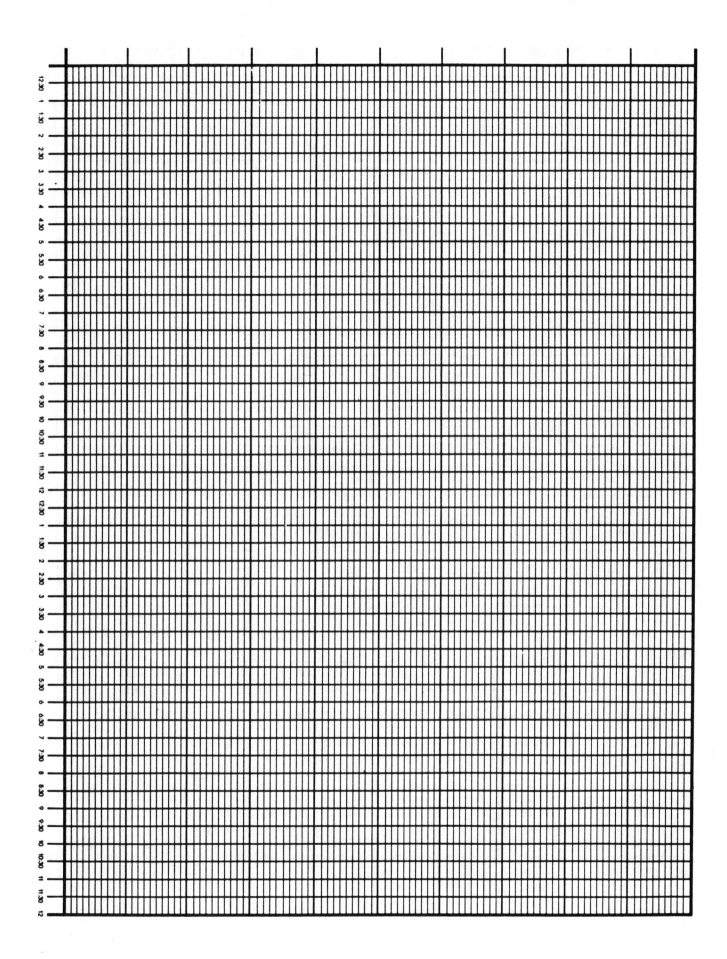

12.30 1 1.30 2 2.30 3 3.30 4 4.30 5 5.30 6 6.30 7 7.30 8 8.30 9 9.30 10 10.30 11 11.30 12 12.30 1 1.30 2 2.30 3 3.30 4 4.30 5 5.30 6 6.30 7 7.30 8 8.30 9 9.30 10 10.30 11 11.30 12

B 405

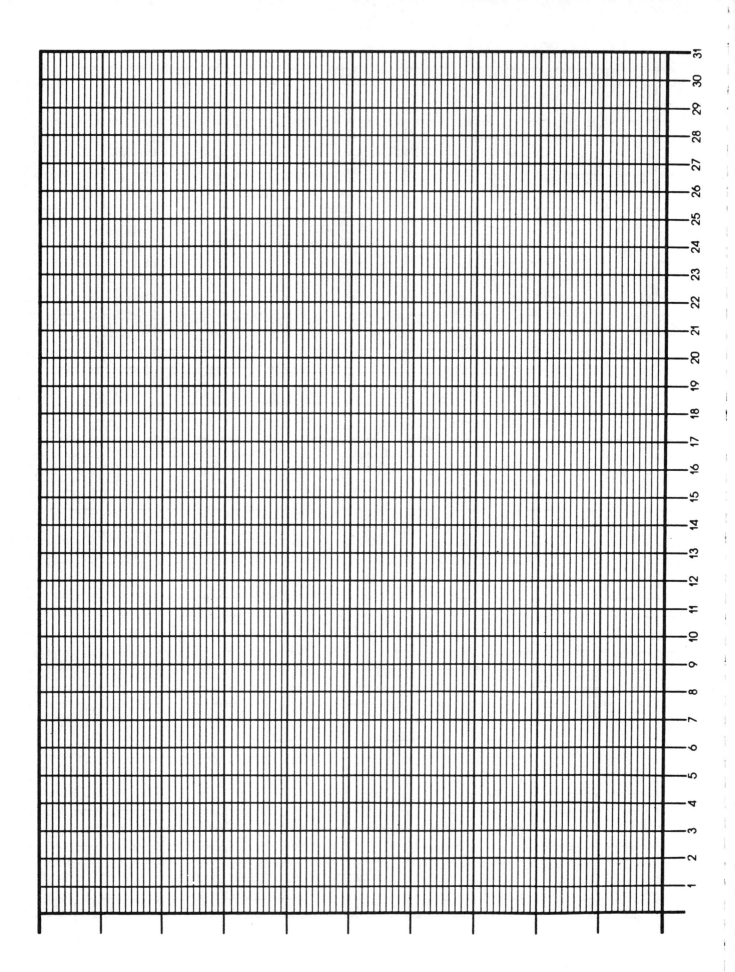

B 406

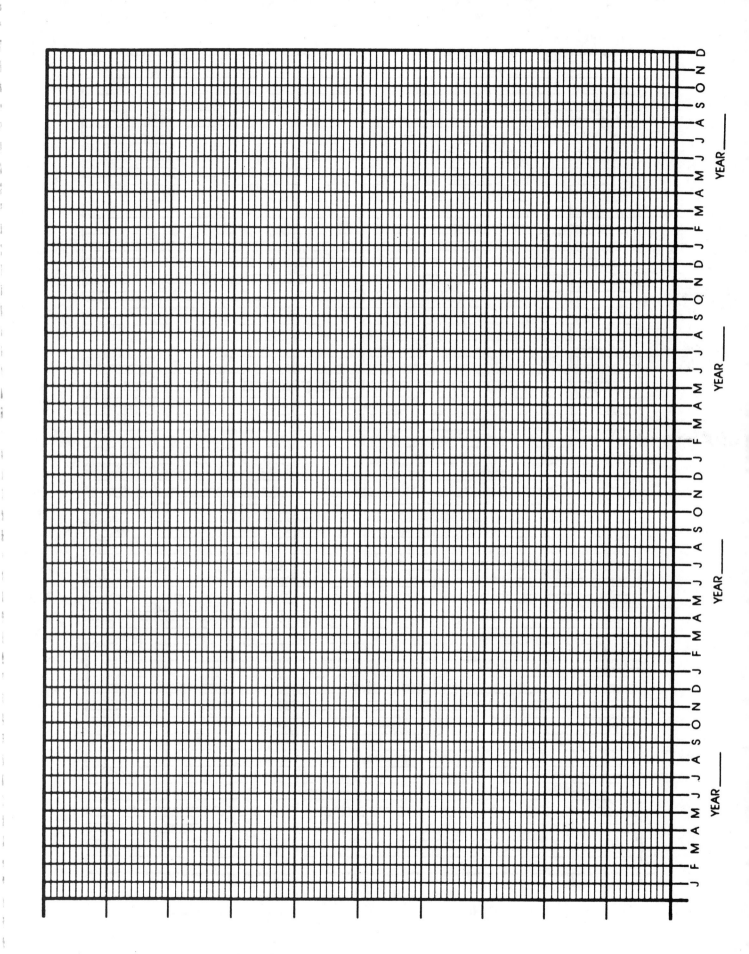

B 407

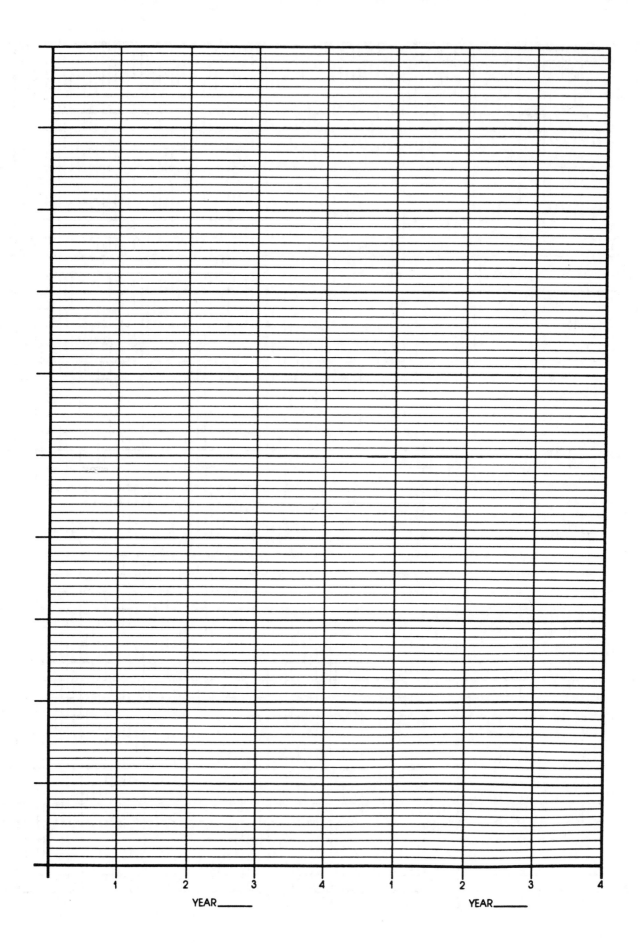

YEAR_____   YEAR_____

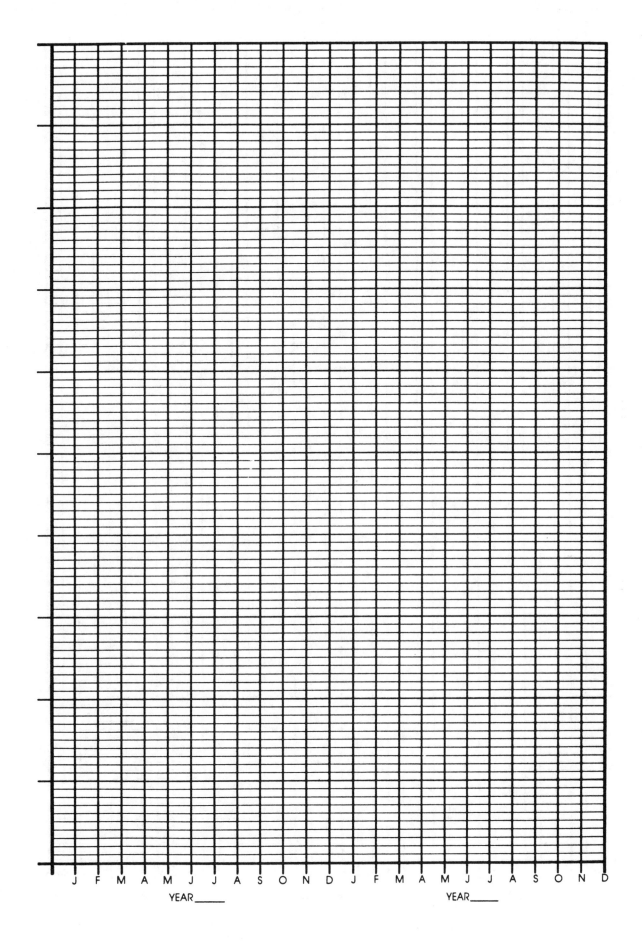

J F M A M J J A S O N D   J F M A M J J A S O N D

YEAR _____   YEAR _____

B 409

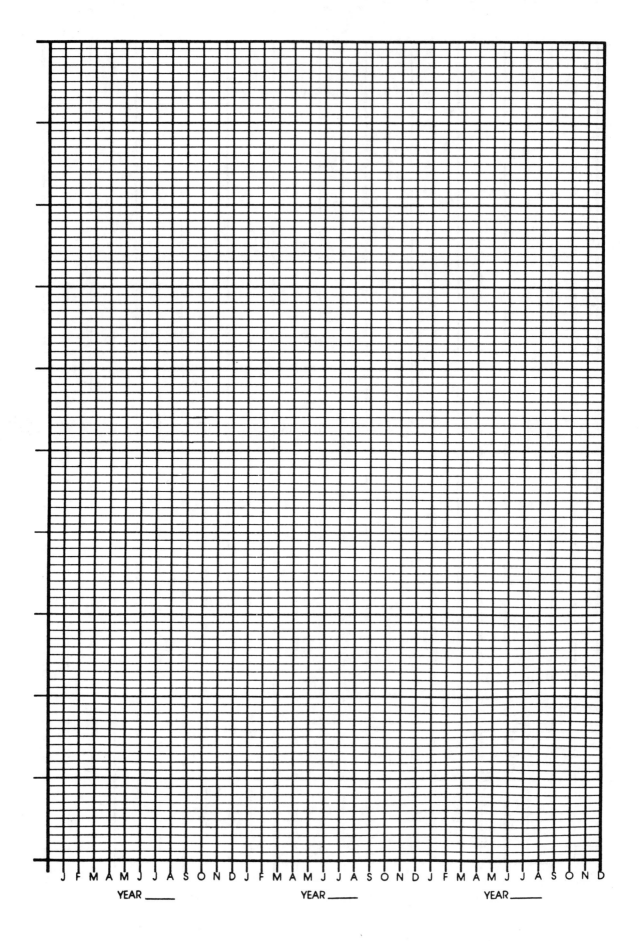

J F M A M J J A S O N D J F M A M J J A S O N D J F M A M J J A S O N D

YEAR _____   YEAR _____   YEAR _____

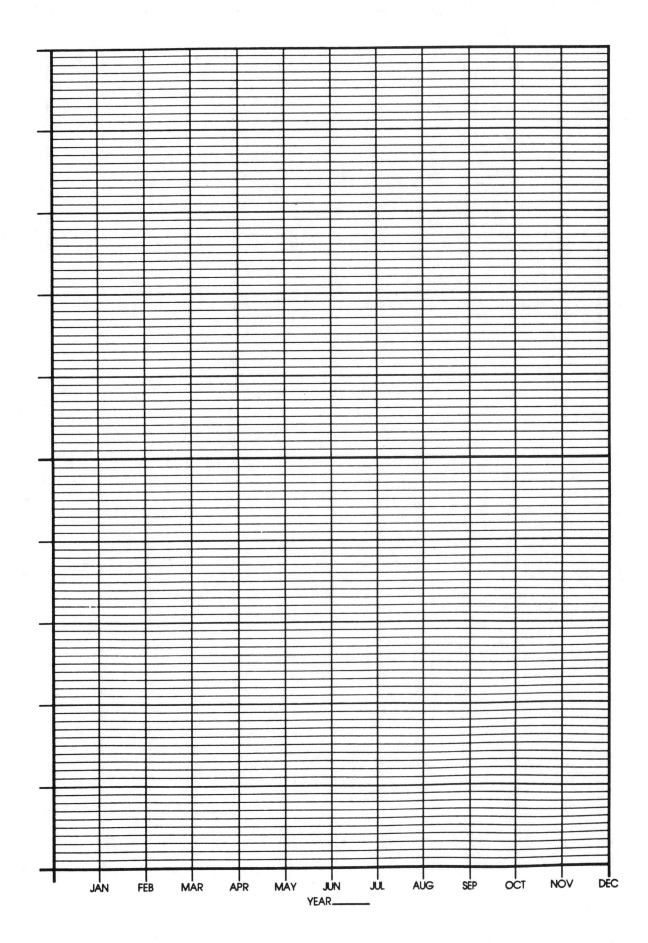

JAN FEB MAR APR MAY JUN JUL AUG SEP OCT NOV DEC

YEAR_____

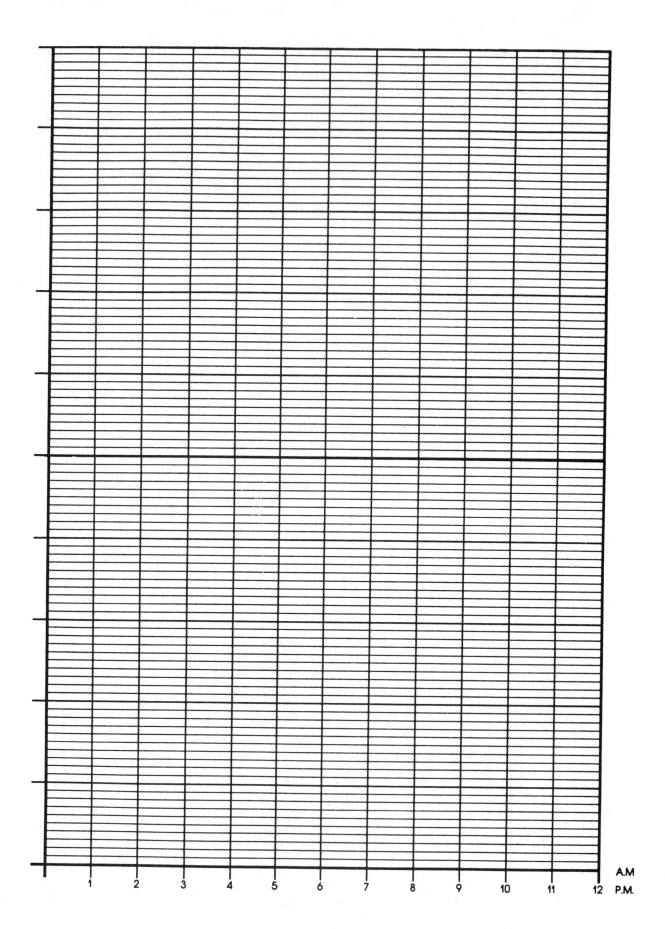

A.M

1 2 3 4 5 6 7 8 9 10 11 12 P.M.

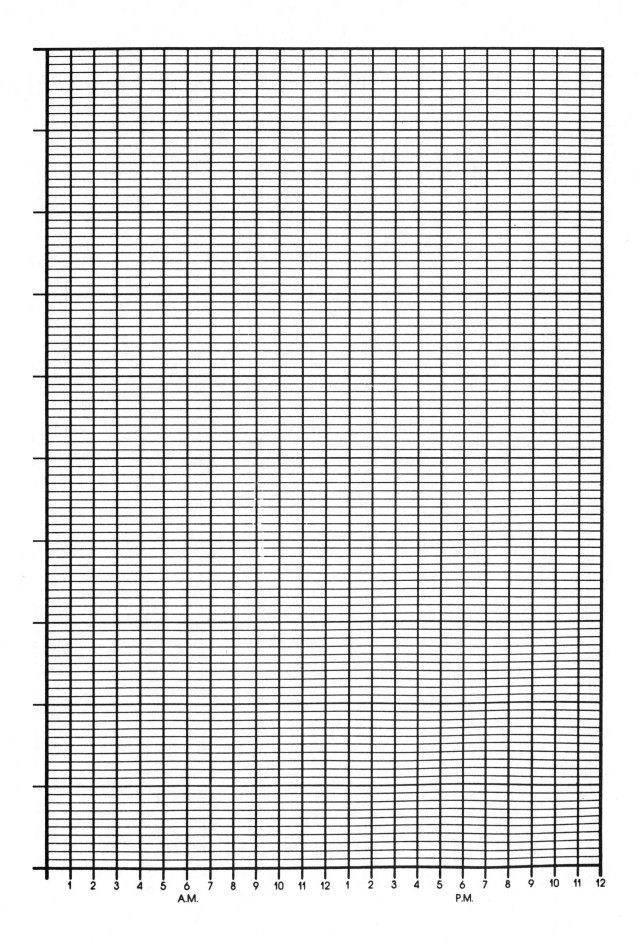

1 2 3 4 5 6 7 8 9 10 11 12 1 2 3 4 5 6 7 8 9 10 11 12

A.M.   P.M.

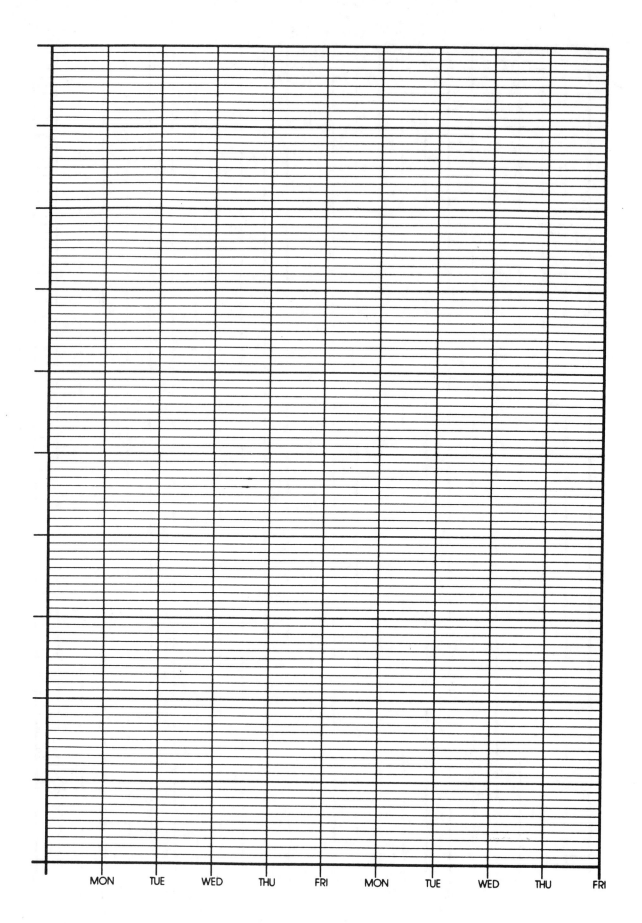

MON   TUE   WED   THU   FRI   MON   TUE   WED   THU   FRI

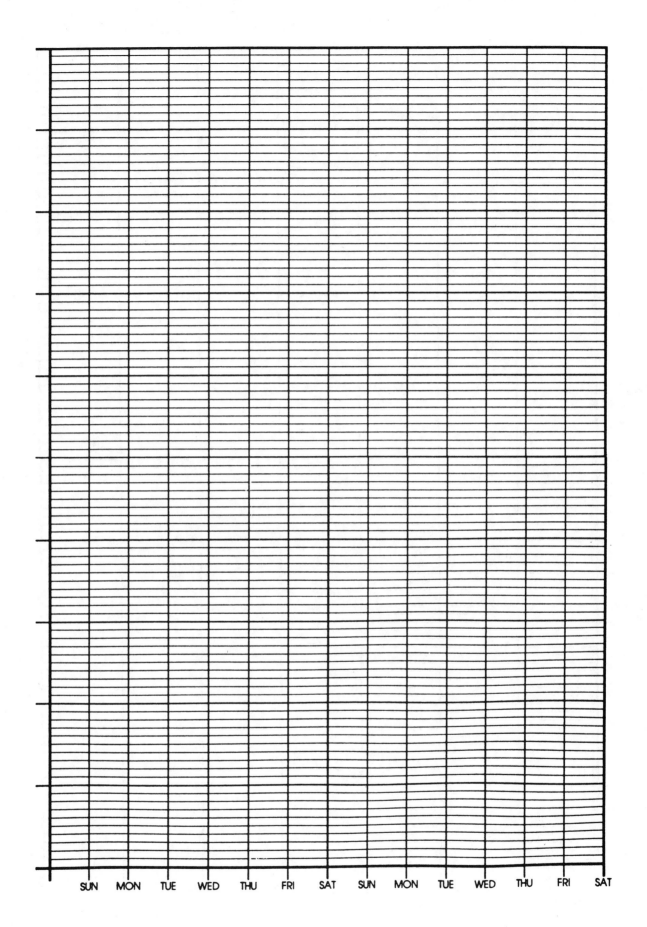

SUN MON TUE WED THU FRI SAT SUN MON TUE WED THU FRI SAT

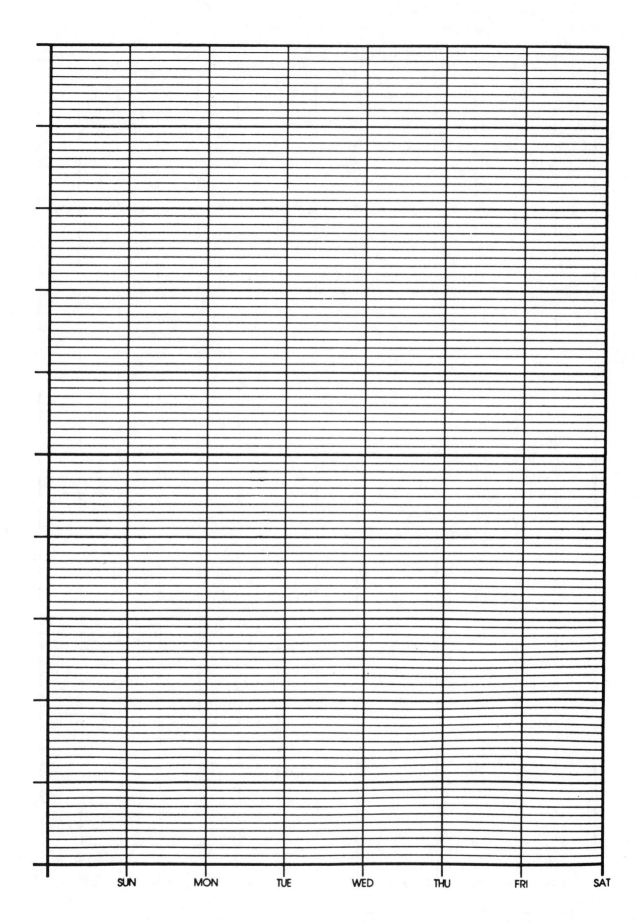

SUN   MON   TUE   WED   THU   FRI   SAT

A.M.

P.M.

JAN   FEB   MAR   APR   MAY   JUN   JUL   AUG   SEP   OCT   NOV   DEC

YEAR————

SUN   MON   TUE   WED   THU   FRI   SAT   SUN   MON   TUE   WED   THU   FRI   SAT

A.M
P.M.

1 2 3 4 5 6 7 8 9 10 11 12

B 421

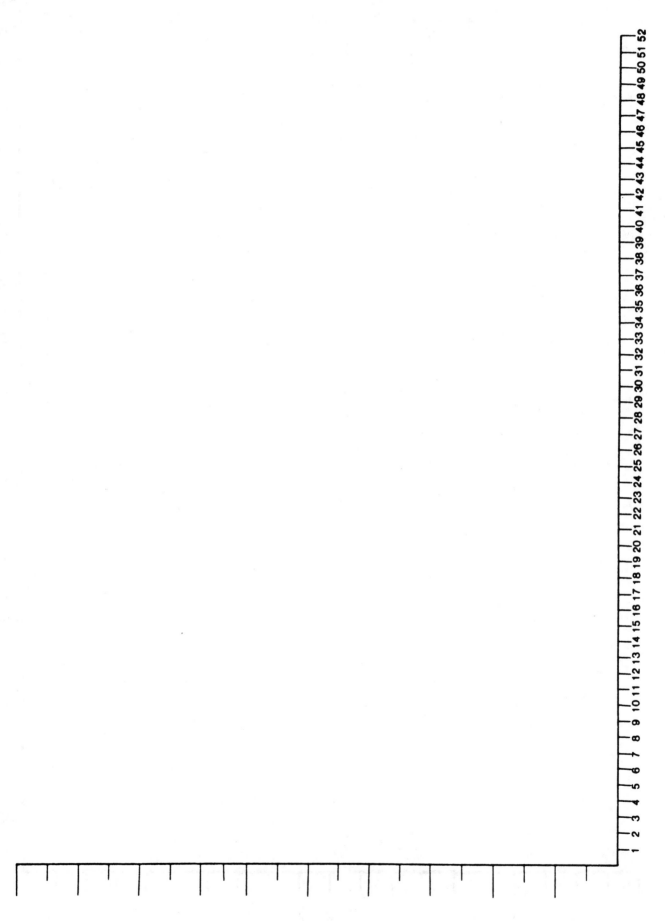

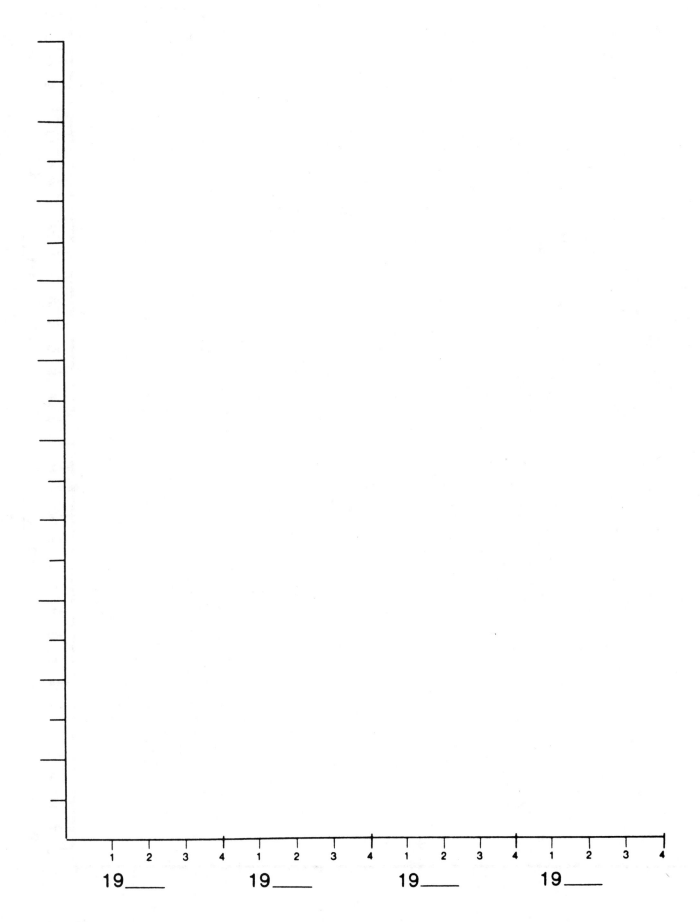

19____   19____   19____   19____

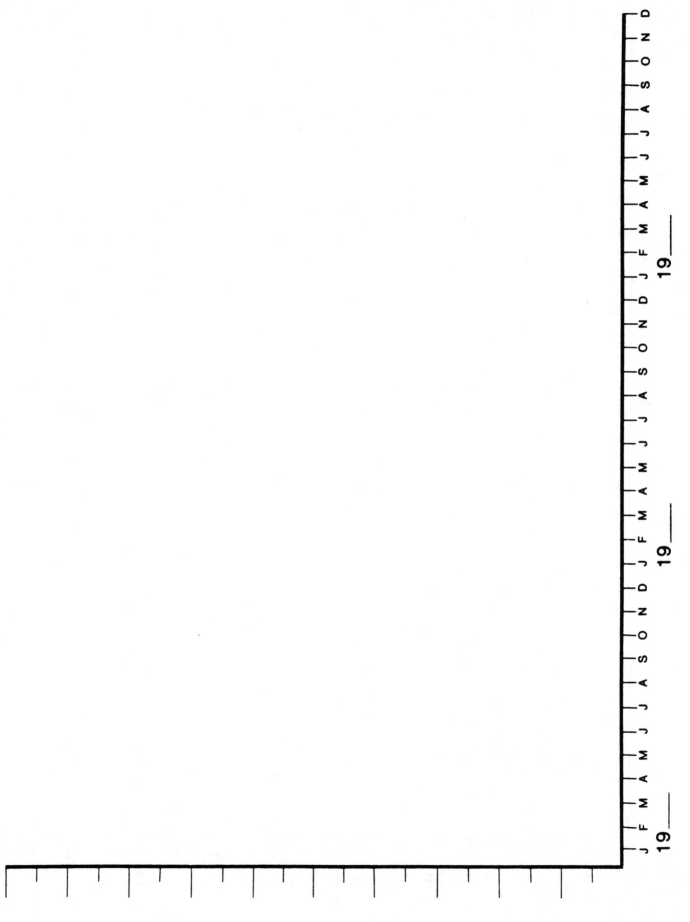

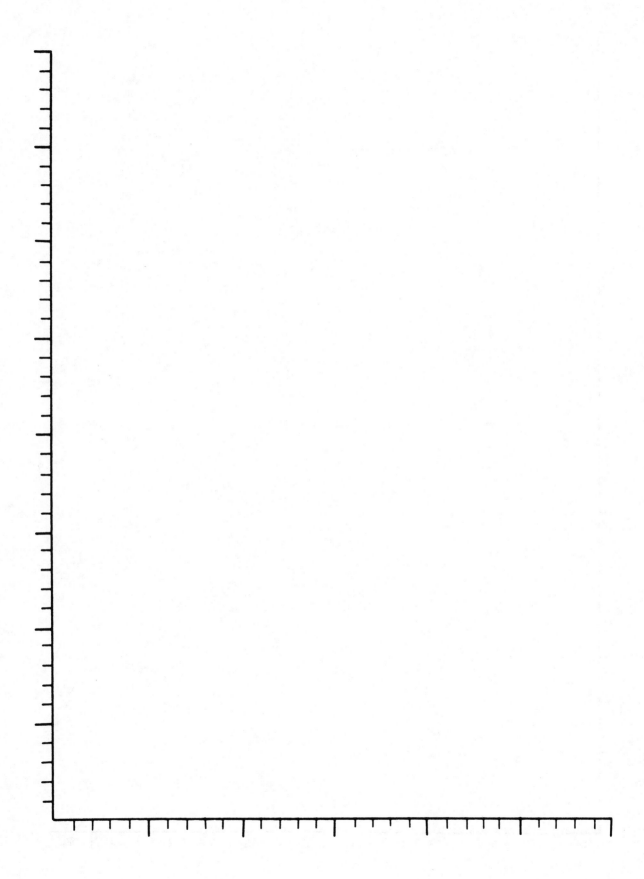

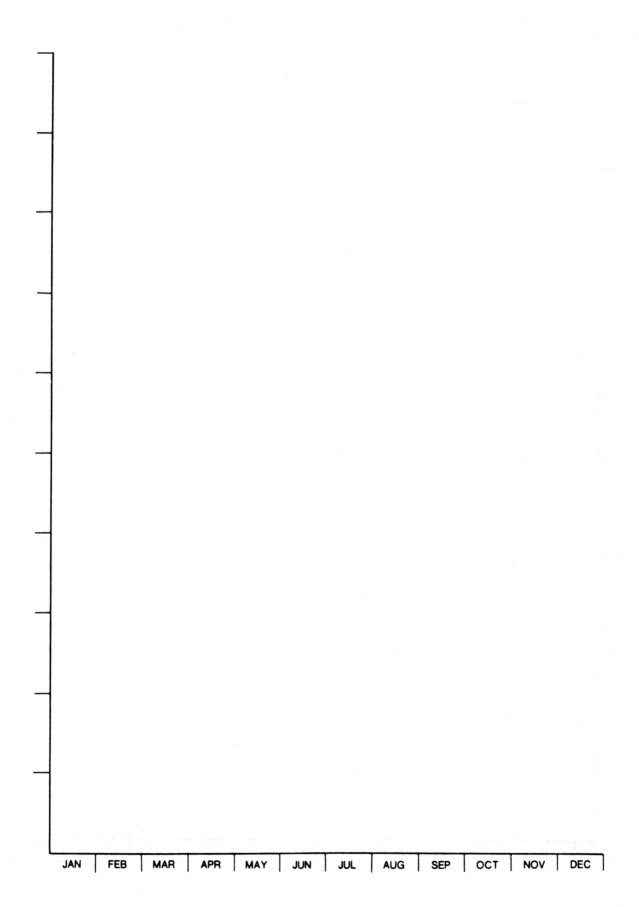

JAN | FEB | MAR | APR | MAY | JUN | JUL | AUG | SEP | OCT | NOV | DEC

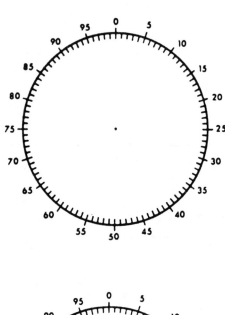

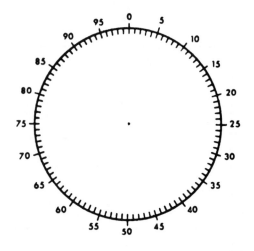

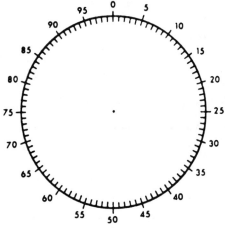

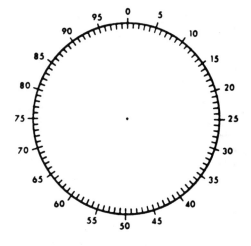

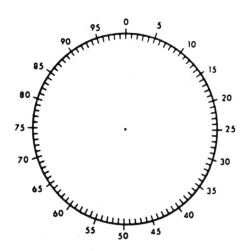

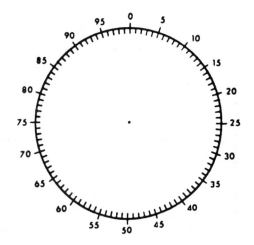

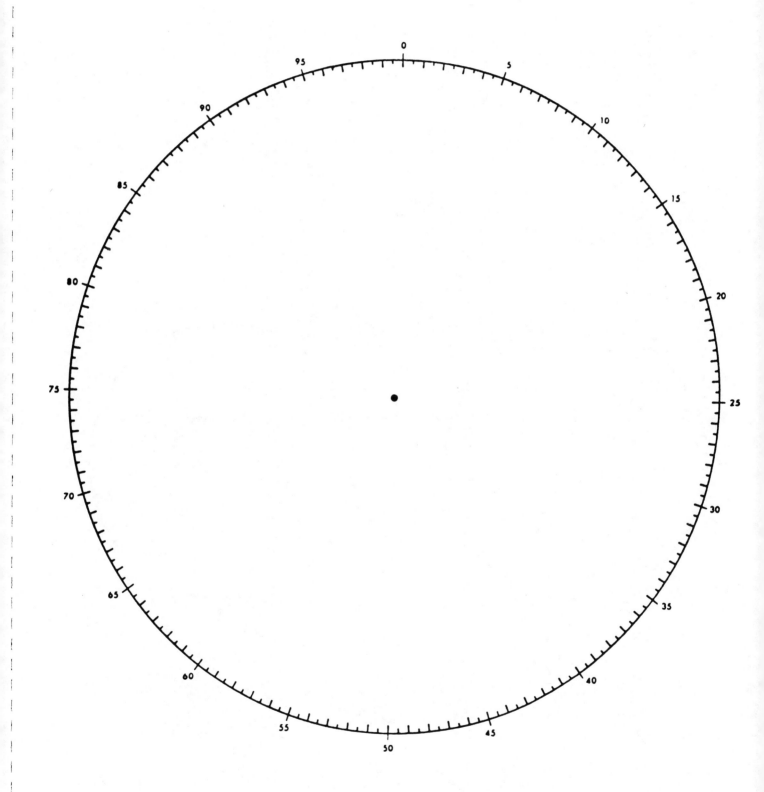

B 429

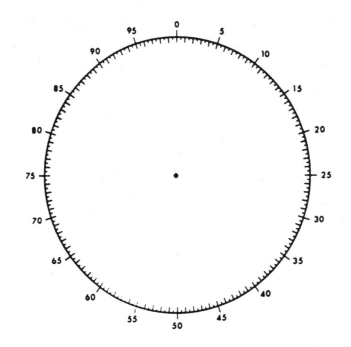

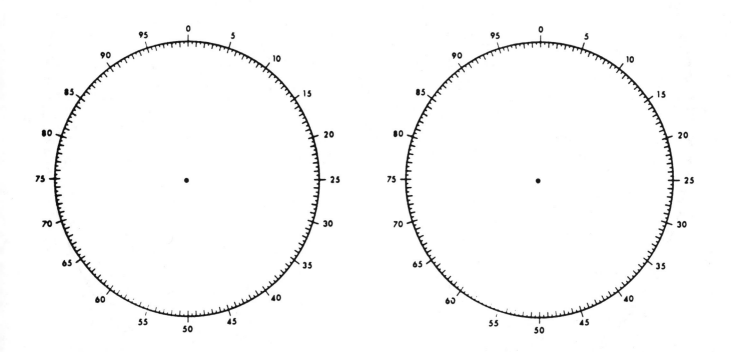

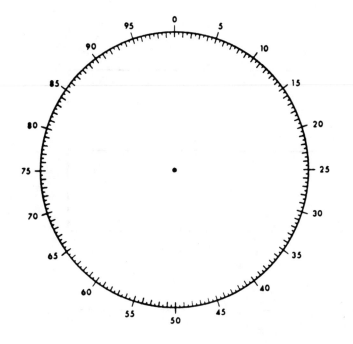
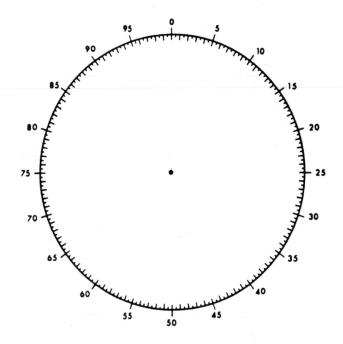
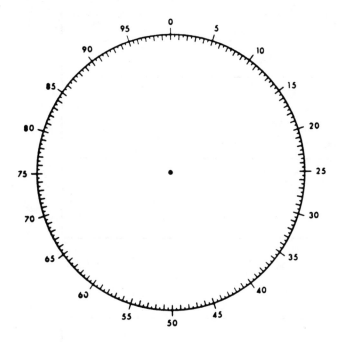
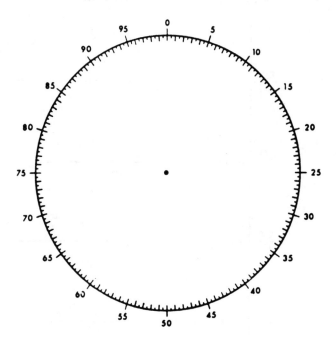

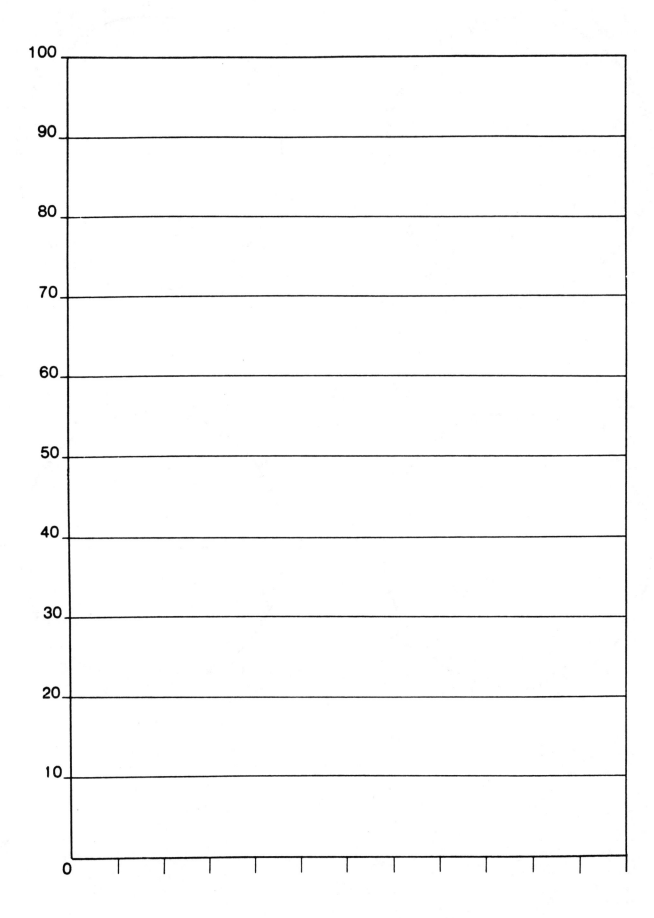

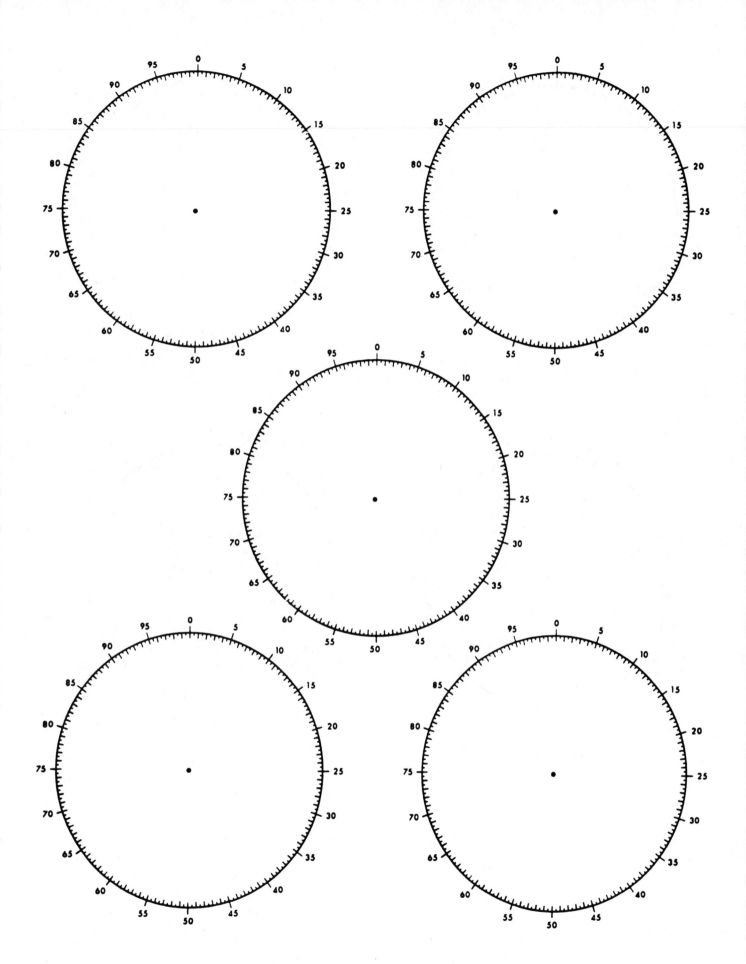

B 433

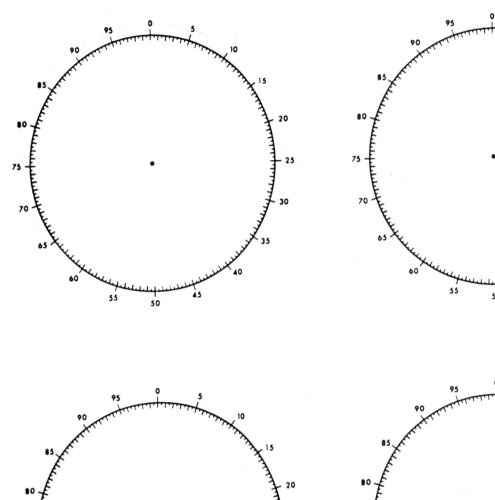

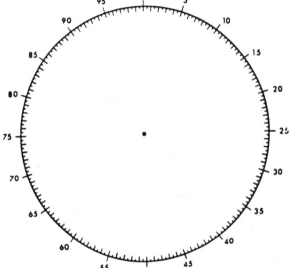

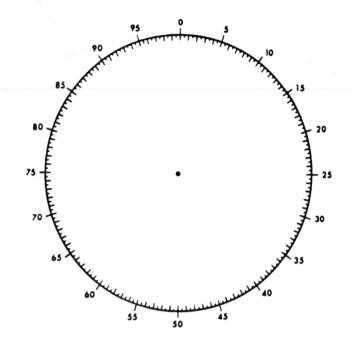

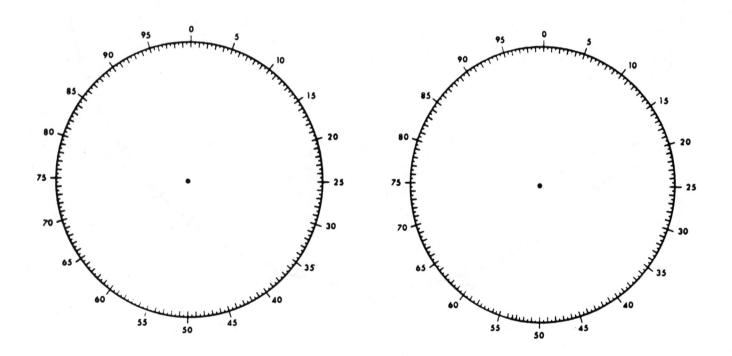

B 435

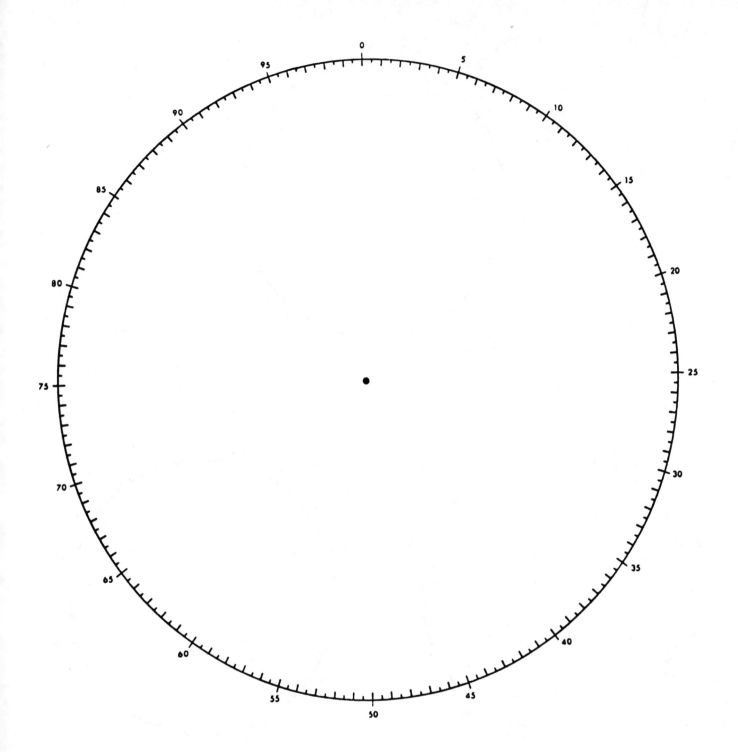

B 436

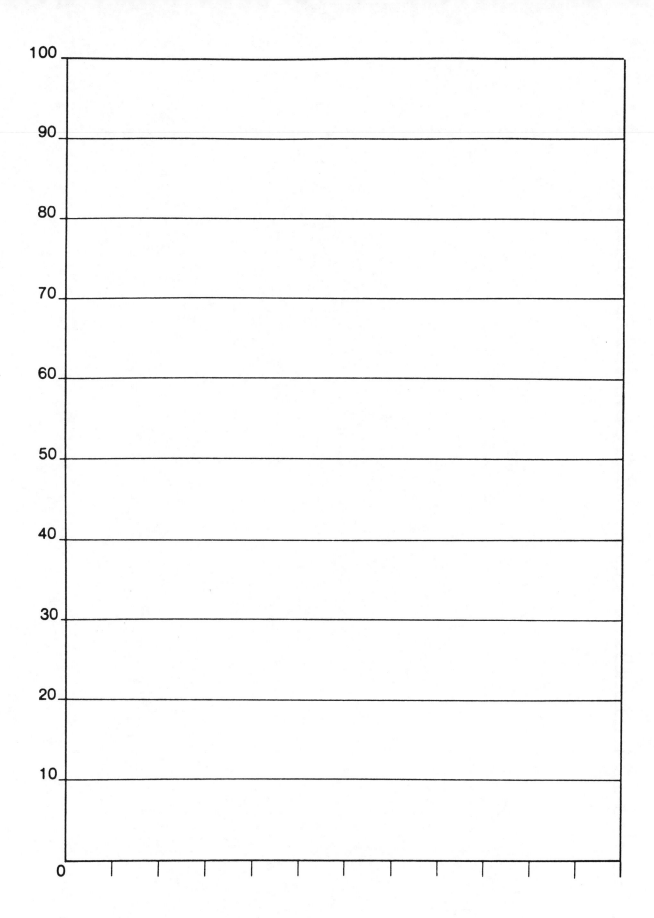

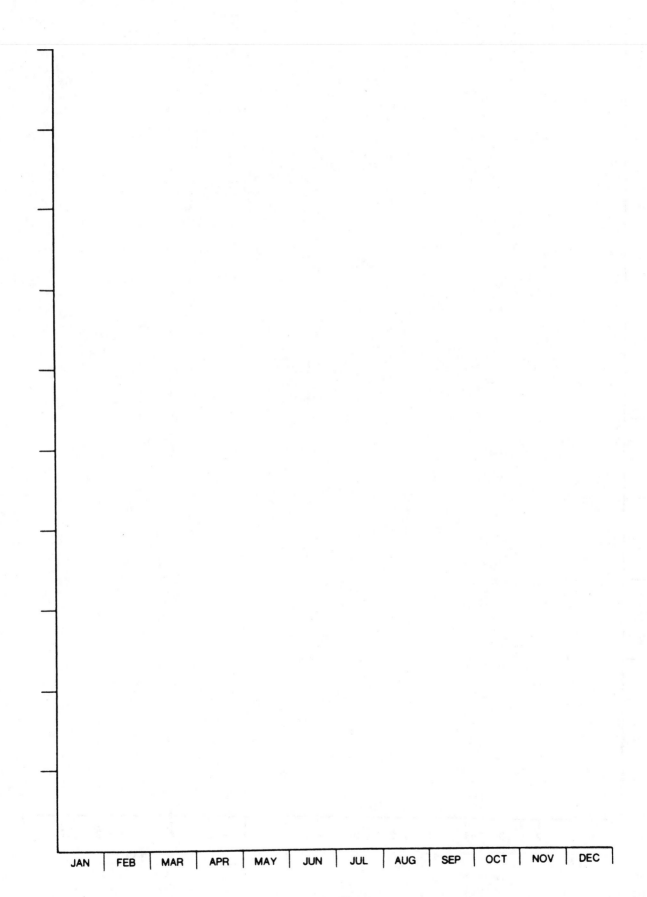

JAN | FEB | MAR | APR | MAY | JUN | JUL | AUG | SEP | OCT | NOV | DEC

1　　2　　3　　4　　1　　2　　3　　4　　1　　2　　3　　4　　1　　2　　3　　4

19_____　　　　　19_____　　　　　19_____　　　　　19_____

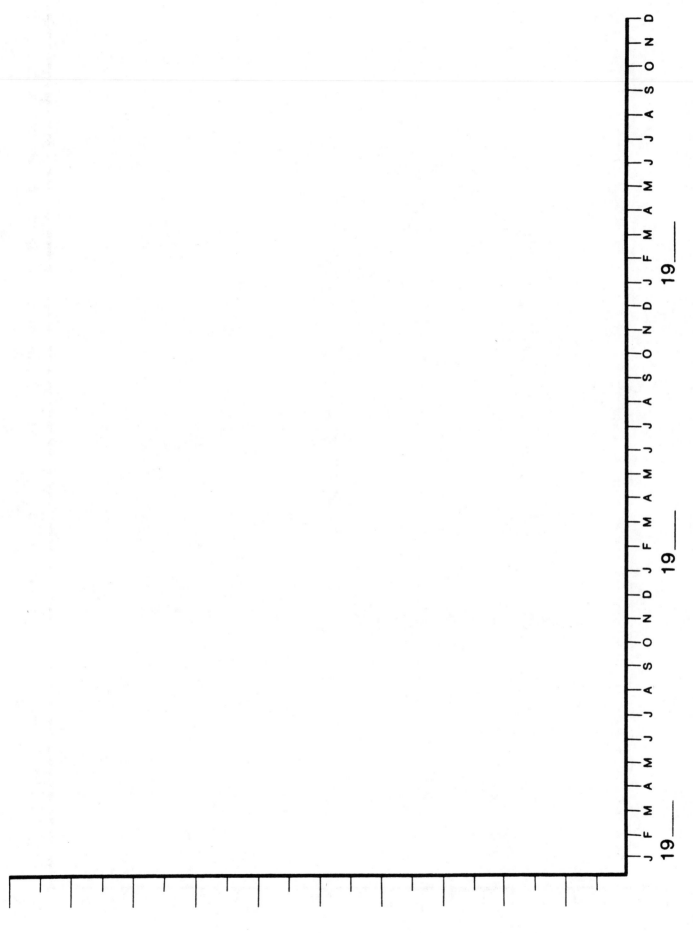

B 442

Maps

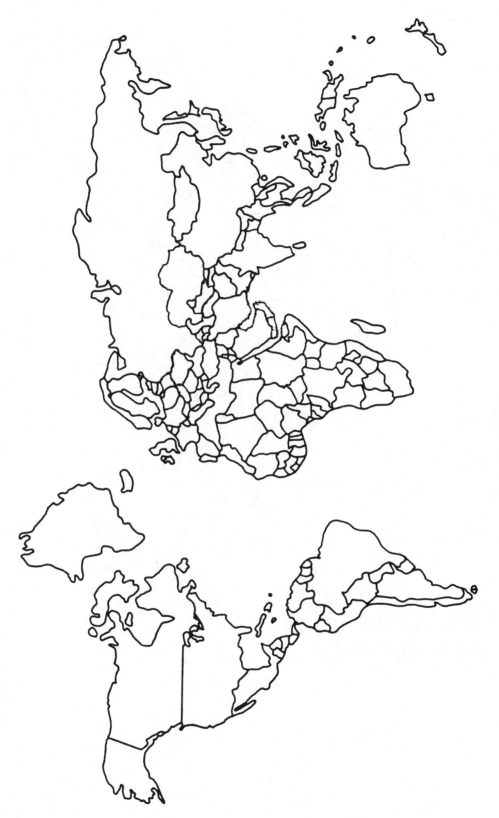

WORLD

**WESTERN
HEMISPHERE**

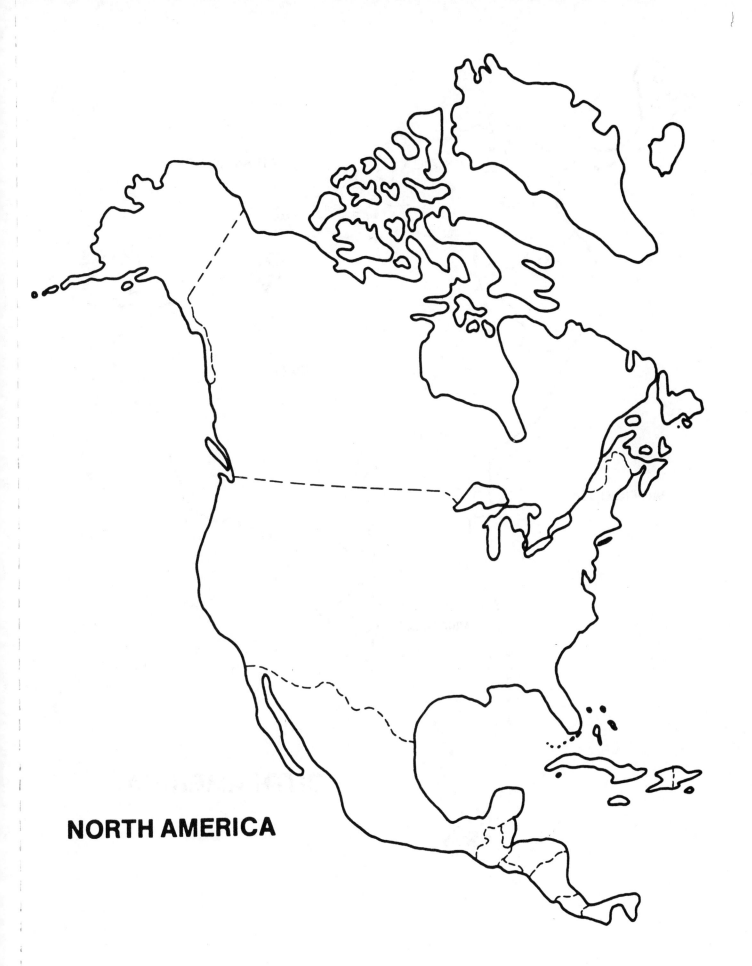

NORTH AMERICA

CENTRAL
AMERICA

VENEZUELA

ATLANTIC OCEAN

COLOMBIA

GUYANA

SURINAME FRENCH
GUYANA

ECUADOR

PERU

BRAZIL

BOLIVIA

PACIFIC OCEAN

CHILE

PARAGUAY

URUGUAY

ARGENTINA

SOUTH AMERICA

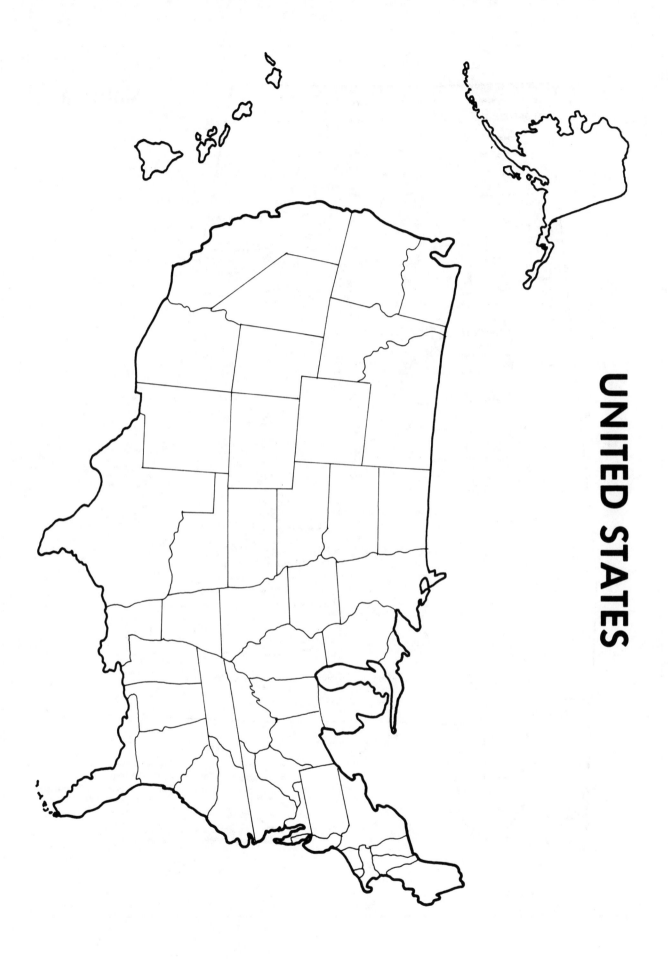

UNITED STATES

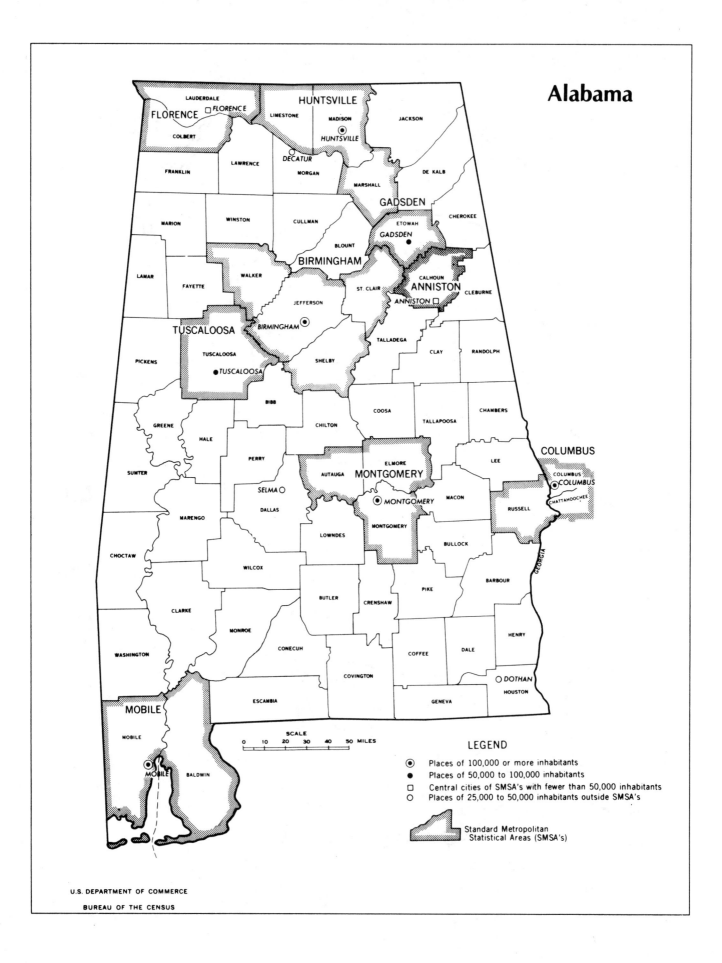

Alabama

LEGEND

⊙ Places of 100,000 or more inhabitants
● Places of 50,000 to 100,000 inhabitants
□ Central cities of SMSA's with fewer than 50,000 inhabitants
○ Places of 25,000 to 50,000 inhabitants outside SMSA's

Standard Metropolitan Statistical Areas (SMSA's)

SCALE
0   10   20   30   40   50 MILES

U.S. DEPARTMENT OF COMMERCE

BUREAU OF THE CENSUS

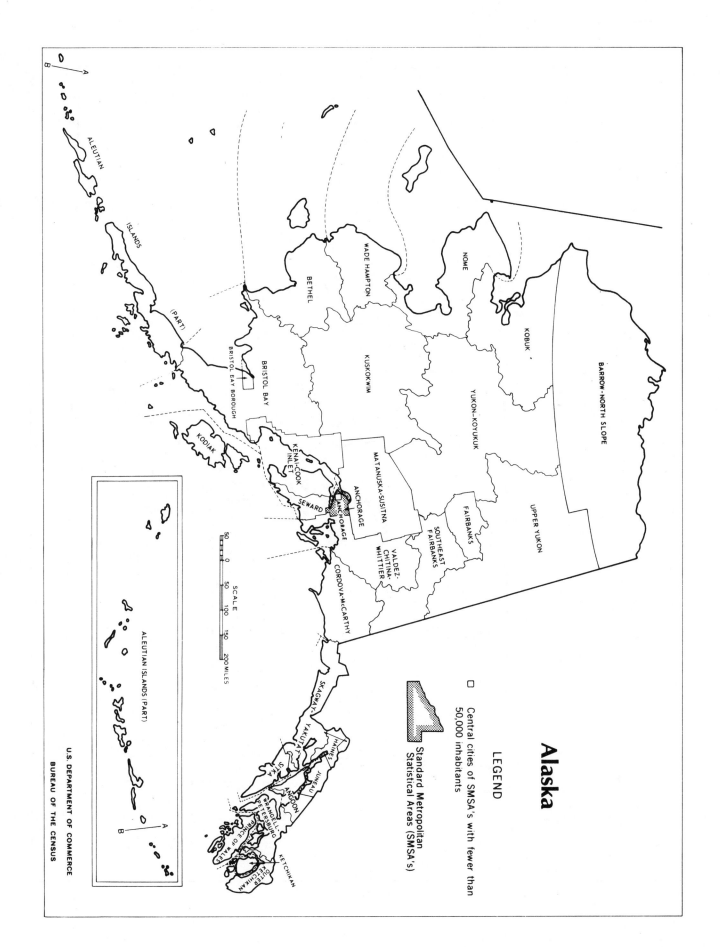

Alaska

LEGEND

☐ Central cities of SMSA's with fewer than 50,000 inhabitants

Standard Metropolitan Statistical Areas (SMSA's)

ALEUTIAN ISLANDS

ALEUTIAN ISLANDS (PART)

(PART)

BRISTOL BAY BOROUGH

BRISTOL BAY

KODIAK

KENAI-COOK INLET

SEWARD

ANCHORAGE

MATANUSKA-SUSITNA

CORDOVA-McCARTHY

VALDEZ-CHITINA-WHITTIER

SOUTHEAST FAIRBANKS

FAIRBANKS

BETHEL

WADE HAMPTON

KUSKOKWIM

NOME

KOBUK

YUKON-KOYUKUK

UPPER YUKON

BARROW-NORTH SLOPE

SKAGWAY-YAKUTAT

HAINES

SITKA

JUNEAU

ANGOON

WRANGELL-PETERSBURG

PRINCE OF WALES

OUTER KETCHIKAN

KETCHIKAN

SCALE

50 0 50 100 150 200 MILES

U.S. DEPARTMENT OF COMMERCE

BUREAU OF THE CENSUS

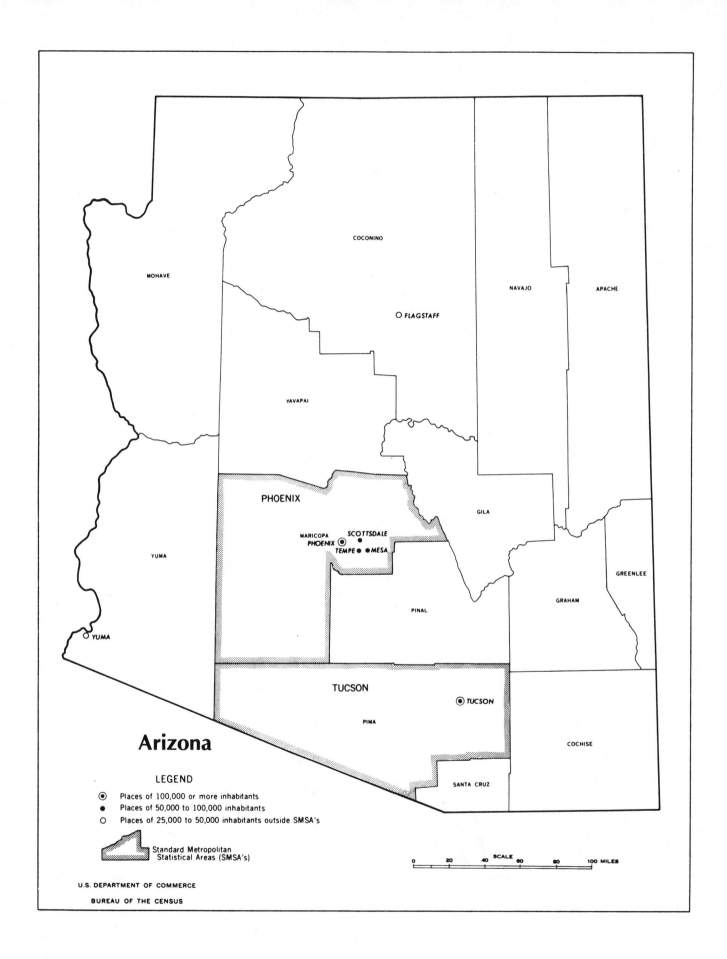

Arizona

LEGEND

⊙ Places of 100,000 or more inhabitants
● Places of 50,000 to 100,000 inhabitants
○ Places of 25,000 to 50,000 inhabitants outside SMSA's

Standard Metropolitan
Statistical Areas (SMSA's)

SCALE
0   20   40   60   80   100 MILES

U.S. DEPARTMENT OF COMMERCE

BUREAU OF THE CENSUS

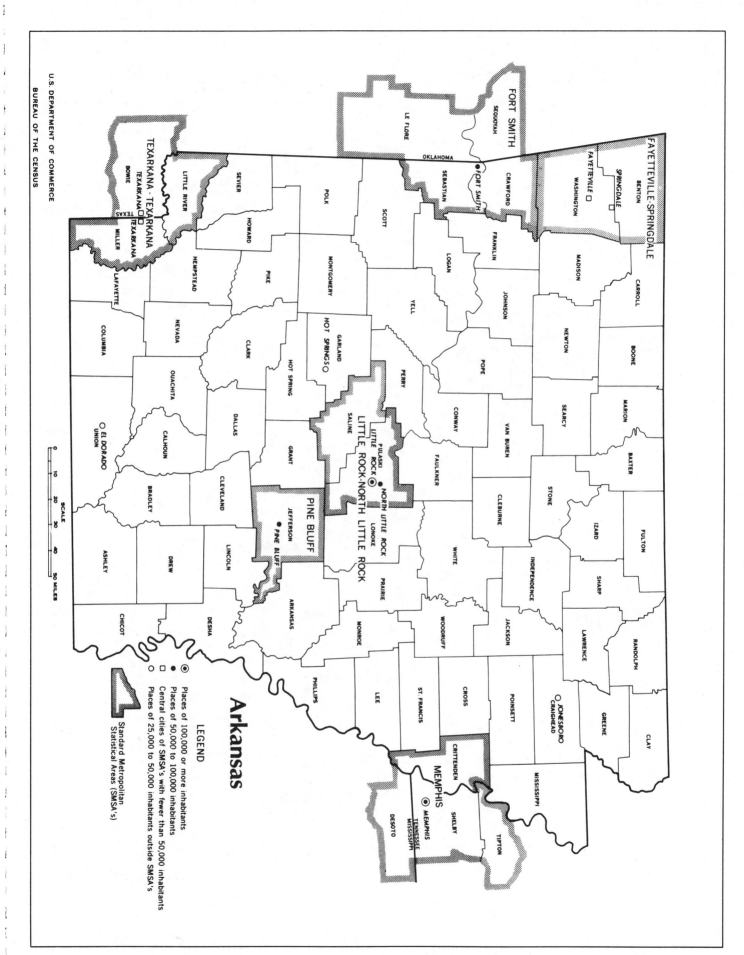

U.S. DEPARTMENT OF COMMERCE
BUREAU OF THE CENSUS

Arkansas

LEGEND

◉ Places of 100,000 or more inhabitants
● Places of 50,000 to 100,000 inhabitants
■ Central cities of SMSA's with fewer than 50,000 inhabitants
○ Places of 25,000 to 50,000 inhabitants outside SMSA's

Standard Metropolitan
Statistical Areas (SMSA's)

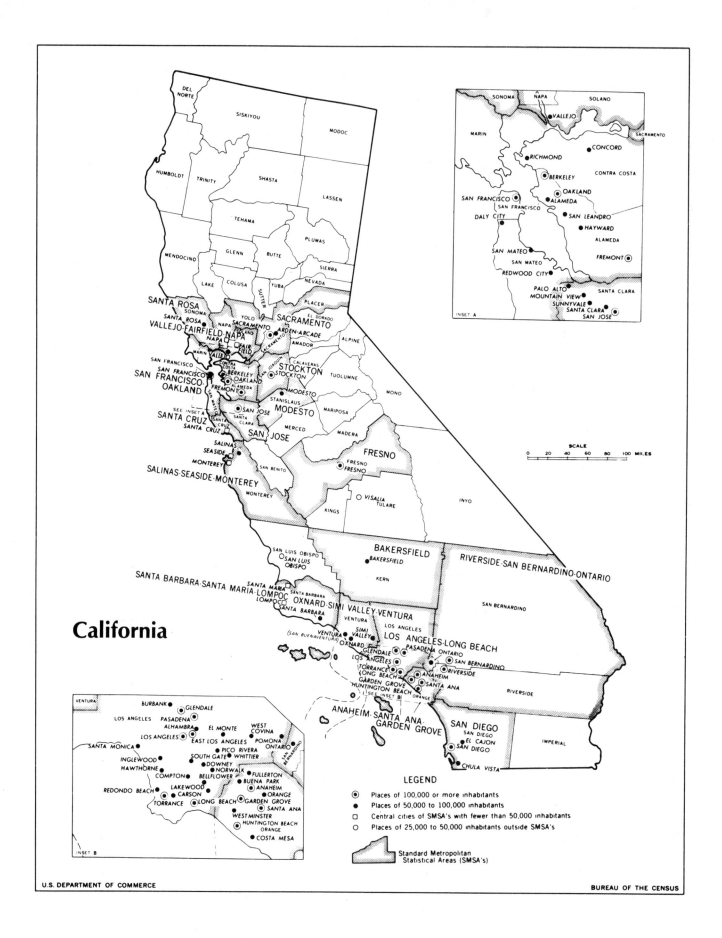

California

LEGEND

⊙ Places of 100,000 or more inhabitants
● Places of 50,000 to 100,000 inhabitants
□ Central cities of SMSA's with fewer than 50,000 inhabitants
○ Places of 25,000 to 50,000 inhabitants outside SMSA's

Standard Metropolitan
Statistical Areas (SMSA's)

SCALE
0 20 40 60 80 100 MILES

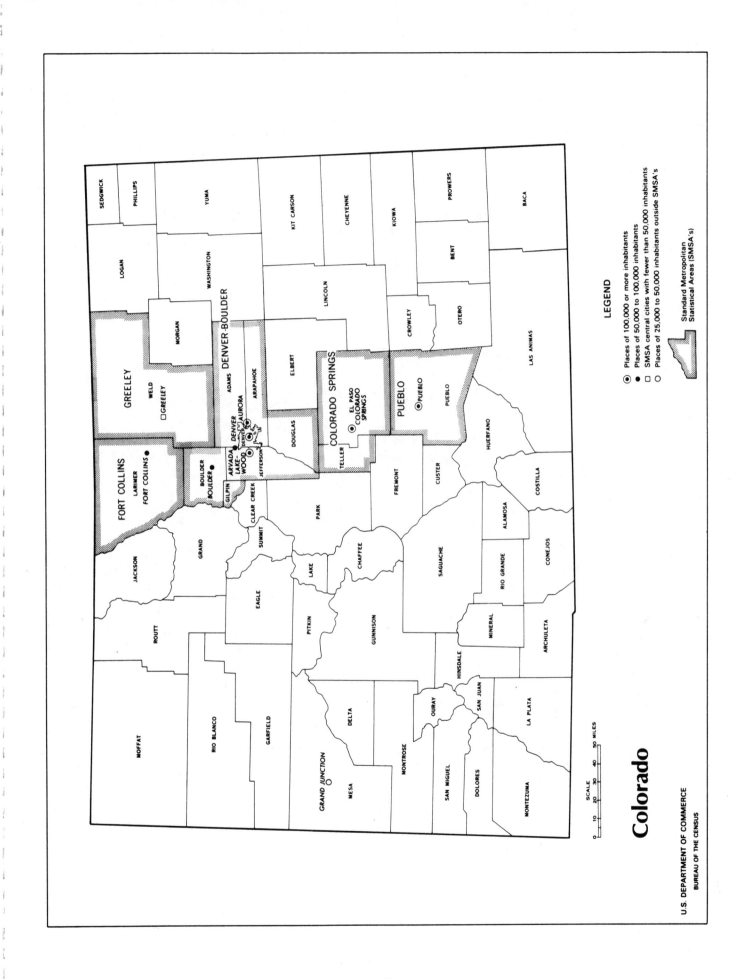

Colorado

U.S. DEPARTMENT OF COMMERCE
BUREAU OF THE CENSUS

LEGEND

⊙ Places of 100,000 or more inhabitants

● Places of 50,000 to 100,000 inhabitants

☐ SMSA central cities with fewer than 50,000 inhabitants

○ Places of 25,000 to 50,000 inhabitants outside SMSA's

Standard Metropolitan
Statistical Areas (SMSA's)

SCALE
0   10   20   30   40   50 MILES

SEDGWICK

PHILLIPS

YUMA

KIT CARSON

CHEYENNE

KIOWA

PROWERS

BACA

LOGAN

WASHINGTON

MORGAN

DENVER-BOULDER

ADAMS

ARAPAHOE

ELBERT

LINCOLN

BENT

CROWLEY

OTERO

LAS ANIMAS

GREELEY

WELD

☐ GREELEY

DENVER

AURORA

DENVER

COLORADO SPRINGS

EL PASO
⊙ COLORADO
SPRINGS

PUEBLO

⊙ PUEBLO

PUEBLO

HUERFANO

FORT COLLINS

LARIMER

FORT COLLINS ●

BOULDER

BOULDER ●

ARVADA
LAKE-
WOOD ●

GILPIN

CLEAR CREEK

JEFFERSON

DOUGLAS

TELLER

FREMONT

CUSTER

COSTILLA

JACKSON

GRAND

SUMMIT

PARK

ALAMOSA

CONEJOS

ROUTT

EAGLE

LAKE

CHAFFEE

SAGUACHE

RIO GRANDE

MINERAL

ARCHULETA

MOFFAT

RIO BLANCO

GARFIELD

PITKIN

GUNNISON

HINSDALE

OURAY

SAN JUAN

LA PLATA

GRAND JUNCTION ○

MESA

DELTA

MONTROSE

SAN MIGUEL

DOLORES

MONTEZUMA

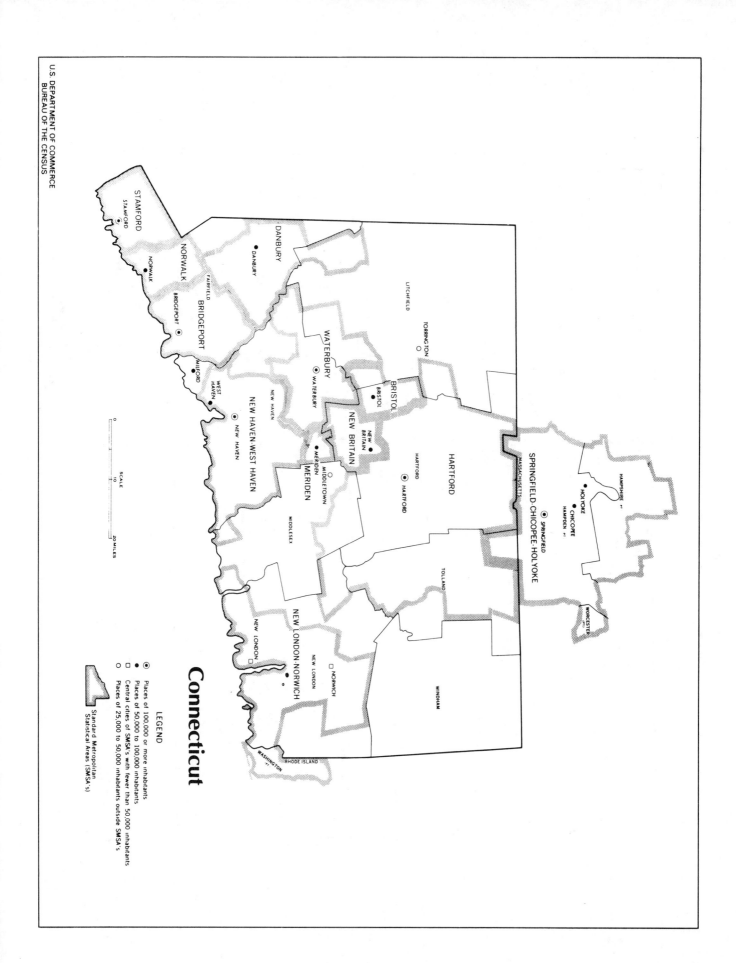

U.S. DEPARTMENT OF COMMERCE
BUREAU OF THE CENSUS

Connecticut

LEGEND

- ◉ Places of 100,000 or more inhabitants
- ● Places of 50,000 to 100,000 inhabitants
- ☐ Central cities of SMSA's with fewer than 50,000 inhabitants
- ○ Places of 25,000 to 50,000 inhabitants outside SMSA's

Standard Metropolitan
Statistical Areas (SMSA's)

SCALE

0

10

20 MILES

STAMFORD

NORWALK

DANBURY

FAIRFIELD

BRIDGEPORT

MILFORD

WEST HAVEN

NEW HAVEN

NEW HAVEN-WEST HAVEN

WATERBURY

LITCHFIELD

TORRINGTON

BRISTOL

NEW BRITAIN

MERIDEN

MIDDLETOWN

MIDDLESEX

HARTFORD

MASSACHUSETTS

SPRINGFIELD-CHICOPEE-HOLYOKE

SPRINGFIELD

HAMPDEN (PT.)

HOLYOKE

CHICOPEE

HAMPSHIRE (PT.)

WORCESTER (PT.)

TOLLAND

WINDHAM

NEW LONDON

NEW LONDON-NORWICH

NORWICH

WASHINGTON (PT.)

RHODE ISLAND

B 456

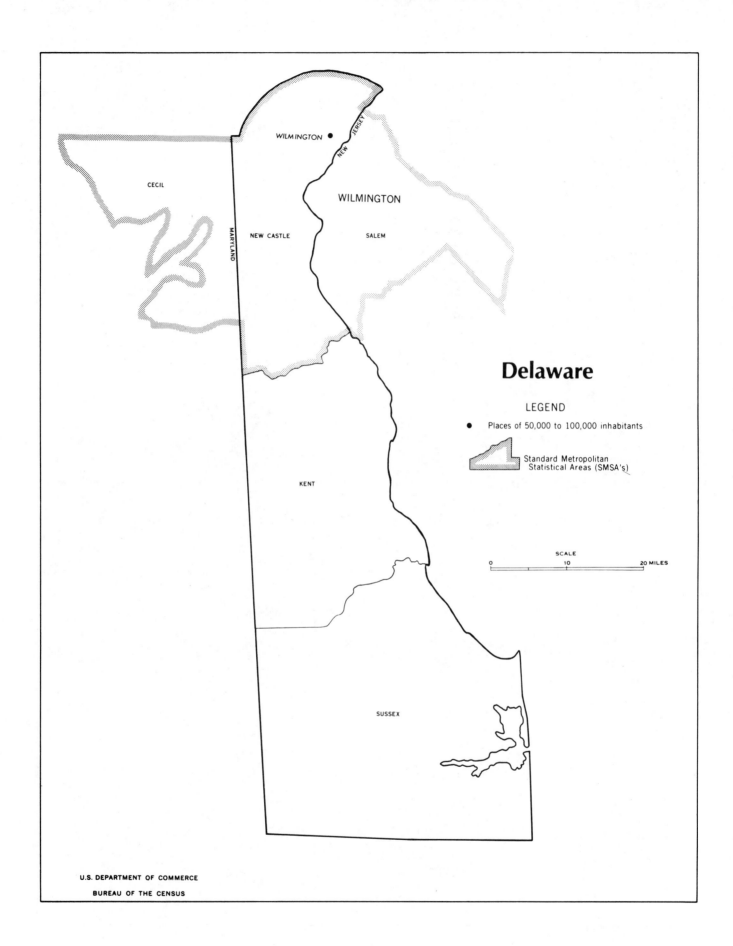

Delaware

LEGEND

● Places of 50,000 to 100,000 inhabitants

Standard Metropolitan
Statistical Areas (SMSA's)

SCALE

0   10   20 MILES

CECIL

WILMINGTON ●

WILMINGTON

NEW JERSEY

MARYLAND

NEW CASTLE

SALEM

KENT

SUSSEX

U.S. DEPARTMENT OF COMMERCE

BUREAU OF THE CENSUS

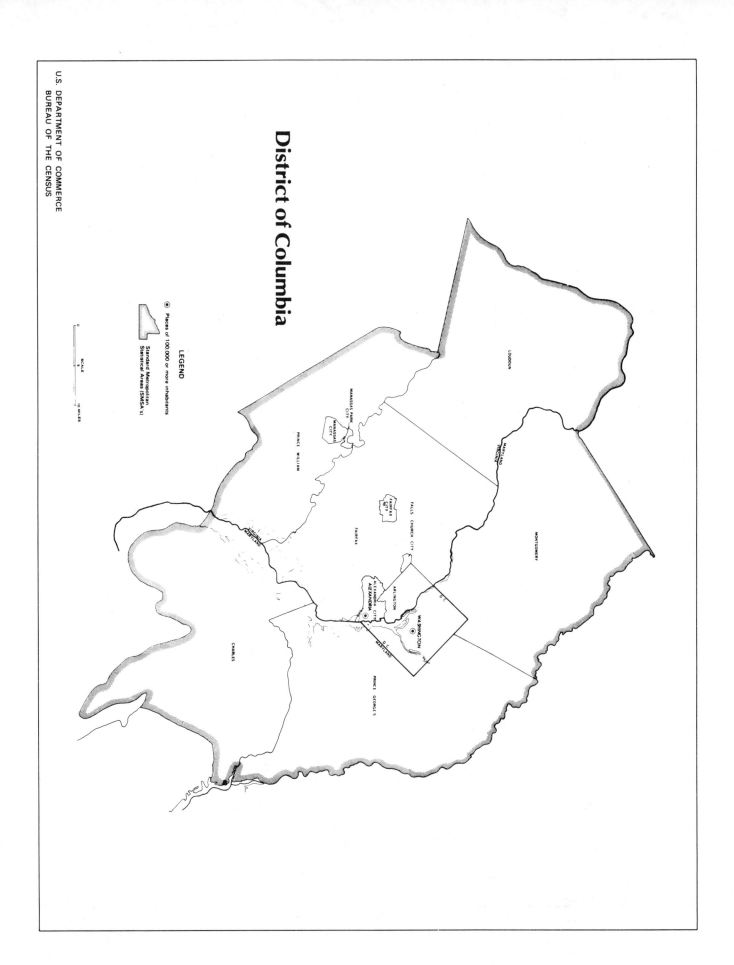

District of Columbia

U.S. DEPARTMENT OF COMMERCE
BUREAU OF THE CENSUS

LEGEND

⊙ Places of 100,000 or more inhabitants

Standard Metropolitan
Statistical Areas (SMSA's)

SCALE

0   5   10 MILES

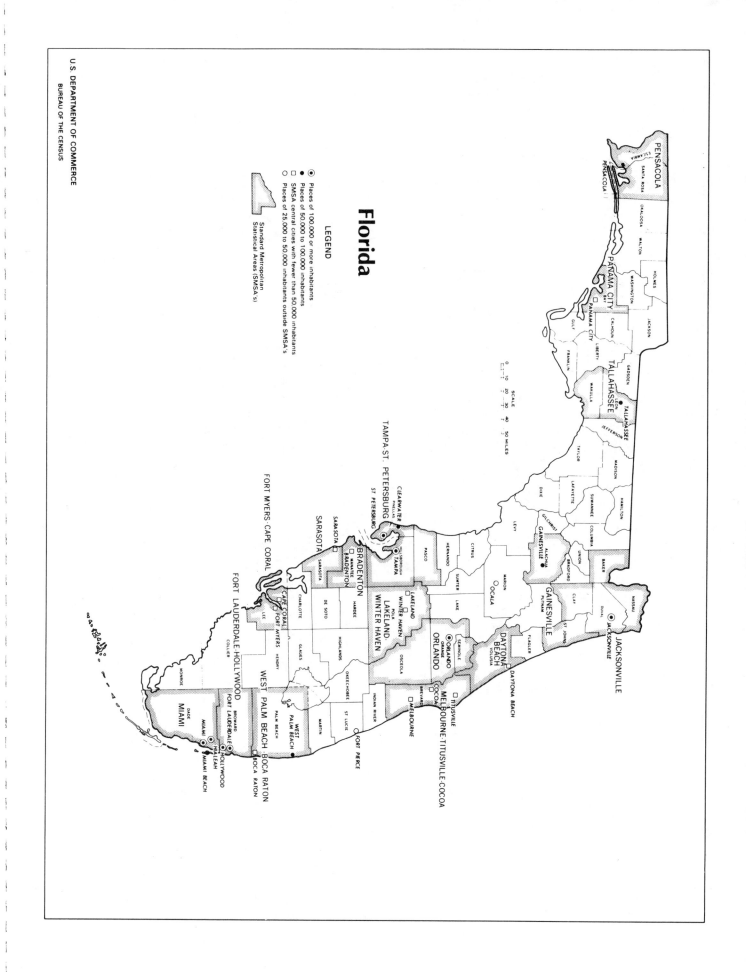

Florida

LEGEND

⊙ Places of 100,000 or more inhabitants
● Places of 50,000 to 100,000 inhabitants
□ SMSA central cities with fewer than 50,000 inhabitants
○ Places of 25,000 to 50,000 inhabitants outside SMSA's

Standard Metropolitan
Statistical Areas (SMSA's)

SCALE
0 10 20 30 40 50 MILES

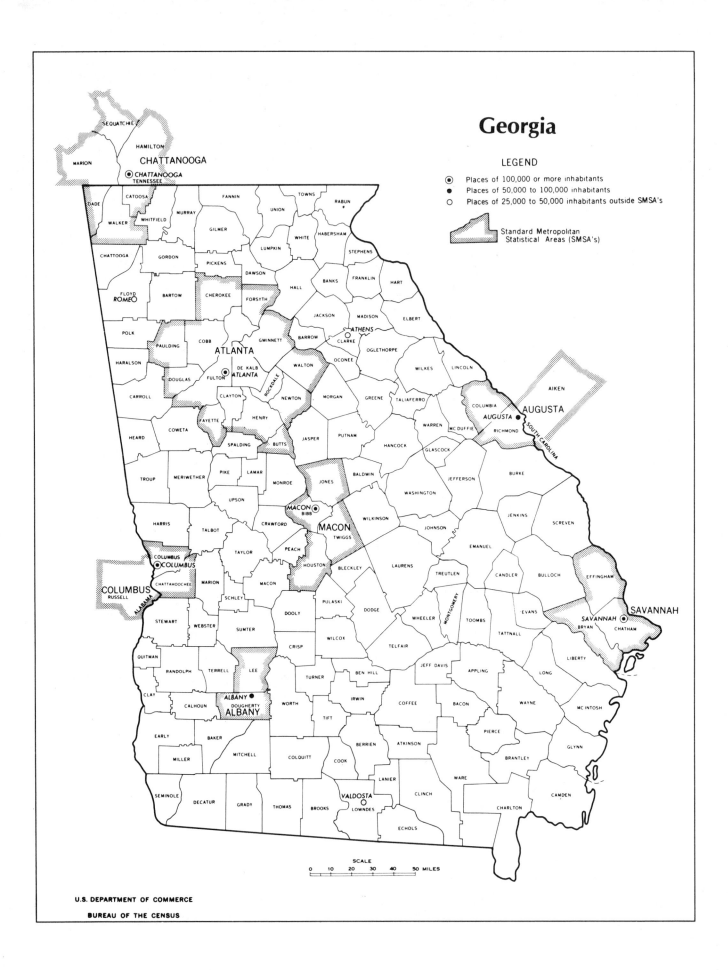

Georgia

LEGEND

⊙ Places of 100,000 or more inhabitants
● Places of 50,000 to 100,000 inhabitants
○ Places of 25,000 to 50,000 inhabitants outside SMSA's

Standard Metropolitan
Statistical Areas (SMSA's)

SEQUATCHIE

HAMILTON

MARION

CHATTANOOGA

⊙ CHATTANOOGA
TENNESSEE

DADE

CATOOSA

FANNIN

TOWNS

RABUN

WALKER

WHITFIELD

MURRAY

GILMER

UNION

WHITE

HABERSHAM

STEPHENS

CHATTOOGA

GORDON

PICKENS

DAWSON

LUMPKIN

HALL

BANKS

FRANKLIN

HART

FLOYD
ROMEO

BARTOW

CHEROKEE

FORSYTH

JACKSON

MADISON

ELBERT

POLK

PAULDING

COBB

GWINNETT

BARROW

○ **ATHENS**
CLARKE

OCONEE

OGLETHORPE

WILKES

LINCOLN

HARALSON

DOUGLAS

ATLANTA

DE KALB
FULTON ⊙ **ATLANTA**

ROCKDALE

WALTON

AIKEN

COLUMBIA

AUGUSTA
● AUGUSTA

CARROLL

CLAYTON

NEWTON

MORGAN

GREENE

TALIAFERRO

WARREN

MCDUFFIE

RICHMOND

SOUTH CAROLINA

COWETA

FAYETTE

HENRY

JASPER

PUTNAM

HANCOCK

GLASCOCK

HEARD

SPALDING

BUTTS

HARRIS

MERIWETHER

PIKE

LAMAR

MONROE

JONES

BALDWIN

WASHINGTON

JEFFERSON

BURKE

TROUP

UPSON

CRAWFORD

WILKINSON

JENKINS

SCREVEN

TALBOT

PEACH

MACON ⊙
BIBB

MACON

TWIGGS

JOHNSON

EMANUEL

CANDLER

BULLOCH

EFFINGHAM

SAVANNAH

COLUMBUS
⊙ COLUMBUS

CHATTAHOOCHEE

MARION

TAYLOR

MACON

HOUSTON

BLECKLEY

LAURENS

TREUTLEN

EVANS

● SAVANNAH ⊙ SAVANNAH

COLUMBUS
RUSSELL

SCHLEY

PULASKI

DODGE

WHEELER

MONTGOMERY

TOOMBS

TATTNALL

BRYAN

CHATHAM

ALABAMA

STEWART

WEBSTER

SUMTER

DOOLY

LIBERTY

QUITMAN

CRISP

WILCOX

TELFAIR

JEFF DAVIS

APPLING

LONG

MC INTOSH

CLAY

RANDOLPH

TERRELL

LEE

TURNER

BEN HILL

IRWIN

COFFEE

BACON

WAYNE

CALHOUN

● **ALBANY**
DOUGHERTY
ALBANY

WORTH

TIFT

PIERCE

GLYNN

EARLY

BAKER

BERRIEN

ATKINSON

BRANTLEY

MILLER

MITCHELL

COLQUITT

COOK

LANIER

WARE

CAMDEN

SEMINOLE

DECATUR

GRADY

THOMAS

BROOKS

VALDOSTA
○ LOWNDES

CLINCH

CHARLTON

ECHOLS

SCALE

0 10 20 30 40 50 MILES

U.S. DEPARTMENT OF COMMERCE

BUREAU OF THE CENSUS

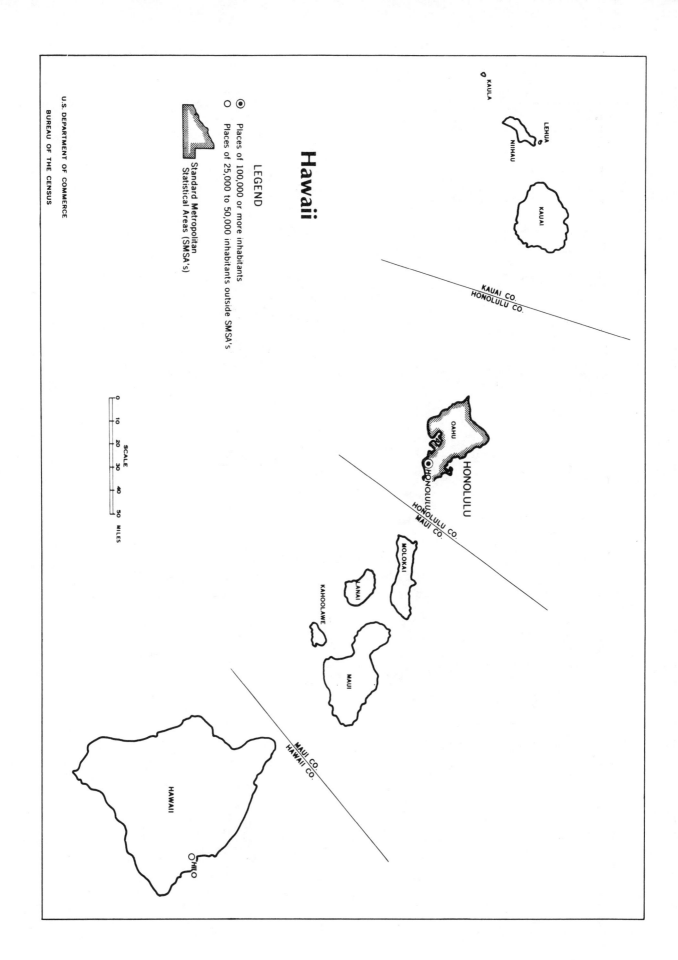

Hawaii

LEGEND

⊙ Places of 100,000 or more inhabitants

○ Places of 25,000 to 50,000 inhabitants outside SMSA's

Standard Metropolitan
Statistical Areas (SMSA's)

SCALE

0
10
20
30
40
50
MILES

U.S. DEPARTMENT OF COMMERCE
BUREAU OF THE CENSUS

KAULA

LEHUA

NIIHAU

KAUAI

KAUAI CO.
HONOLULU CO.

OAHU

HONOLULU

HONOLULU CO.
MAUI CO.

MOLOKAI

LANAI

KAHOOLAWE

MAUI

MAUI CO.
HAWAII CO.

HAWAII

HILO

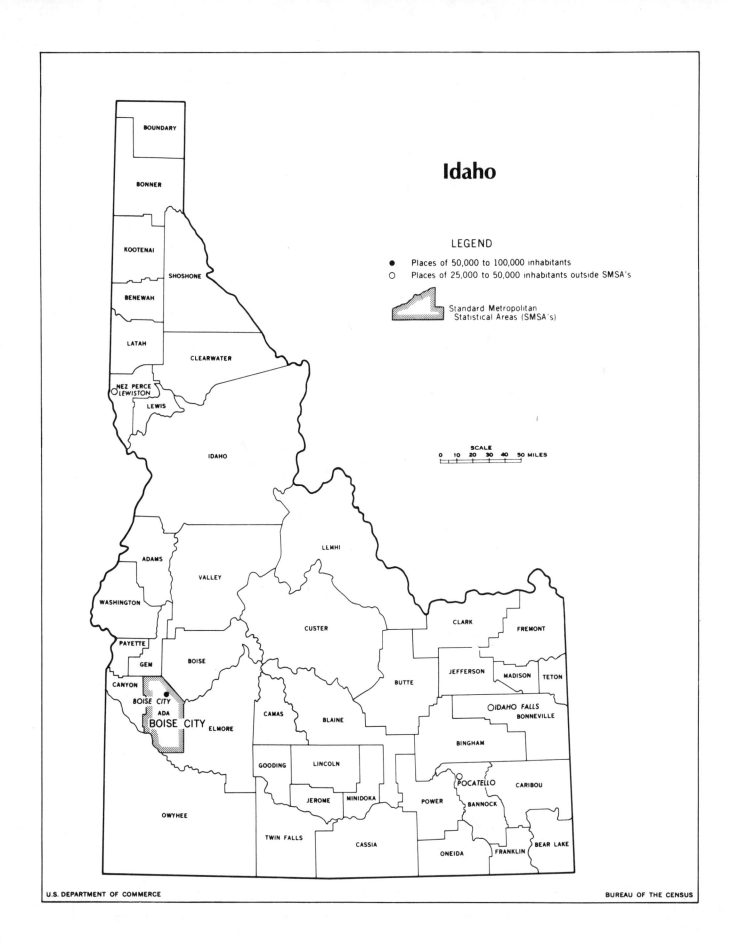

Idaho

LEGEND

● Places of 50,000 to 100,000 inhabitants

○ Places of 25,000 to 50,000 inhabitants outside SMSA's

Standard Metropolitan Statistical Areas (SMSA's)

SCALE
0 10 20 30 40 50 MILES

BOUNDARY

BONNER

KOOTENAI

SHOSHONE

BENEWAH

LATAH

CLEARWATER

NEZ PERCE
○LEWISTON

LEWIS

IDAHO

ADAMS

VALLEY

LEMHI

WASHINGTON

CUSTER

CLARK

FREMONT

PAYETTE

GEM

BOISE

JEFFERSON

MADISON

TETON

CANYON

BUTTE

BOISE CITY ●

ADA

BOISE CITY

ELMORE

CAMAS

BLAINE

○IDAHO FALLS

BONNEVILLE

BINGHAM

GOODING

LINCOLN

POCATELLO ○

CARIBOU

JEROME

MINIDOKA

POWER

BANNOCK

OWYHEE

TWIN FALLS

CASSIA

ONEIDA

FRANKLIN

BEAR LAKE

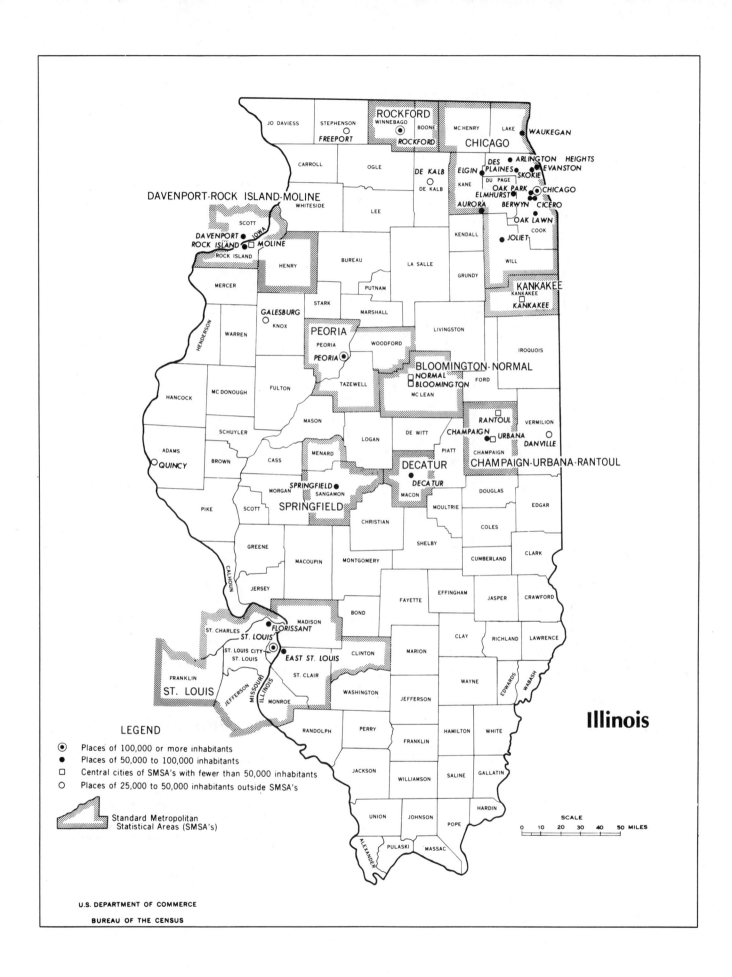

Illinois

LEGEND

⊙   Places of 100,000 or more inhabitants
●   Places of 50,000 to 100,000 inhabitants
□   Central cities of SMSA's with fewer than 50,000 inhabitants
○   Places of 25,000 to 50,000 inhabitants outside SMSA's

Standard Metropolitan
Statistical Areas (SMSA's)

SCALE
0   10   20   30   40   50 MILES

Indiana

LEGEND

- ⊙ Places of 100,000 or more inhabitants
- ● Places of 50,000 to 100,000 inhabitants
- ☐ SMSA central cities with fewer than 50,000 inhabitants
- ○ Places of 25,000 to 50,000 inhabitants outside SMSA's

Standard Metropolitan
Statistical Areas (SMSA's)

U.S. DEPARTMENT OF COMMERCE

BUREAU OF THE CENSUS

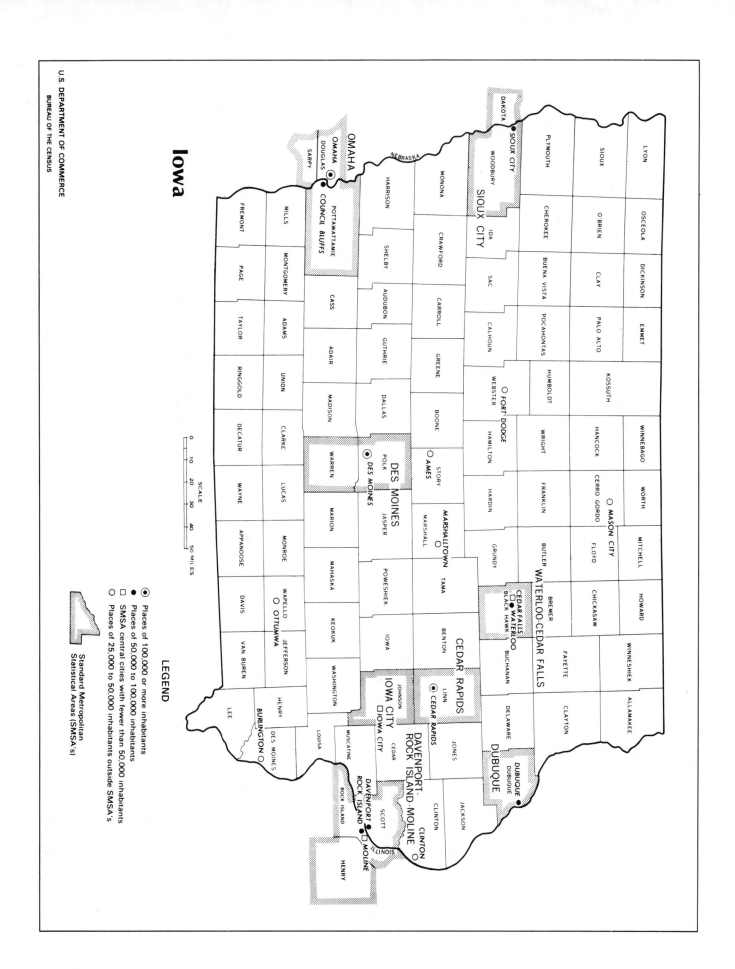

Iowa

U.S. DEPARTMENT OF COMMERCE
BUREAU OF THE CENSUS

SCALE

0
10
20
30
40
50 MILES

LEGEND

◉ Places of 100,000 or more inhabitants
● Places of 50,000 to 100,000 inhabitants
□ SMSA central cities with fewer than 50,000 inhabitants
○ Places of 25,000 to 50,000 inhabitants outside SMSA's

Standard Metropolitan
Statistical Areas (SMSA's)

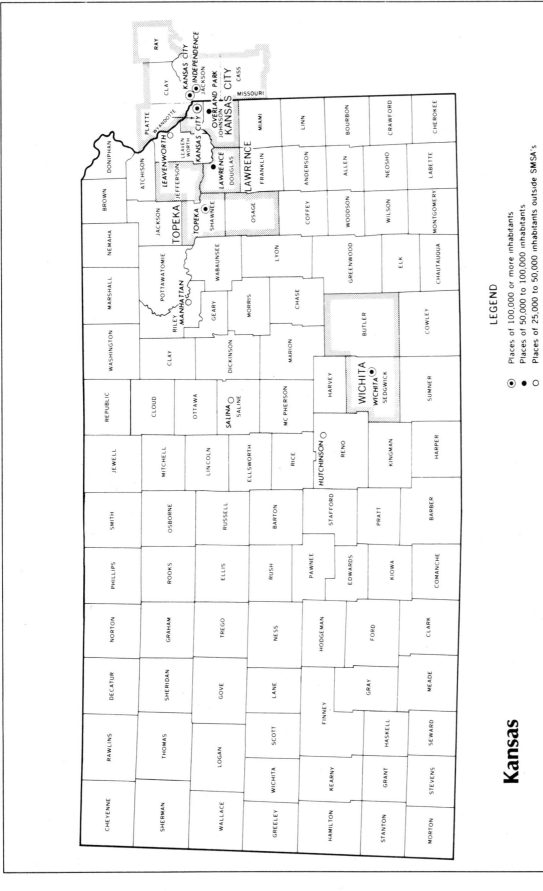

Kansas

LEGEND

⊙ Places of 100,000 or more inhabitants

● Places of 50,000 to 100,000 inhabitants

○ Places of 25,000 to 50,000 inhabitants outside SMSA's

 Standard Metropolitan
Statistical Areas (SMSA's)

SCALE

0   10   20   30   40   50 MILES

U.S. DEPARTMENT OF COMMERCE
BUREAU OF THE CENSUS

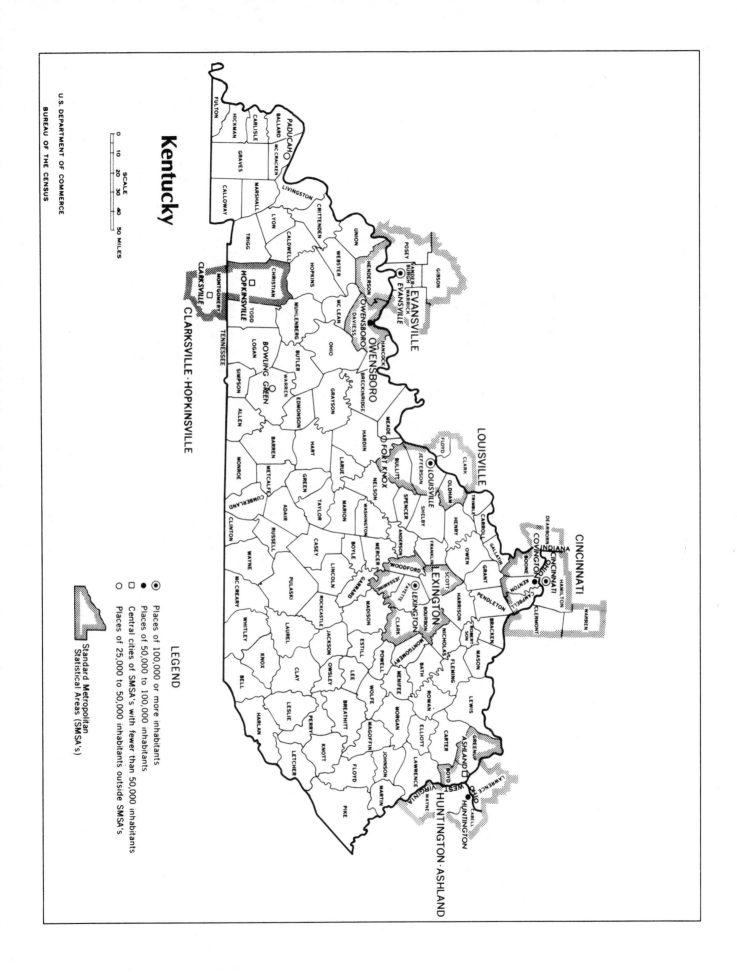

Kentucky

U.S. DEPARTMENT OF COMMERCE
BUREAU OF THE CENSUS

SCALE
0 10 20 30 40 50 MILES

LEGEND

⊙ Places of 100,000 or more inhabitants
● Places of 50,000 to 100,000 inhabitants
□ Central cities of SMSA's with fewer than 50,000 inhabitants
○ Places of 25,000 to 50,000 inhabitants outside SMSA's

Standard Metropolitan
Statistical Areas (SMSA's)

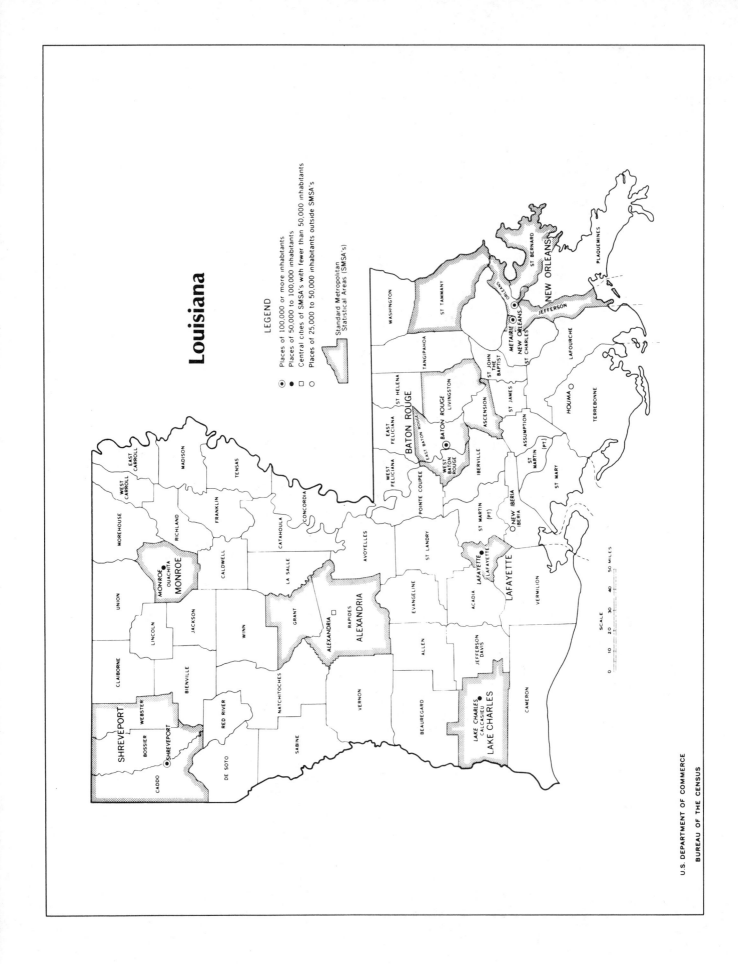

Louisiana

U.S. DEPARTMENT OF COMMERCE

BUREAU OF THE CENSUS

B 468

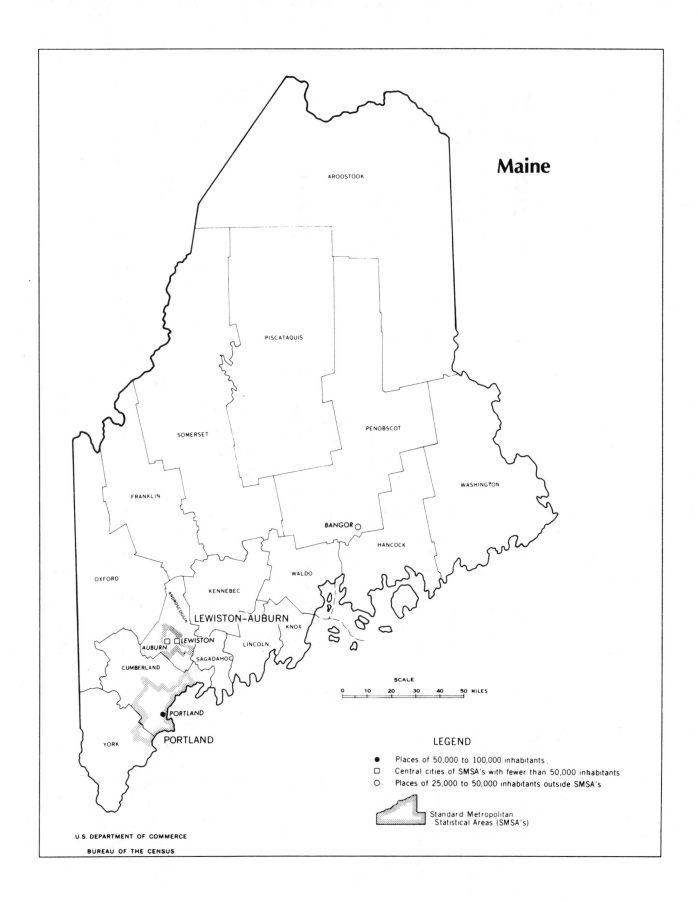

Maine

AROOSTOOK

PISCATAQUIS

SOMERSET

PENOBSCOT

FRANKLIN

WASHINGTON

BANGOR ○

HANCOCK

OXFORD

KENNEBEC

WALDO

ANDROSCOGGIN

LEWISTON–AUBURN

KNOX

□ LEWISTON

LINCOLN

AUBURN □

SAGADAHOC

CUMBERLAND

SCALE

● PORTLAND

PORTLAND

YORK

0 10 20 30 40 50 MILES

LEGEND

●   Places of 50,000 to 100,000 inhabitants

□   Central cities of SMSA's with fewer than 50,000 inhabitants

○   Places of 25,000 to 50,000 inhabitants outside SMSA's

Standard Metropolitan
Statistical Areas (SMSA's)

U.S. DEPARTMENT OF COMMERCE

BUREAU OF THE CENSUS

Maryland

U.S. DEPARTMENT OF COMMERCE
BUREAU OF THE CENSUS

LEGEND

- ◉ Places of 100,000 or more inhabitants
- ● Places of 50,000 to 100,000 inhabitants
- ○ Places of 25,000 to 50,000 inhabitants outside SMSA's

▨ Standard Metropolitan
Statistical Areas (SMSA's)

SCALE
0   10   20   30 MILES

SCALE
0   10   20   30 MILES

GARRETT

CUMBERLAND
ALLEGANY

HAGERSTOWN

WASHINGTON

FREDERICK

WASHINGTON

VIRGINIA

LOUDOUN

MONTGOMERY

FAIRFAX CITY
MANASSAS
PARK CITY
MANASSAS CITY
PRINCE WILLIAM
FALLS CHURCH CITY
ARLINGTON
ALEXANDRIA CITY
FAIRFAX
ALEXANDRIA

WASHINGTON

PRINCE GEORGES

CARROLL

HOWARD

BALTIMORE

BALTIMORE

BALTIMORE CITY

ANNE ARUNDEL

HARFORD

CECIL

CHARLES

ST MARYS

CALVERT

KENT

QUEEN ANNES

TALBOT

CAROLINE

DORCHESTER

WICOMICO

SOMERSET

WORCESTER

WILMINGTON
NEW CASTLE
DELAWARE

NEW JERSEY

SALEM

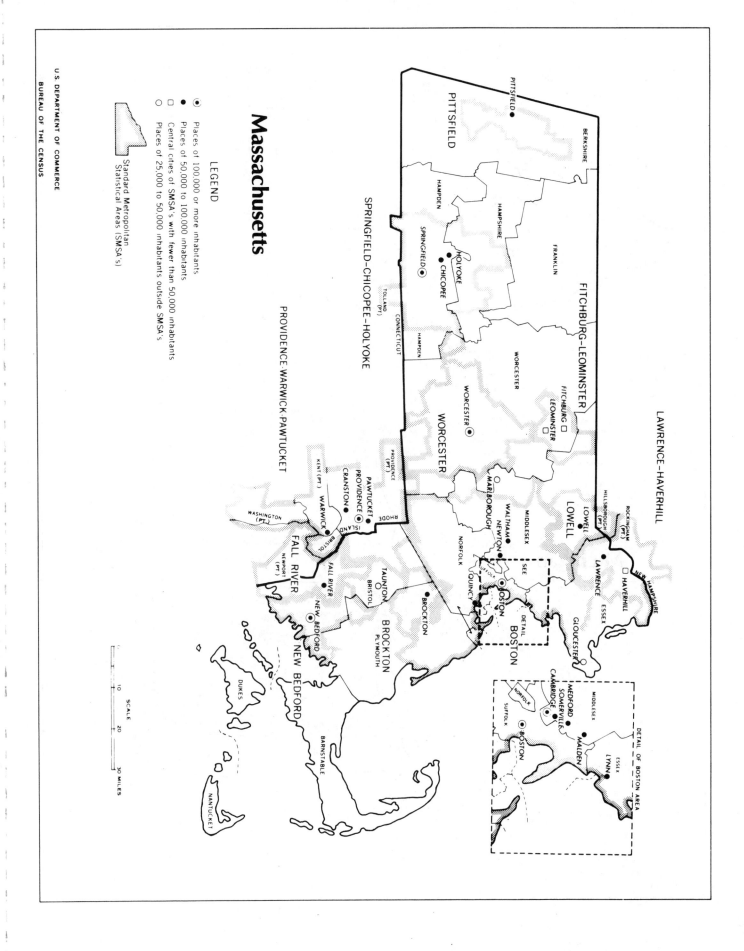

Massachusetts

U.S. DEPARTMENT OF COMMERCE
BUREAU OF THE CENSUS

LEGEND

⊙ Places of 100,000 or more inhabitants

● Places of 50,000 to 100,000 inhabitants

□ Central cities of SMSA's with fewer than 50,000 inhabitants

○ Places of 25,000 to 50,000 inhabitants outside SMSA's

Standard Metropolitan
Statistical Areas (SMSA's)

SCALE

0   10   20   30 MILES

PITTSFIELD

SPRINGFIELD-CHICOPEE-HOLYOKE

FITCHBURG-LEOMINSTER

LAWRENCE-HAVERHILL

PROVIDENCE-WARWICK-PAWTUCKET

FALL RIVER

NEW BEDFORD

WORCESTER

BROCKTON

DETAIL OF BOSTON AREA

SEE DETAIL BOSTON

BERKSHIRE

HAMPDEN

HAMPSHIRE

FRANKLIN

WORCESTER

HILLSBOROUGH (PT)

ROCKINGHAM (PT)

NEW HAMPSHIRE

ESSEX

MIDDLESEX

NORFOLK

SUFFOLK

PLYMOUTH

BRISTOL

RHODE ISLAND

CONNECTICUT

TOLLAND (PT)

HAMPDEN

PROVIDENCE (PT)

KENT (PT)

WASHINGTON (PT)

NEWPORT (PT)

BRISTOL

GLOUCESTER

DUKES

NANTUCKET

BARNSTABLE

PITTSFIELD

SPRINGFIELD ⊙
HOLYOKE ●
CHICOPEE ●

FITCHBURG □
LEOMINSTER □

WORCESTER ⊙

MARLBOROUGH ○
WALTHAM ●
NEWTON ●
LOWELL ●
LAWRENCE ●
HAVERHILL □

QUINCY ●
BOSTON

PROVIDENCE ⊙
PAWTUCKET ●
CRANSTON ●
WARWICK ●

FALL RIVER ●
NEW BEDFORD ⊙

TAUNTON ○
BROCKTON ●

MEDFORD
SOMERVILLE
CAMBRIDGE ⊙
MALDEN ●
LYNN ●
BOSTON ⊙

NORFOLK
SUFFOLK
MIDDLESEX
ESSEX

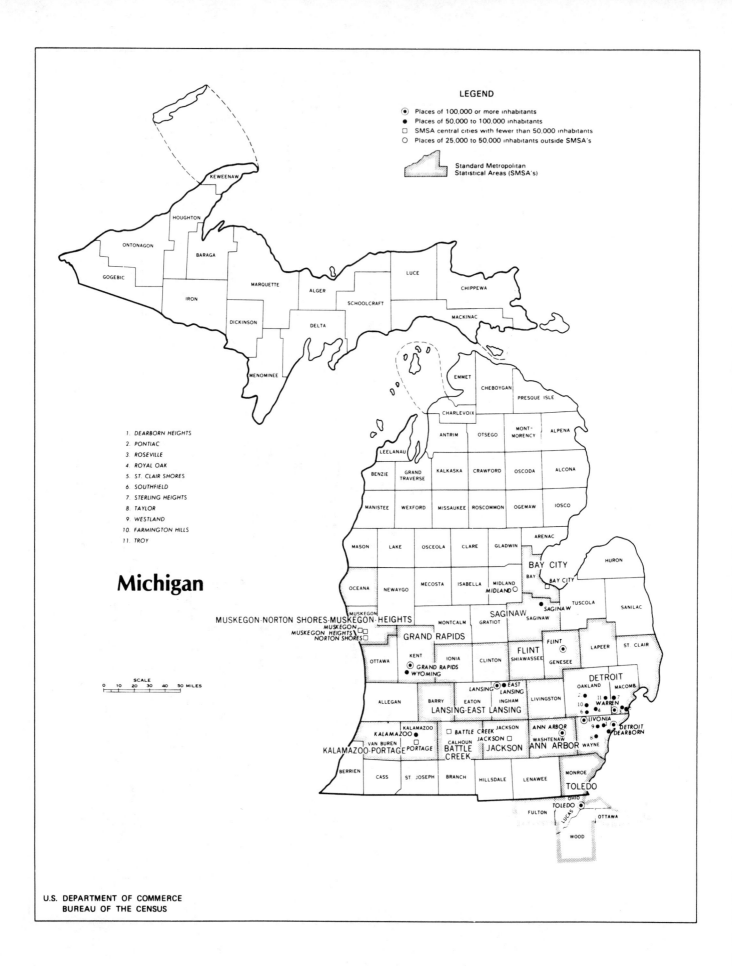

LEGEND

- ⊙ Places of 100,000 or more inhabitants
- ● Places of 50,000 to 100,000 inhabitants
- ☐ SMSA central cities with fewer than 50,000 inhabitants
- ○ Places of 25,000 to 50,000 inhabitants outside SMSA's

Standard Metropolitan
Statistical Areas (SMSA's)

1. DEARBORN HEIGHTS
2. PONTIAC
3. ROSEVILLE
4. ROYAL OAK
5. ST. CLAIR SHORES
6. SOUTHFIELD
7. STERLING HEIGHTS
8. TAYLOR
9. WESTLAND
10. FARMINGTON HILLS
11. TROY

Michigan

SCALE
0 10 20 30 40 50 MILES

U.S. DEPARTMENT OF COMMERCE
BUREAU OF THE CENSUS

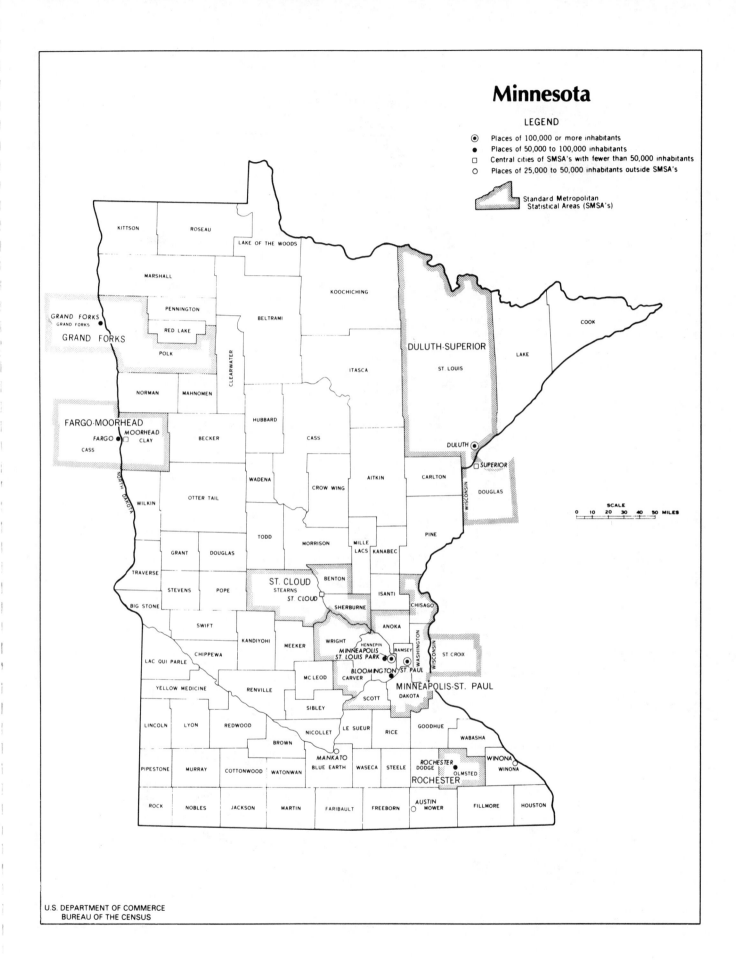

Minnesota

LEGEND

⊙ Places of 100,000 or more inhabitants

● Places of 50,000 to 100,000 inhabitants

☐ Central cities of SMSA's with fewer than 50,000 inhabitants

○ Places of 25,000 to 50,000 inhabitants outside SMSA's

Standard Metropolitan Statistical Areas (SMSA's)

KITTSON

ROSEAU

LAKE OF THE WOODS

MARSHALL

KOOCHICHING

GRAND FORKS

GRAND FORKS

PENNINGTON

RED LAKE

BELTRAMI

COOK

GRAND FORKS

POLK

CLEARWATER

ITASCA

DULUTH-SUPERIOR

ST. LOUIS

LAKE

NORMAN

MAHNOMEN

HUBBARD

FARGO-MOORHEAD

MOORHEAD

FARGO

CLAY

BECKER

CASS

DULUTH

CASS

WADENA

CROW WING

AITKIN

CARLTON

SUPERIOR

DOUGLAS

WILKIN

OTTER TAIL

NORTH DAKOTA

PINE

WISCONSIN

TODD

MORRISON

MILLE LACS

KANABEC

TRAVERSE

GRANT

DOUGLAS

BENTON

ST. CLOUD

STEARNS

ST. CLOUD

ISANTI

STEVENS

POPE

CHISAGO

BIG STONE

SHERBURNE

SCALE
0 10 20 30 40 50 MILES

SWIFT

KANDIYOHI

MEEKER

WRIGHT

ANOKA

HENNEPIN

MINNEAPOLIS

ST. LOUIS PARK

RAMSEY

ST. CROIX

WASHINGTON

WISCONSIN

LAC QUI PARLE

CHIPPEWA

BLOOMINGTON

ST. PAUL

MC LEOD

CARVER

YELLOW MEDICINE

RENVILLE

MINNEAPOLIS-ST. PAUL

SCOTT

DAKOTA

SIBLEY

LINCOLN

LYON

REDWOOD

NICOLLET

LE SUEUR

RICE

GOODHUE

WABASHA

BROWN

MANKATO

BLUE EARTH

WASECA

STEELE

ROCHESTER

DODGE

WINONA

WINONA

PIPESTONE

MURRAY

COTTONWOOD

WATONWAN

OLMSTED

ROCHESTER

ROCK

NOBLES

JACKSON

MARTIN

FARIBAULT

FREEBORN

AUSTIN

MOWER

FILLMORE

HOUSTON

U.S. DEPARTMENT OF COMMERCE
BUREAU OF THE CENSUS

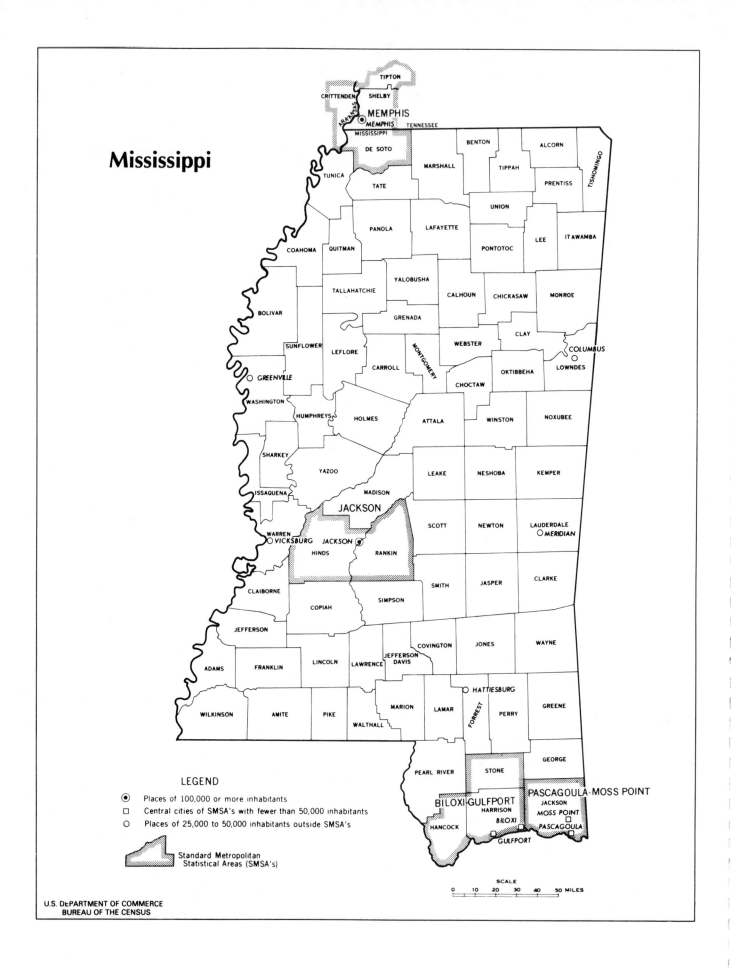

Mississippi

LEGEND

- ⊙ Places of 100,000 or more inhabitants
- ☐ Central cities of SMSA's with fewer than 50,000 inhabitants
- ○ Places of 25,000 to 50,000 inhabitants outside SMSA's

Standard Metropolitan Statistical Areas (SMSA's)

SCALE
0   10   20   30   40   50 MILES

U.S. DEPARTMENT OF COMMERCE
BUREAU OF THE CENSUS

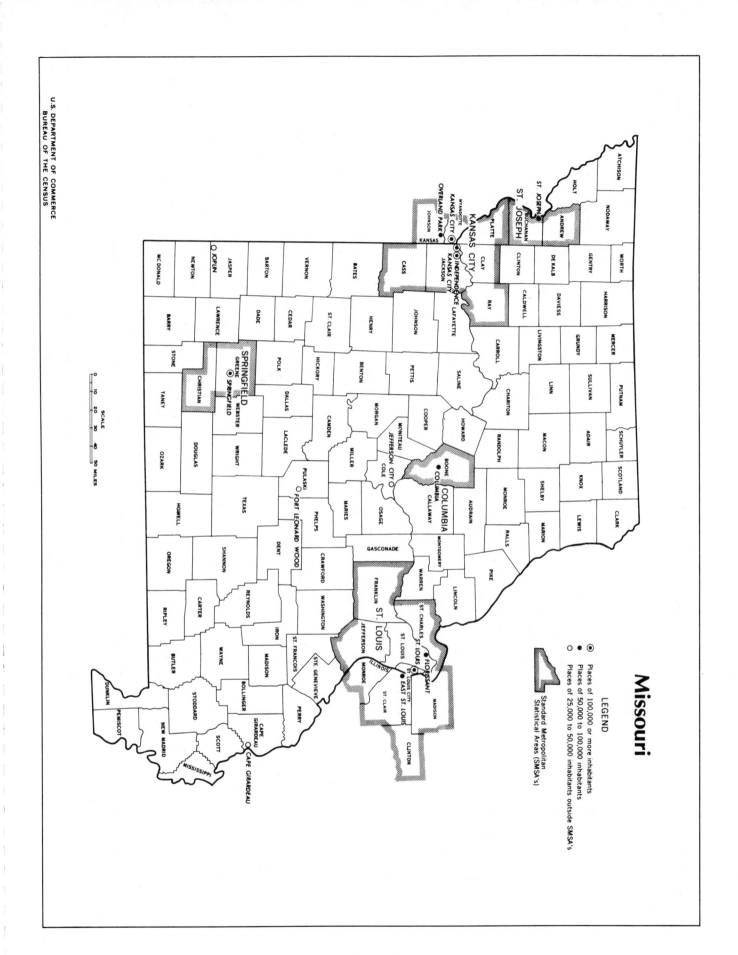

Missouri

LEGEND

⊙ Places of 100,000 or more inhabitants
● Places of 50,000 to 100,000 inhabitants
○ Places of 25,000 to 50,000 inhabitants outside SMSA's

◤ Standard Metropolitan
Statistical Areas (SMSA's)

U.S. DEPARTMENT OF COMMERCE
BUREAU OF THE CENSUS

SCALE
0
10
20
30
40
50 MILES

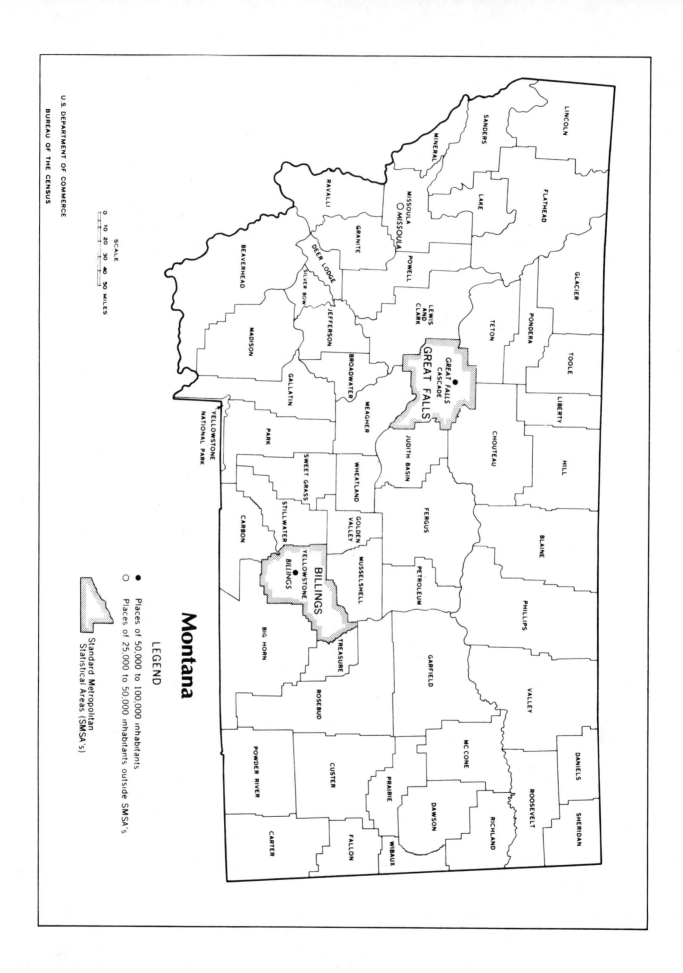

Montana

LEGEND

● Places of 50,000 to 100,000 inhabitants

○ Places of 25,000 to 50,000 inhabitants outside SMSA's

Standard Metropolitan
Statistical Areas (SMSA's)

U.S. DEPARTMENT OF COMMERCE
BUREAU OF THE CENSUS

SCALE

0 10 20 30 40 50 MILES

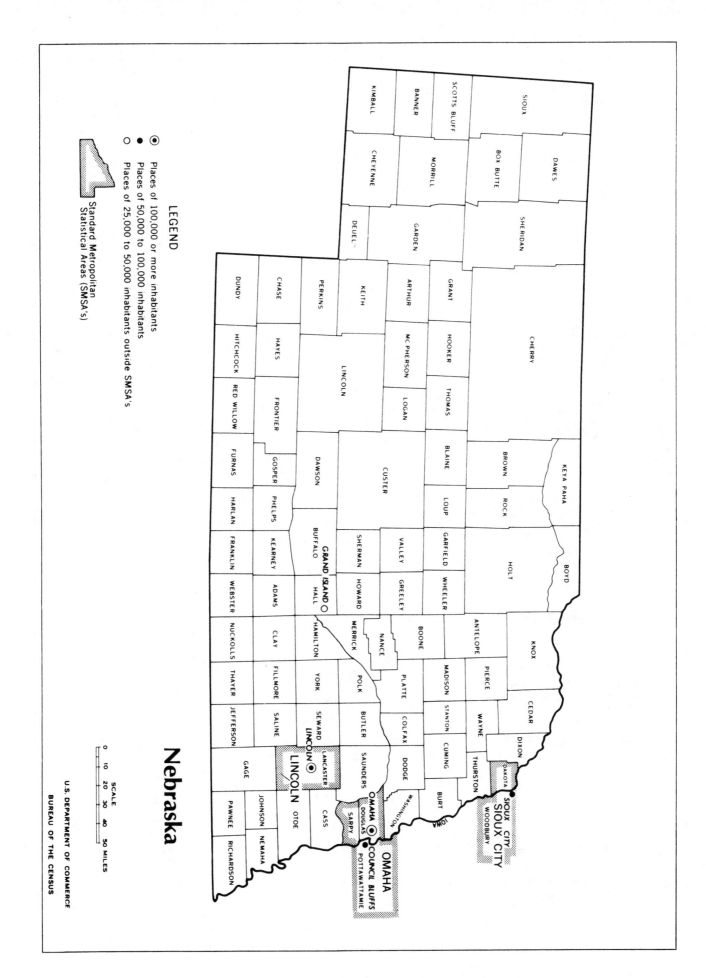

Nebraska

LEGEND

⊙ Places of 100,000 or more inhabitants

● Places of 50,000 to 100,000 inhabitants

○ Places of 25,000 to 50,000 inhabitants outside SMSA's

Standard Metropolitan
Statistical Areas (SMSA's)

SCALE
0 10 20 30 40 50 MILES

U.S. DEPARTMENT OF COMMERCE
BUREAU OF THE CENSUS

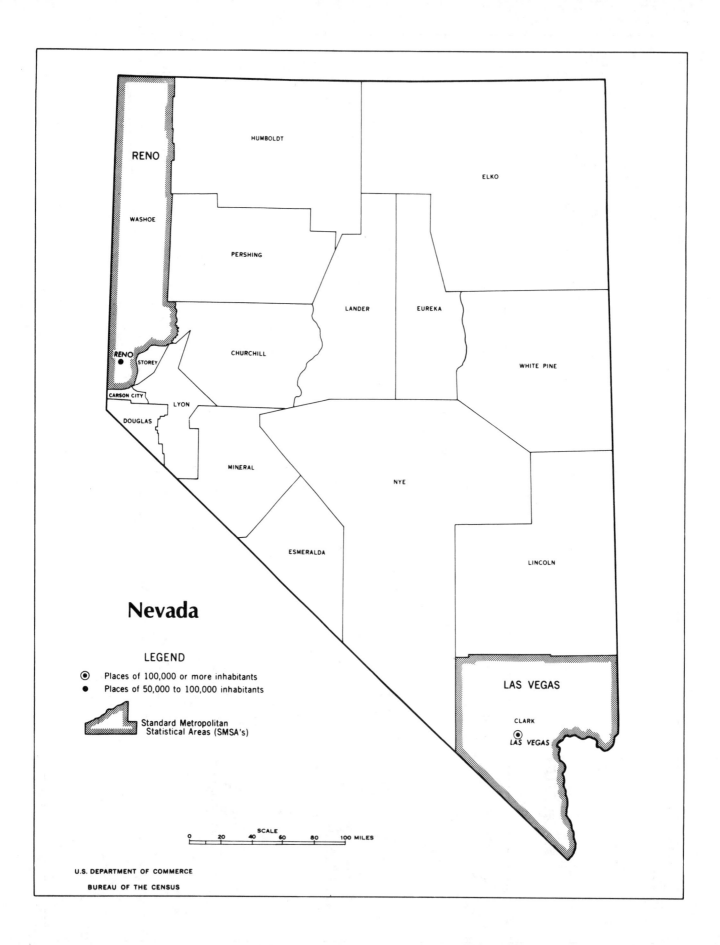

Nevada

LEGEND

⊙   Places of 100,000 or more inhabitants

●   Places of 50,000 to 100,000 inhabitants

Standard Metropolitan
Statistical Areas (SMSA's)

SCALE

0   20   40   60   80   100 MILES

U.S. DEPARTMENT OF COMMERCE

BUREAU OF THE CENSUS

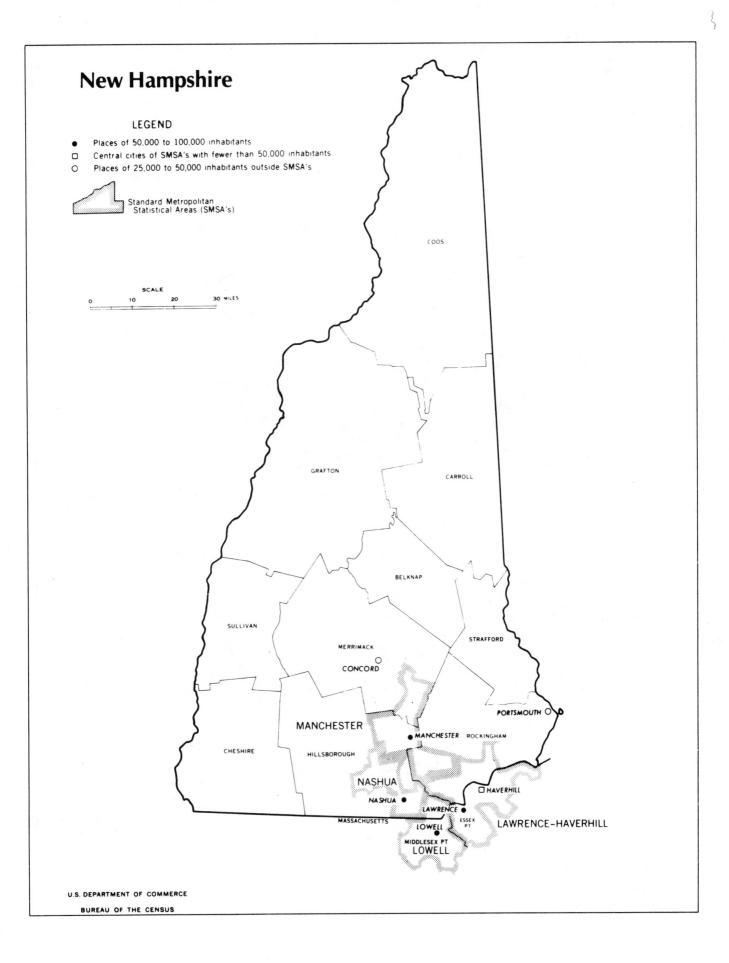

New Hampshire

LEGEND

● Places of 50,000 to 100,000 inhabitants
□ Central cities of SMSA's with fewer than 50,000 inhabitants
○ Places of 25,000 to 50,000 inhabitants outside SMSA's

Standard Metropolitan
Statistical Areas (SMSA's)

SCALE

0   10   20   30 MILES

COOS

GRAFTON

CARROLL

BELKNAP

SULLIVAN

MERRIMACK

STRAFFORD

○ CONCORD

PORTSMOUTH ○

MANCHESTER

● MANCHESTER   ROCKINGHAM

CHESHIRE

HILLSBOROUGH

NASHUA

□ HAVERHILL

NASHUA ●

LAWRENCE

LAWRENCE ●

MASSACHUSETTS

LOWELL ●   ESSEX PT

LAWRENCE-HAVERHILL

MIDDLESEX PT

LOWELL

U.S. DEPARTMENT OF COMMERCE

BUREAU OF THE CENSUS

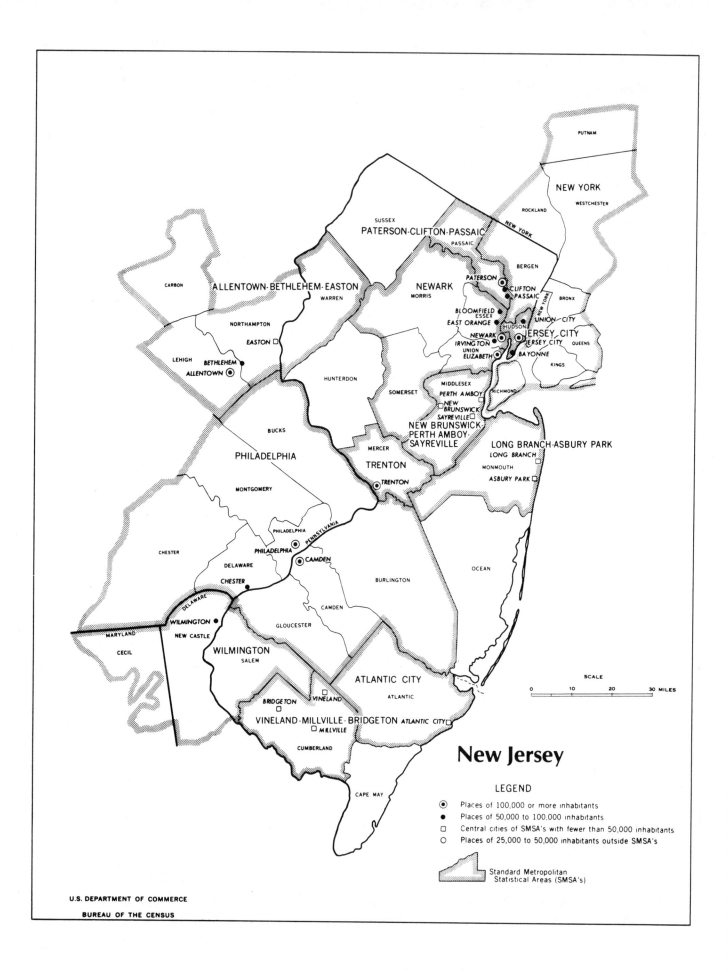

New Jersey

LEGEND

⊙ Places of 100,000 or more inhabitants

● Places of 50,000 to 100,000 inhabitants

□ Central cities of SMSA's with fewer than 50,000 inhabitants

○ Places of 25,000 to 50,000 inhabitants outside SMSA's

Standard Metropolitan
Statistical Areas (SMSA's)

PATERSON·CLIFTON·PASSAIC

ALLENTOWN·BETHLEHEM·EASTON

NEWARK

JERSEY CITY

NEW BRUNSWICK·
PERTH AMBOY·
SAYREVILLE

LONG BRANCH·ASBURY PARK

PHILADELPHIA

TRENTON

WILMINGTON

ATLANTIC CITY

VINELAND·MILLVILLE·BRIDGETON

SCALE

0   10   20   30 MILES

U.S. DEPARTMENT OF COMMERCE

BUREAU OF THE CENSUS

B 480

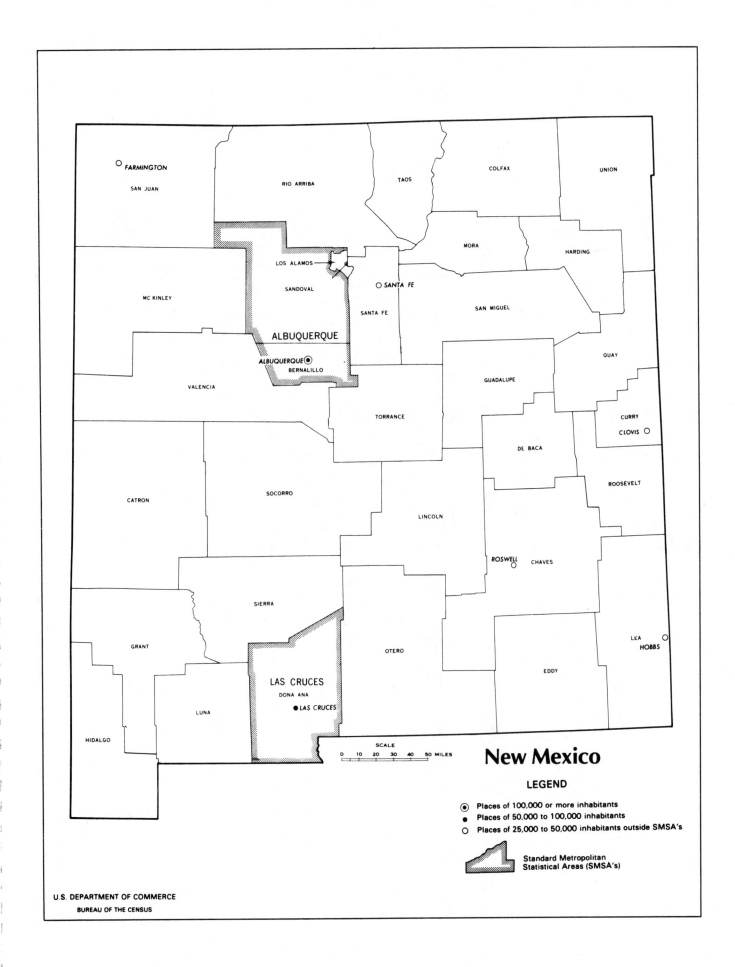

FARMINGTON

SAN JUAN

RIO ARRIBA

TAOS

COLFAX

UNION

MORA

HARDING

LOS ALAMOS

MC KINLEY

SANDOVAL

SANTA FE

SAN MIGUEL

ALBUQUERQUE

SANTA FE

ALBUQUERQUE
BERNALILLO

QUAY

VALENCIA

GUADALUPE

TORRANCE

CURRY
CLOVIS

DE BACA

ROOSEVELT

CATRON

SOCORRO

LINCOLN

ROSWELL
CHAVES

SIERRA

LEA
HOBBS

GRANT

OTERO

LAS CRUCES
DONA ANA
LAS CRUCES

EDDY

LUNA

HIDALGO

SCALE
0 10 20 30 40 50 MILES

New Mexico

LEGEND

⊙ Places of 100,000 or more inhabitants

● Places of 50,000 to 100,000 inhabitants

○ Places of 25,000 to 50,000 inhabitants outside SMSA's

Standard Metropolitan
Statistical Areas (SMSA's)

U.S. DEPARTMENT OF COMMERCE

BUREAU OF THE CENSUS

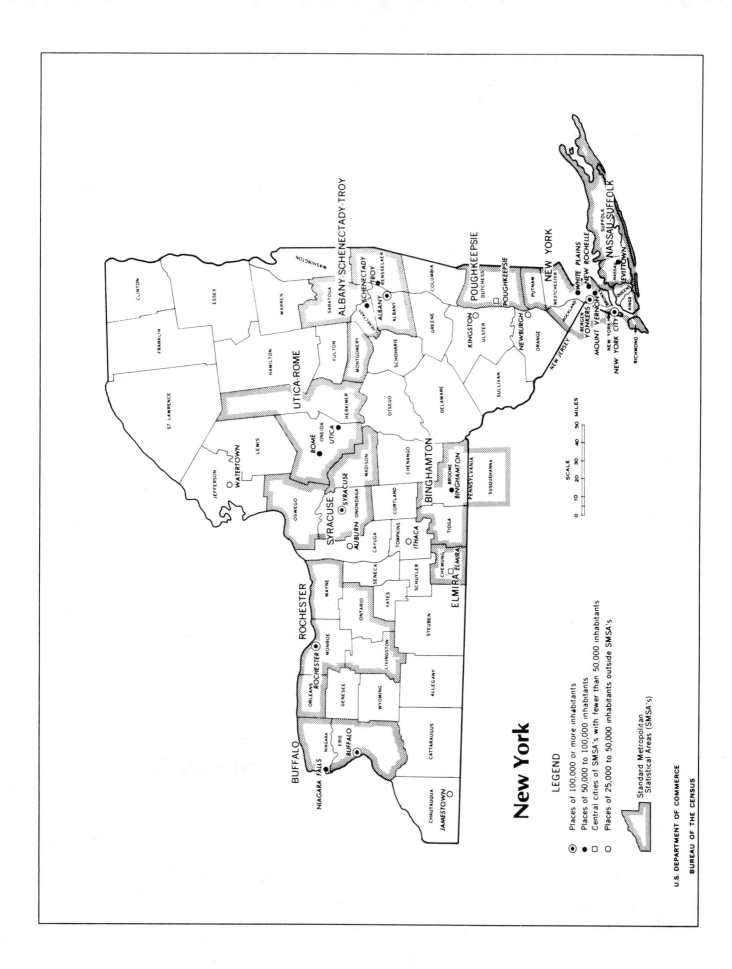

New York

LEGEND

⊙ Places of 100,000 or more inhabitants

● Places of 50,000 to 100,000 inhabitants

□ Central cities of SMSA's with fewer than 50,000 inhabitants

○ Places of 25,000 to 50,000 inhabitants outside SMSA's

Standard Metropolitan
Statistical Areas (SMSA's)

U.S. DEPARTMENT OF COMMERCE

BUREAU OF THE CENSUS

SCALE

0 10 20 30 40 50 MILES

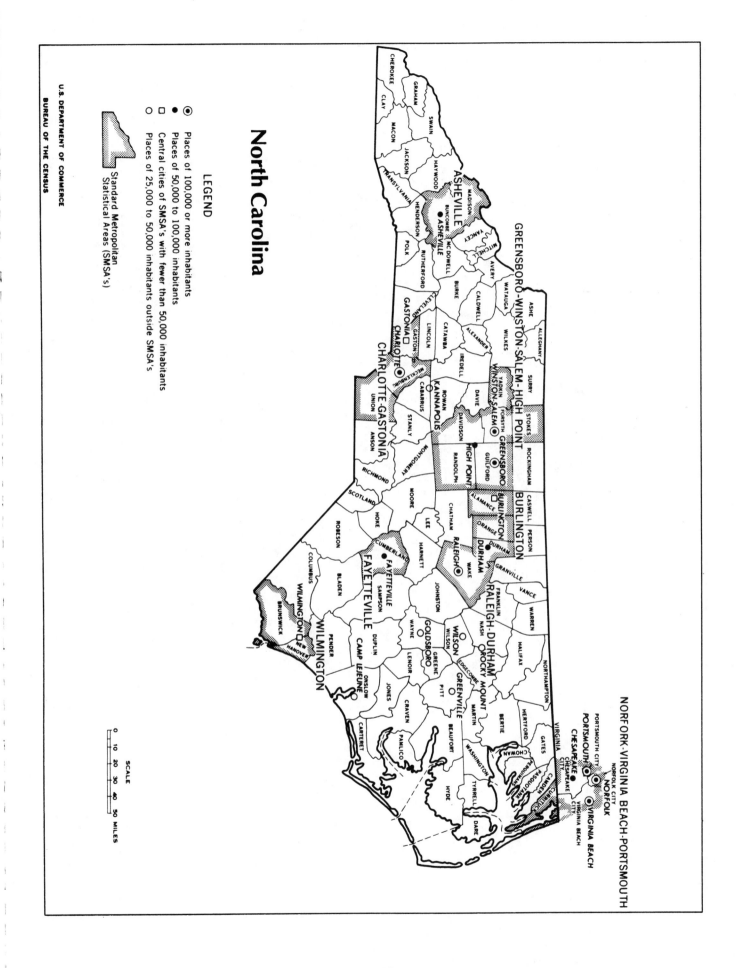

North Carolina

LEGEND

◉ Places of 100,000 or more inhabitants

● Places of 50,000 to 100,000 inhabitants

□ Central cities of SMSA's with fewer than 50,000 inhabitants

○ Places of 25,000 to 50,000 inhabitants outside SMSA's

Standard Metropolitan
Statistical Areas (SMSA's)

U.S. DEPARTMENT OF COMMERCE
BUREAU OF THE CENSUS

SCALE

0 10 20 30 40 50 MILES

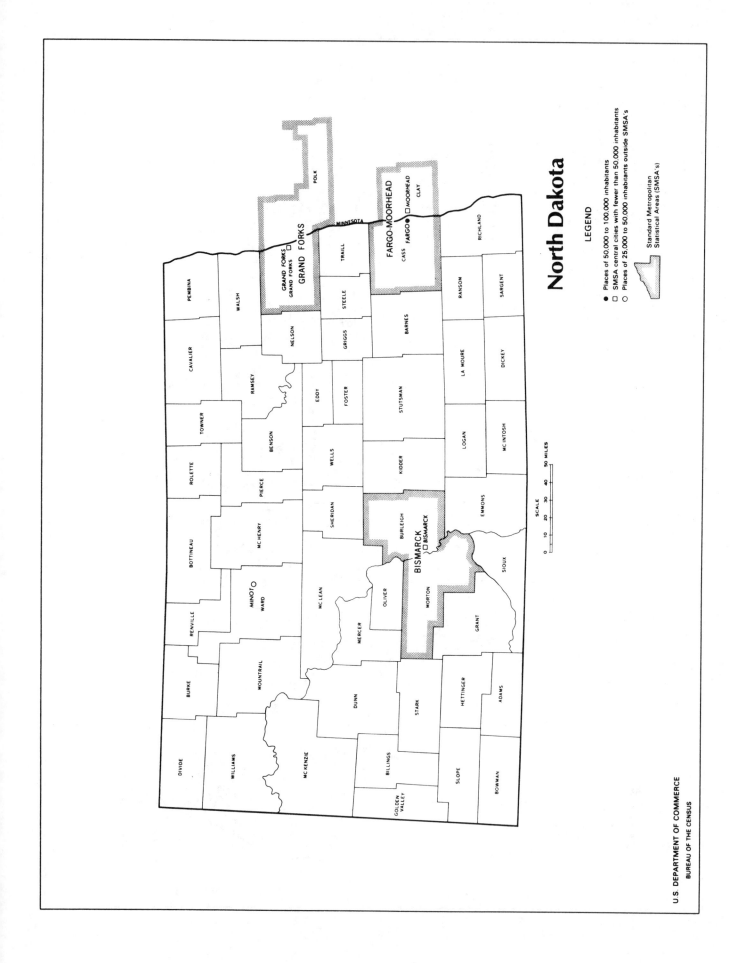

North Dakota

LEGEND

● Places of 50,000 to 100,000 inhabitants
□ SMSA central cities with fewer than 50,000 inhabitants
○ Places of 25,000 to 50,000 inhabitants outside SMSA's

Standard Metropolitan
Statistical Areas (SMSA's)

U.S. DEPARTMENT OF COMMERCE
BUREAU OF THE CENSUS

Ohio

LEGEND

⊙ Places of 100,000 or more inhabitants
● Places of 50,000 to 100,000 inhabitants
□ SMSA central cities with fewer than 50,000 inhabitants
○ Places of 25,000 to 50,000 inhabitants outside SMSA's

Standard Metropolitan
Statistical Areas (SMSA's)

U.S. DEPARTMENT OF COMMERCE

BUREAU OF THE CENSUS

SCALE

0   10   20   30   40   50 MILES

B 485

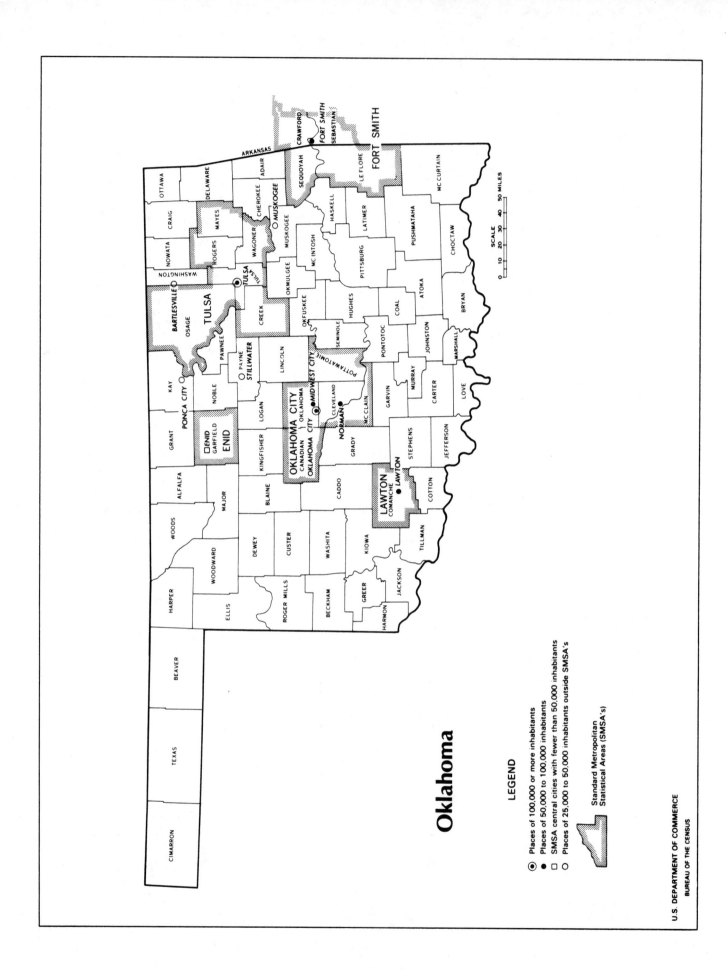

Oklahoma

LEGEND

- ◉ Places of 100,000 or more inhabitants
- ● Places of 50,000 to 100,000 inhabitants
- □ SMSA central cities with fewer than 50,000 inhabitants
- ○ Places of 25,000 to 50,000 inhabitants outside SMSA's

Standard Metropolitan
Statistical Areas (SMSA's)

U.S. DEPARTMENT OF COMMERCE
BUREAU OF THE CENSUS

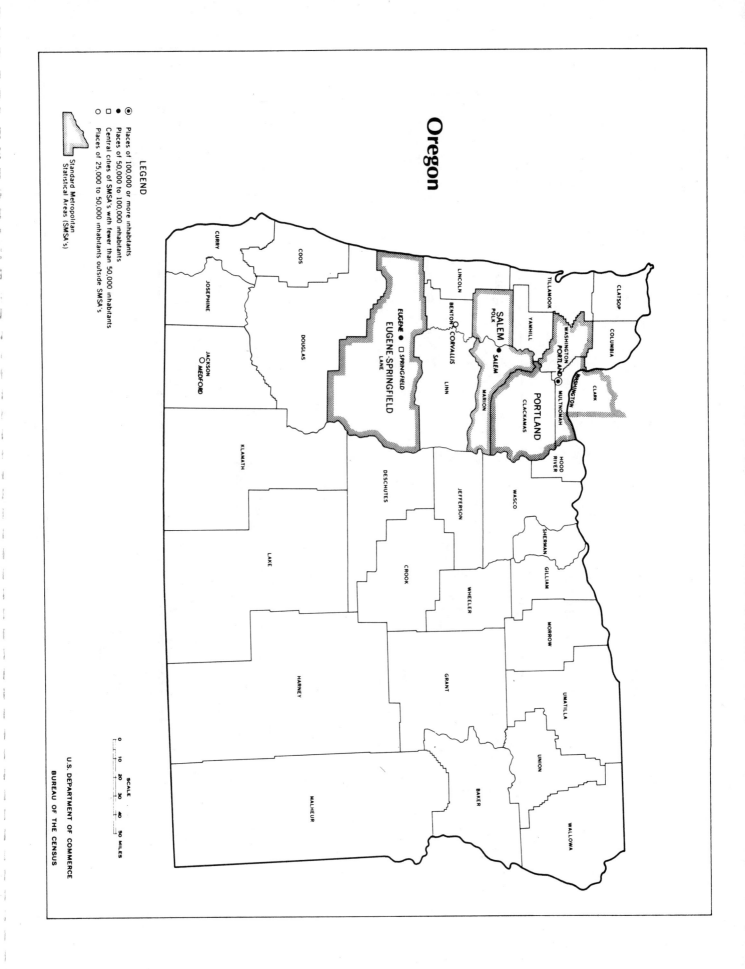

Oregon

LEGEND

⊙ Places of 100,000 or more inhabitants

● Places of 50,000 to 100,000 inhabitants

■ Central cities of SMSA's with fewer than 50,000 inhabitants

○ Places of 25,000 to 50,000 inhabitants outside SMSA's

Standard Metropolitan
Statistical Areas (SMSA's)

SCALE

0 10 20 30 40 50 MILES

U.S. DEPARTMENT OF COMMERCE
BUREAU OF THE CENSUS

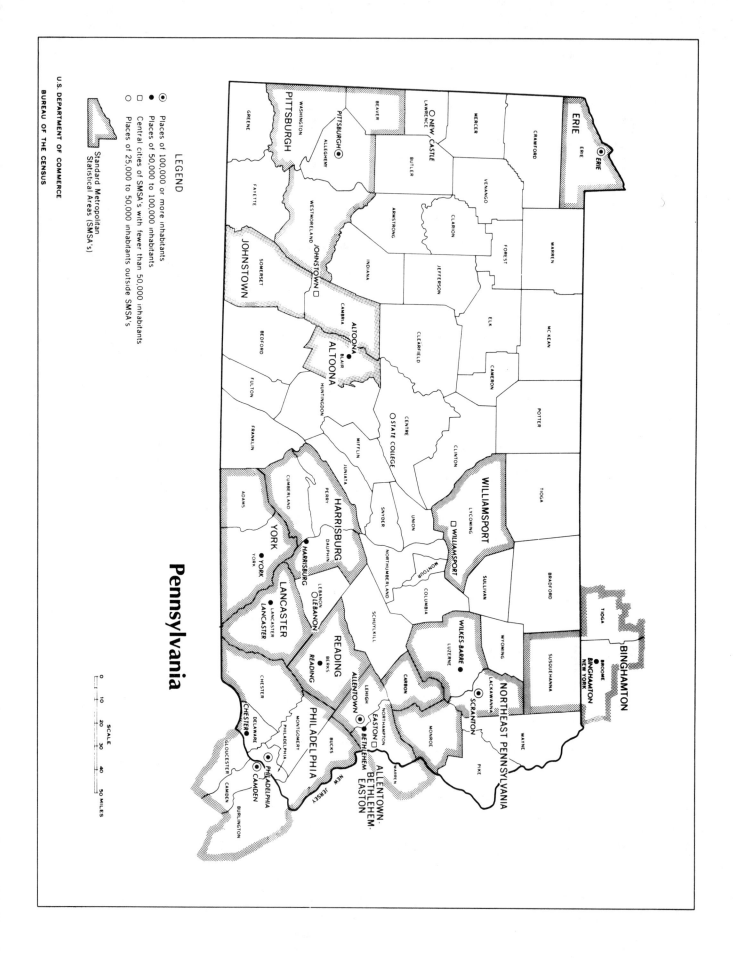

Pennsylvania

U.S. DEPARTMENT OF COMMERCE

BUREAU OF THE CENSUS

LEGEND

⦿ Places of 100,000 or more inhabitants

● Places of 50,000 to 100,000 inhabitants

□ Central cities of SMSA's with fewer than 50,000 inhabitants

○ Places of 25,000 to 50,000 inhabitants outside SMSA's

Standard Metropolitan
Statistical Areas (SMSA's)

SCALE

0   10   20   30   40   50 MILES

Rhode Island

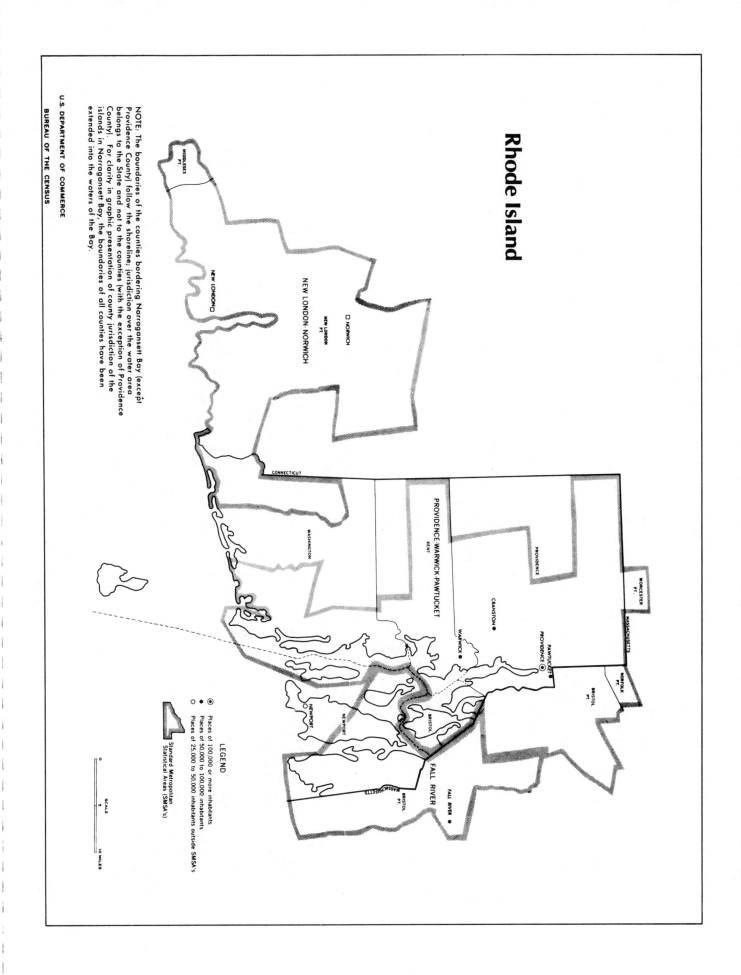

NOTE: The boundaries of the counties bordering Narragansett Bay (except Providence County) follow the shoreline; jurisdiction over the water area belongs to the State and not to the counties (with the exception of Providence County). For clarity in graphic presentation of county jurisdiction of the islands in Narragansett Bay, the boundaries of all counties have been extended into the waters of the Bay.

U.S. DEPARTMENT OF COMMERCE
BUREAU OF THE CENSUS

LEGEND

⊙ Places of 100,000 or more inhabitants
● Places of 50,000 to 100,000 inhabitants
○ Places of 25,000 to 50,000 inhabitants

Standard Metropolitan
Statistical Areas (SMSA's)

SCALE

0   5   10 MILES

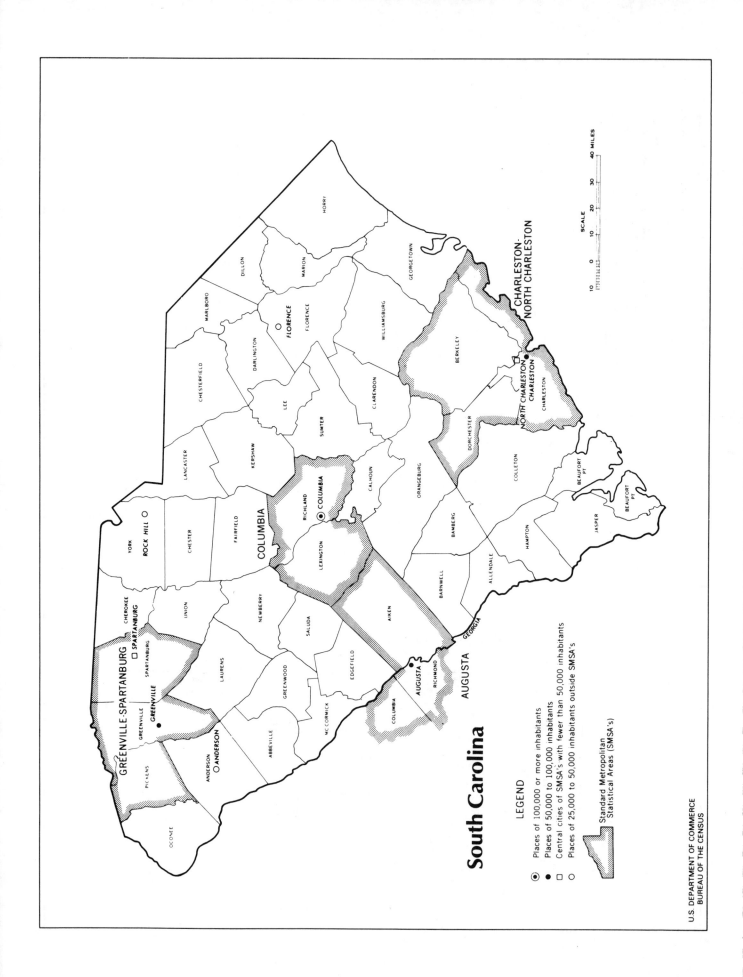

South Carolina

LEGEND

⊙ Places of 100,000 or more inhabitants

● Places of 50,000 to 100,000 inhabitants

□ Central cities of SMSA's with fewer than 50,000 inhabitants

○ Places of 25,000 to 50,000 inhabitants outside SMSA's

Standard Metropolitan
Statistical Areas (SMSA's)

SCALE

40 MILES

30

20

10

0

10

CHARLESTON-
NORTH CHARLESTON

HORRY

DILLON

MARION

MARLBORO

GEORGETOWN

FLORENCE

FLORENCE

WILLIAMSBURG

BERKELEY

CHESTERFIELD

DARLINGTON

CLARENDON

LEE

DORCHESTER

NORTH CHARLESTON

CHARLESTON

CHARLESTON

LANCASTER

KERSHAW

SUMTER

CALHOUN

ORANGEBURG

COLLETON

BEAUFORT
PT

YORK

ROCK HILL

CHESTER

FAIRFIELD

RICHLAND

COLUMBIA

COLUMBIA

LEXINGTON

BAMBERG

HAMPTON

JASPER

BEAUFORT
PT

BARNWELL

ALLENDALE

CHEROKEE

SPARTANBURG

UNION

NEWBERRY

SALUDA

AIKEN

GREENVILLE-SPARTANBURG

SPARTANBURG

SPARTANBURG

LAURENS

GREENWOOD

EDGEFIELD

GEORGIA

AUGUSTA

GREENVILLE

GREENVILLE

GREENVILLE

ANDERSON

ABBEVILLE

MC CORMICK

COLUMBIA

AUGUSTA

RICHMOND

AUGUSTA

PICKENS

ANDERSON

OCONEE

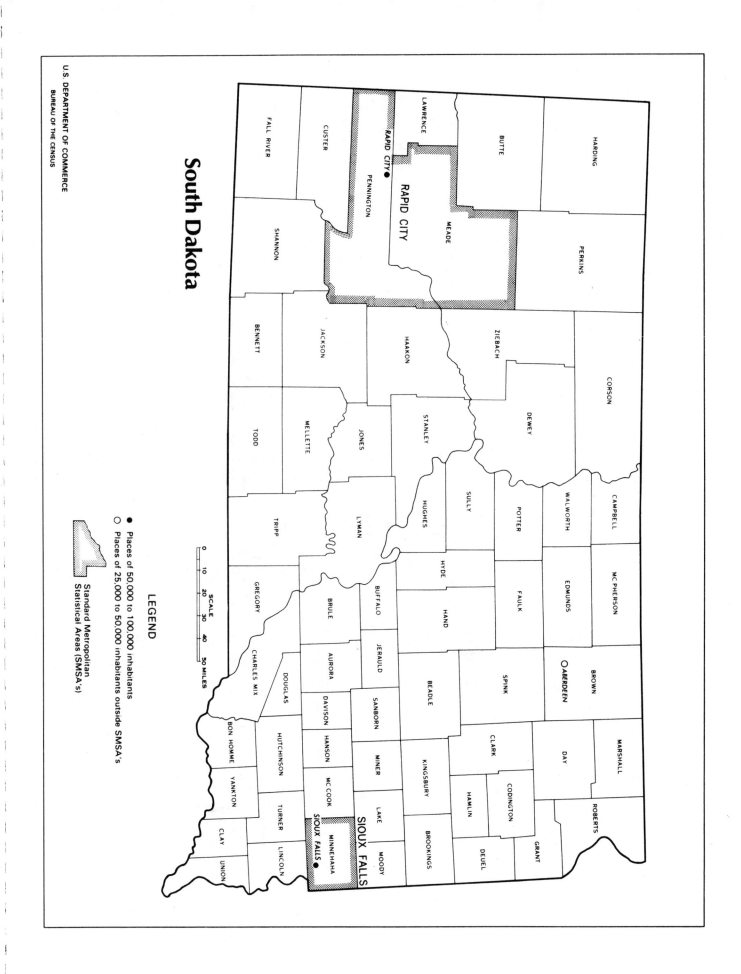

South Dakota

U.S. DEPARTMENT OF COMMERCE
BUREAU OF THE CENSUS

LEGEND

● Places of 50,000 to 100,000 inhabitants
○ Places of 25,000 to 50,000 inhabitants outside SMSA's

Standard Metropolitan
Statistical Areas (SMSA's)

SCALE
0
10
20
30
40
50 MILES

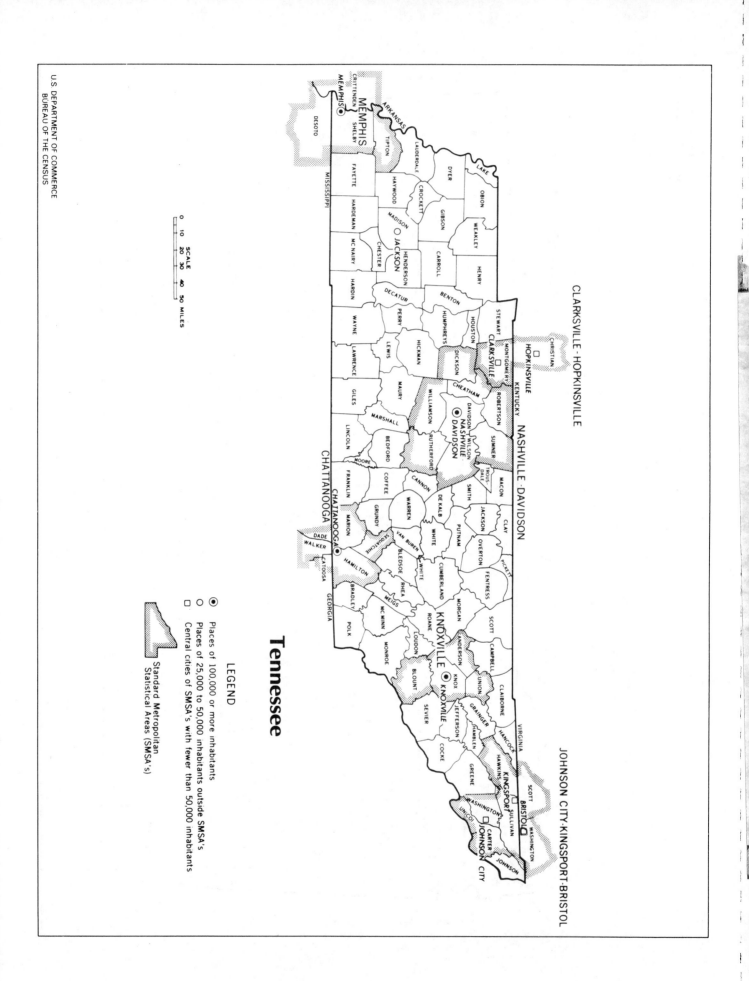

Tennessee

LEGEND

- ◉ Places of 100,000 or more inhabitants
- ◯ Places of 25,000 to 50,000 inhabitants outside SMSA's
- ◻ Central cities of SMSA's with fewer than 50,000 inhabitants

◢ Standard Metropolitan
Statistical Areas (SMSA's)

U.S. DEPARTMENT OF COMMERCE
BUREAU OF THE CENSUS

SCALE
0 10 20 30 40 50 MILES

CLARKSVILLE-HOPKINSVILLE

JOHNSON CITY-KINGSPORT-BRISTOL

NASHVILLE-DAVIDSON

CHATTANOOGA

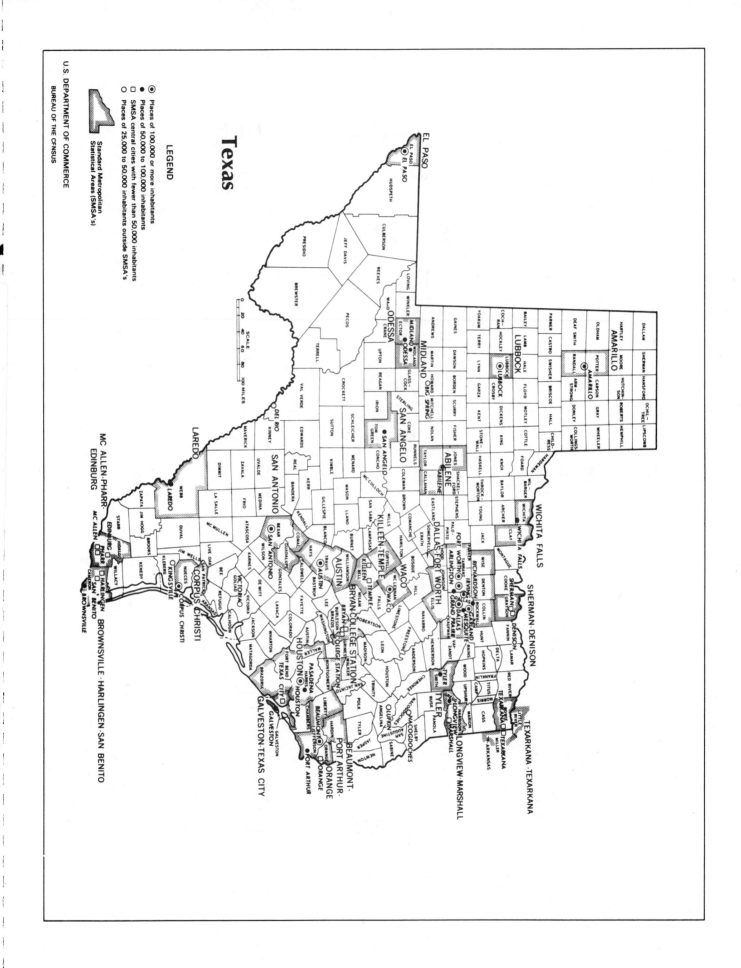

Texas

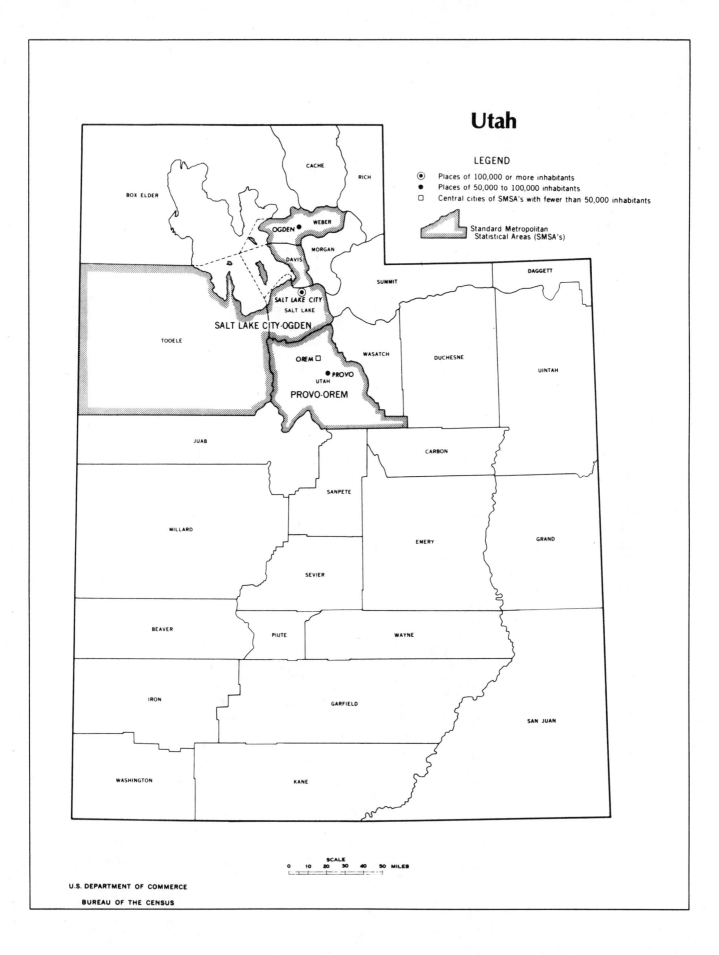

Utah

LEGEND

⊙ Places of 100,000 or more inhabitants
● Places of 50,000 to 100,000 inhabitants
□ Central cities of SMSA's with fewer than 50,000 inhabitants

Standard Metropolitan
Statistical Areas (SMSA's)

BOX ELDER

CACHE

RICH

WEBER

OGDEN ●

MORGAN

DAVIS

SUMMIT

DAGGETT

SALT LAKE CITY ⊙

SALT LAKE

SALT LAKE CITY-OGDEN

TOOELE

WASATCH

DUCHESNE

UINTAH

OREM □

● PROVO

UTAH

PROVO-OREM

JUAB

CARBON

SANPETE

MILLARD

EMERY

GRAND

SEVIER

BEAVER

PIUTE

WAYNE

IRON

GARFIELD

SAN JUAN

WASHINGTON

KANE

SCALE
0 10 20 30 40 50 MILES

U.S. DEPARTMENT OF COMMERCE

BUREAU OF THE CENSUS

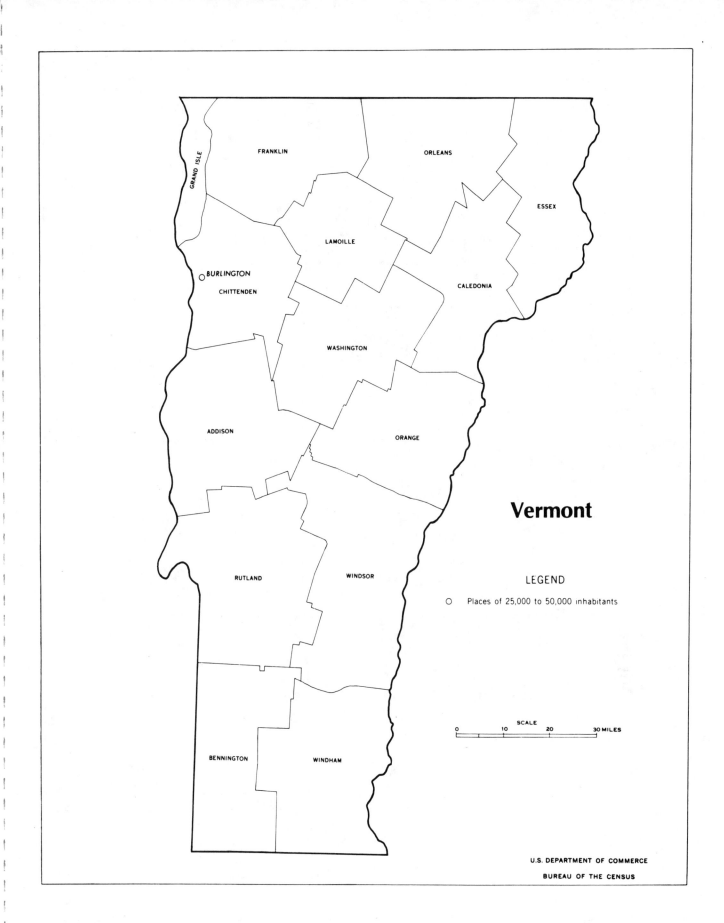

Vermont

LEGEND

○ Places of 25,000 to 50,000 inhabitants

SCALE

0 ... 10 ... 20 ... 30 MILES

U.S. DEPARTMENT OF COMMERCE

BUREAU OF THE CENSUS

B 495

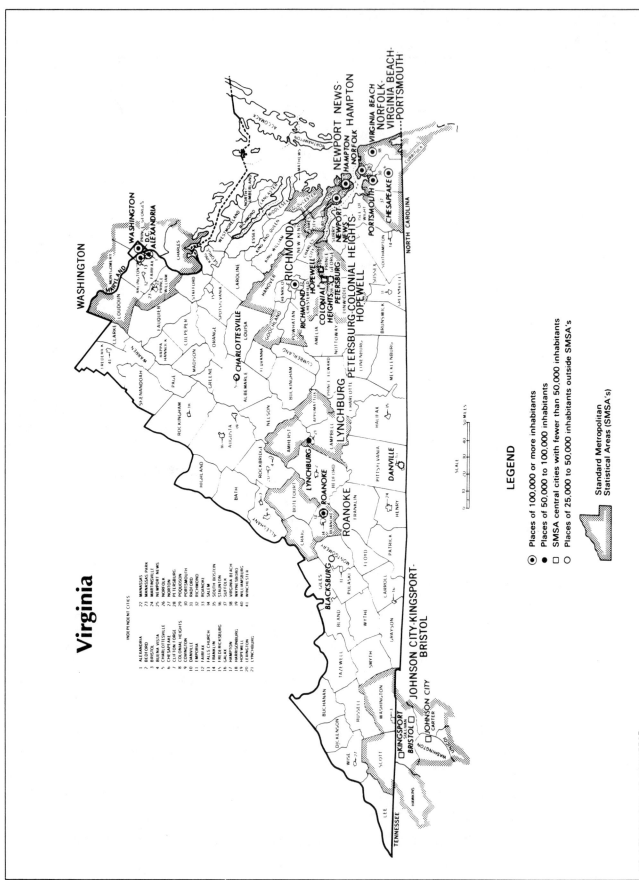

Virginia

INDEPENDENT CITIES

1	ALEXANDRIA	22	MANASSAS
2	BEDFORD	23	MANASSAS PARK
3	BRISTOL	24	MARTINSVILLE
4	BUENA VISTA	25	NEWPORT NEWS
5	CHARLOTTESVILLE	26	NORFOLK
6	CHESAPEAKE	27	NORTON
7	CLIFTON FORGE	28	PETERSBURG
8	COLONIAL HEIGHTS	29	POQUOSON
9	COVINGTON	30	PORTSMOUTH
10	DANVILLE	31	RADFORD
11	EMPORIA	32	RICHMOND
12	FAIRFAX	33	ROANOKE
13	FALLS CHURCH	34	SALEM
14	FRANKLIN	35	SOUTH BOSTON
15	FREDERICKSBURG	36	STAUNTON
16	GALAX	37	SUFFOLK
17	HAMPTON	38	VIRGINIA BEACH
18	HARRISONBURG	39	WAYNESBORO
19	HOPEWELL	40	WILLIAMSBURG
20	LEXINGTON	41	WINCHESTER
21	LYNCHBURG		

LEGEND

⊙ Places of 100,000 or more inhabitants

● Places of 50,000 to 100,000 inhabitants

□ SMSA central cities with fewer than 50,000 inhabitants

○ Places of 25,000 to 50,000 inhabitants outside SMSA's

Standard Metropolitan
Statistical Areas (SMSA's)

U.S. DEPARTMENT OF COMMERCE
BUREAU OF THE CENSUS

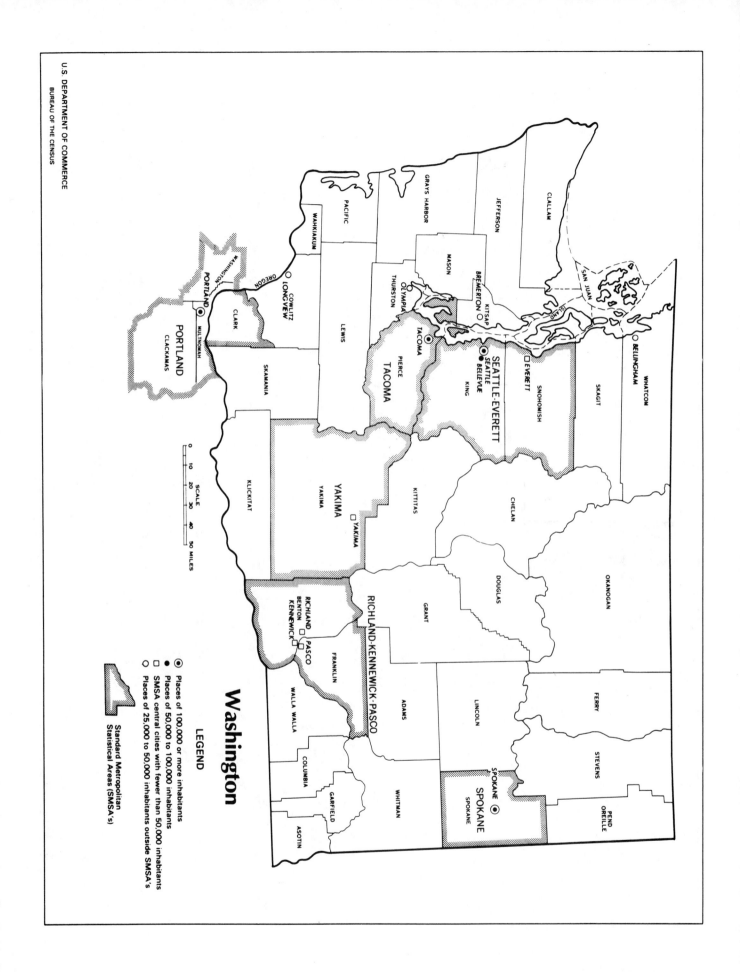

Washington

LEGEND

⊙ Places of 100,000 or more inhabitants
● Places of 50,000 to 100,000 inhabitants
□ SMSA central cities with fewer than 50,000 inhabitants
○ Places of 25,000 to 50,000 inhabitants outside SMSA's

Standard Metropolitan
Statistical Areas (SMSA's)

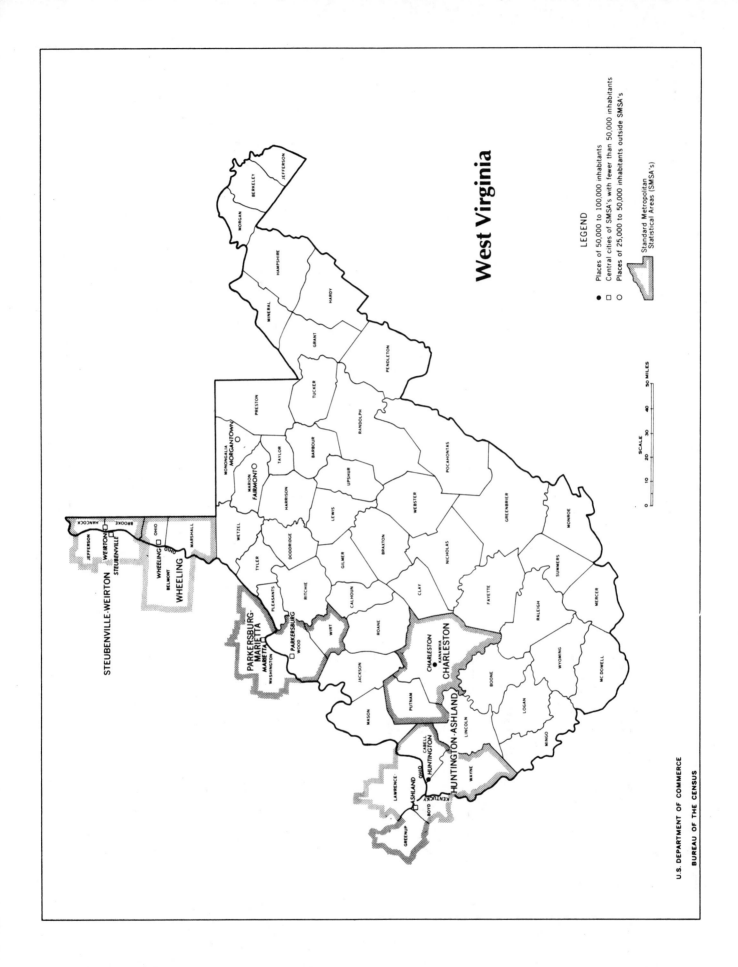

West Virginia